The Californian

Wildlife Region

*Turn the pages and meet the plants
and animals living in our region.*

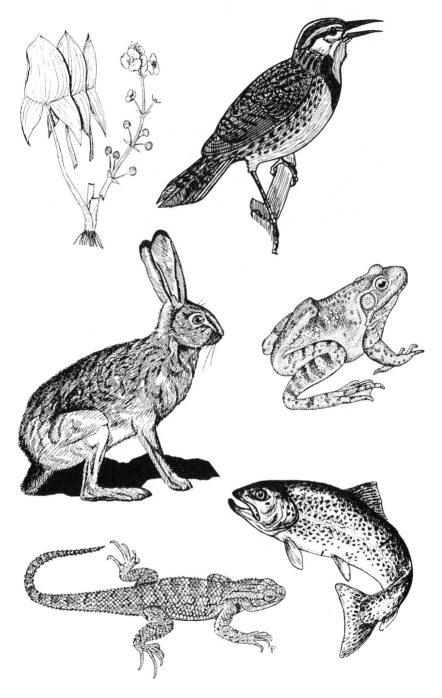

The
Californian
Wildlife Region

Third Revised and Expanded Edition

by Vinson Brown

Major illustrators:
Plants: Janet Coyle and Emily Reid
Mammals: Byron Alexander
Birds: Janet Coyle
Reptiles and Amphibians: Byron Alexander and Phyllis Thompson
Fishes: Byron Alexander and Rune Hapness

Naturegraph Publishers

Library of Congress Cataloging-in-Publication Data
Brown, Vinson, 1912-1991
    The Californian wildlife region / by Vinson Brown ; major illustrators,
Janet Coyle ... [et al.]. -- 3rd rev. and expanded ed.
        p.   cm.
    Includes bibliographical references (p.   ).
    ISBN 0-87961-201-0
    1. Natural history--California.   I. Title.
QH105.C2B675   1999   99-14521
578'.09794—dc21   CIP

ISBN 0-87961-201-0

Cover design by Av-tec, photo by Brooking Tatum

Naturegraph Publishers has been publishing books on
natural history, Native Americans, and outdoor subjects
since 1946. Please write for our free catalog.

Naturegraph Publishers, Inc.
3543 Indian Creek Road
Happy Camp, CA 96039
(530) 493-5353

Books for a better world

Preface and Acknowledgments

The common and scientific names of the plants and animals in this 1999 revised field guide as well as the species descriptions have been updated using recent authoritative references. For example, for the plants *The Jepson Manual, Higher Plants of California* (Berkeley: University of California Press, 1993) was referred to. The list of suggested references at the end of this book includes sources used for updating the descriptions. The 1999 edition of *The Californian Wildlife Region* is enlarged by the addition of nearly 100 common plant species not included in earlier editions, and the text is enhanced with added species information and many new plant and wildlife illustrations.

Many people have assisted in various ways over the years to the revisions and improvement of this book since it was first published in 1957. For the first edition, Dr. John C. Briggs of Stanford University reviewed the section on fishes; Dr. Robert Stebbins and Dr. A. Starker Leopold of the University of California gave general and specific criticisms; Mrs. L. S. Cook of the Santa Barbara Natural History Museum and Mrs. Helen Sharsmith of the University of California Botany Department made valuable suggestions in regard to the plants; Miss Helen Hefferman, Mrs. Ester Nelson, and Mr. Lloyd Bevans of the State Department of Education offered helpful suggestions on the book's organization.

Dr. George Lawrence of California State University at Bakersfield assisted Mr. Brown with the book's second revision in 1965. The current edition was started in 1985, but unfortunately Vinson Brown passed away in 1991 while still valiantly trying to complete this revision. His daughter, Roxana Hodges, on leave from work at the birth of a son, organized her father's work and researched all the animal chapters. A couple years later, while working toward his Ph.D, Keven Brown, completed his father's work on the plants. Again the work sat. For the final stage his wife, Barbara Brown, added information to the animal chapters, secured the numerous illustrations, and prepared the work for publishing. Even so the book would still be in limbo were it not for the help of Faith Crowder who painstakingly arranged the many pages of illustrations; April Krammer for putting many rewrites of text and the index in the computer, and Albert Vanderhoof for finalizing typeset pages for printing.

Barbara Brown, Publisher

Artists

For wildlife identification the old saying that "a picture takes the place of a thousand words" is especially true. So to the artists, whose work complements and clarifies the descriptions, we extend a special thank you for making this field guide practical to use.

Except where all the illustrations for a chapter, or an particular section, are by the same artist, all other illustrations are identified by the following initials.

BA   Byron Alexander (mammals, reptiles, amphibians, fish, and all hawks)
JC   Janet Coyle (plants and all birds other than water birds and hawks)
FC   Faith Crowder (fish)
RH   Rune Hapness (fish)
ER   Emily Reid (plants)
RS   Robert Stebbins (reptiles and amphibians)
LT   Linda Thompson (all water birds)
PT   Phyllis Thompson (reptiles, amphibians and fish)
CY   Charles Yocom (plants)

Contents

About the Region

Wildlife regions, such as the Californian wildlife region, are distinctive, natural geographic areas of similar climate and topography, which tend to have certain typical animals and plants within their boundaries. There is, however, much overlapping between wildlife regions so that their boundaries are never rigid. The Californian wildlife region, as explained here, has the geographical area shown on the map on page 10, plus some small extensions northward into the valleys around Grants Pass and Medford in Oregon. The region covers most of lowland and foothill California except for the deserts and the northwest coast forest of redwoods and firs, which borders it on the northwest. It is bordered on the east by the Sierra Nevadan wildlife region, and on the southeast by the arid Mohave and Sonoran deserts.

The region includes: the blue oak-pine woodland and the chaparral of the **South Coast Ranges**, the savanna and shrubland of the **interior valleys of southern California**, and the chaparral and oak woodland of the **Transverse and Peninsular ranges**. It includes grassland and dry, desertlike areas in the **Central Valley**, i. e. the Sacramento and San Joaquin valleys, and blue oak-pine woodland and chaparral in the **foothills of the surrounding inner North Coast Ranges, Cascade Range, and the Sierra Nevada**, as well as the **San Francisco Bay**

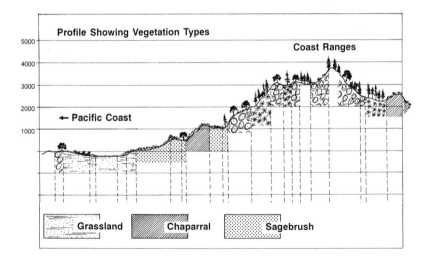

area and the coastal scrub of the **central California Coast** from Marin Co. south to Point Conception. It also includes the **southern California Coast** from Point Conception to Baja, Mexico, which extends farther inland than the central coast, and has both coastal sage scrub and chaparral. The mixed evergreen forest of the North Coast Ranges, which extends as far south as the Santa Cruz Mountains, is not covered in this book.

The region's climate is mild. Most of the year is frost-free, and its rainfall ranges from near 8 inches in the dry grasslands to as much as 40 inches or more in the oak woodlands. High summer temperatures prevail inland (up to 115 degrees F.), but near the coast, the influence of the ocean maintains a milder temperature most of the year. Since the major part of the region's rainfall comes in the winter and early spring, and there are sometimes dry years with little rain, most of the plant and animal life has adapted to live through many months of dryness. Unlike the perennials, which have the hardiness to survive, annual plants dry up and die in the summer, but spread their seeds in readiness for the coming rains. Animals avoid the extreme dryness by either migrating to moister areas, such as the mountains, or going into a kind of summer sleep called estivation. In the southern San Joaquin Valley and neighboring inner Coast Ranges and valleys the dryness is sometimes so great that many desert animals and plants are found there as well.

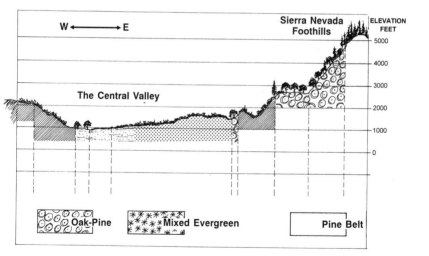

Californian Wildlife Region Map

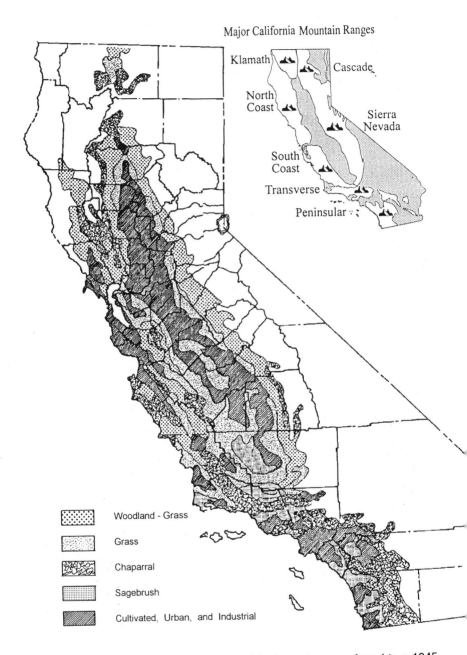

Major California Mountain Ranges

Klamath

Cascade

North Coast

Sierra Nevada

South Coast

Transverse

Peninsular

Woodland - Grass

Grass

Chaparral

Sagebrush

Cultivated, Urban, and Industrial

To indicate vegetation type areas within the region we referred to a 1945 U.S. Forest Service, Forest Survey Map.

How to Use this Book

This book introduces a large number of the common wild plants and animals of the Californian wildlife region, and provides basic descriptions for their identification. First, study the descriptions and pictures of the principal wildlife habitats, or plant communities, found in the Californian wildlife region so that you will recognize them when you see them. Then, study the lists of common plants and animals found in each plant community. There are certain immensely successful plants in each wildlife habitat that help to identify it. These are called indicator species. In the streamside woodland, for example, the willows, alders, and cottonwoods are prominent; in the chaparral, the manzanita, chamise, and wild lilac; and in the oak woodland, the live oaks, foothill pine, and California walnut. Next, review Chapter 2, which has a glossary of the plant terms used in this book and illustrations for helping to identify plants. You are now ready to commence identification.

For example, let us suppose that you are hiking and you come into a chaparral plant community, which you identify from the picture and description of such a habitat given in this book. After finding a plant you wish to identify, read through the list of common chaparral plants and study their descriptions and illustrations in Chapter 3. If the plant is a herb, turn to the section on herbs; if it is a tree or shrub, turn section covering trees, shrubs, and vines; and so forth. You will notice, as you study the Common Plants chapter, that many other species of plants besides those listed as indicator species also grow in the chaparral. These are shown by the bold print words in brackets. For example, if you are in an oak woodland and discover a fern not listed among the common indicator plants for that habitat, turn to the section on ferns in Chapter 3 to see which ferns include the oak woodland as a potential habitat. Be sure to read the habitat and range information at the end of each species description to determine if that plant could be in your location. If no geographical range is given, this means that the plant or animal is found in all parts of the Californian wildlife region.

Even if you are not able to identify the exact species, you should be able to identify the plant's genus or family. Most of the plants described in this book are common, though a few less common species have been included because they are good indicator species. Some genera, such as *Carex* and *Scirpus* have so many common members that it was only possible to list one or two representative species. The species included, however, include the majority of the plants you are likely to encounter. For more detailed information on particular species or rarer species, the reader can refer to the books listed in the Suggested References. Use the same method to identify animals found in each habitat area.

Streamside woodland. Photo by Moulin Studios

1.

Habitats of the Californian Wildlife Region

The animals shown in silhouette are: A—Tree Swallow; B—Great Blue Heron; C—Horned Owl; D—Yellow-legged Frog; E—Raccoon; F—Western Garter Snake; G—Audubon Cottontail; H—Mule Deer; I—Virginia Opossum; J —Striped Skunk; K—California Newt.

The Streamside Woodland

The shade, thick cover, great number of leaves, and usual abundance of water found in the streamside woodland make this habitat a popular home for wild animals. In northern California the trees usually grow fairly close together with numerous undershrubs, but in the drier areas of southern California, where the California sycamore and the cottonwoods are most numerous, the trees may be spaced in widely separated clumps. Because of the shade, the temperature in the streamside woodland is likely to be lower than in neighboring grassland or shrubland. Many animals move to this streamside environment during the heat of a summer day. The plants included here may be found in more than one plant community, but they are especially common along streams or river banks.

The Oak Woodland

California black oak. Photo by F.G. Plummer, courtesy U.S. Forest Service.

The oak woodland is divided into three types: The first is the **Oregon or northern oak woodland**, where the Oregon oak and the California black oak are important indicator species and the plant undergrowth is fairly open. It includes the North Coast Ranges east of the fir and redwood forests from Humboldt and Trinity counties as far south as Napa County. The second is the **foothill woodland** of central California, in which the live oaks, the blue oak, and the foothill and Coulter pines are principal trees and the undergrowth is either dense or open. This woodland includes the inner Coast Ranges from Trinity Co. to Santa Barbara Co., the western Sierra Nevada foothills south to northwestern Los Angeles Co., and the inner part of the outer South Coast Ranges. The third is the **southern oak woodland**, where the coast live oak, the mesa oak, and the California walnut are indicator species, and there is very little undergrowth, but chiefly grass. It includes the valleys and foothills of interior southern California, ascending to about 5,000 feet in some places, from Los Angeles Co. south to San Diego Co.

In the south, the oak woodlands are in sheltered valleys or along the north-facing sides of canyons. In the north, they are more on hilltops or in wide valleys. They form a good shelter for many animals and their shade keeps the temperature lower than in the surrounding grasslands or chaparral. The oak woodlands have the highest annual rainfall (15–40 inches) and the lowest average temperature (29–42 degrees F. in winter) of any wildlife area in the region. Coniferous forest animals often come here.

The animals shown in silhouette are: A—Screech Owl; B—Gray Squirrel; C—Hoary Bat; D—Acorn Woodpecker; E—Mountain Quail; F—Gray Fox; G—Dusky-footed Woodrat; H—Long-tailed Weasel; I—Western Skink.

Southern oak woodland in Santa Barbara County with mostly grass growing under Blue and Live Oaks. Photo by Josef Muench, from National Audubon Society.

The Shrubland

There are at least three distinct kinds of shrubland in the Californian wildlife region. The **true chaparral** is found on dry slopes or ridges of the Coast Ranges, in the western foothills of the Sierra Nevada below the yellow pine forest, and in the mountains of southern California. It is made up of stiff-branched, small-leaved shrubs from 3–10 feet high that are adapted to survive the long, hot summer months. Chamise and buckthorn are two indicator species. This wildlife area attracts about 14–25 inches of rainfall per year.

Another kind of shrubland is the **northern coastal scrub**, found near the coast from Monterey county north, usually below 500 feet between the coast and the redwood forest. It is dominated by rather low shrubs (usually under 6 feet), such as chaparral broom and monkeyflower, often with large areas of grassland growing in between. Fog, wind, and rain prevail here, with 25–75 inches of average rainfall and a much lower average summer temperature. Properly speaking, this shrubland belongs more with the Pacific Coastal wildlife region than with the Californian.

The third kind of shrubland is the **coastal sage scrub** of the South Coast Ranges near the ocean, below 3,000 ft., continuing south on the southern California coastal plain from Point Conception to Mexico. The plants are generally from 1–6 feet tall and less dense than in the chaparral which occurs above it on the hotter, more inland slopes. Sagebrush is one of the predominant species here. The annual rainfall is 10–20 inches, but more fog makes the summer cooler.

The animals shown in silhouette are: A—Red-tailed Hawk; B—Wildcat;
C—California Thrasher; D—Spotted Skunk; E—Western Fence Lizard;
F—Coast Horned Lizard; G—Western Rattlesnake; H—California Quail;
I—California Striped Racer; J—Ring-tailed Cat.

Common Indicator Plants

Chaparral

manzanitas	65-67
chaparral pea	69
scrub oak	71
woolly bluecurls	77
Whipple's yucca	79
ceanothus spp.	83-85
buckthorn spp.	85
chamise/greasewood	87
birchleaf mt. mahogany	87
toyon/Christmas berry	87
holly-leaved cherry	87
fremontia/flannelbush	91

Coastal Sage Scrub

lemonade berry	55
California sagebrush	57
California encelia	57
golden yarrow	57
goldenbushes	57-59
bladderpod	61
white sage	77
purple sage	77
black sage	77
California buckwheat	83

wedge-leaved horkelia 123

Northern Coastal Scrub (includes coastal grassland)

wild oats	49
California oatgrass	51
common velvetgrass	51
chaparral broom	57
coyote brush	57
seaside sunflower	59
particolor lupine	69
California blackberry	89
bush monkeyflower	91
cow parsnip	93
pearly everlasting	95
seaside daisy	99

Common Animals

Mammals

opossum	131
most bats	133-37
ring-tailed cat	137
long-tailed weasel	139
badger	139
spotted skunk	141
gray fox	141
coyote	141
mountain lion	143
bobcat	145
Calif. ground squirrel	145
pocket gopher	147
pocket mice	149
most kangaroo rats	149
woodrats	151
white-footed mice	153
brush rabbit	159
black-tailed jackrabbit	159
deer	159
wild boar	159

Birds

turkey vulture	185
California condor	185
red-tailed hawk	187
great horned owl	193
mountain quail	195
California quail	195
roadrunner	197
most hummingbirds	201-03
poorwill	203
ash-throated flycatcher	205
scrub jay	209
bushtit	211
house wren	213

20 Californian Wildlife Region

Chaparral covered hillsides. Photo courtesy U.S. Forest Service.

The Savanna

The savanna is a halfway country, halfway between oak woodland and grassland, and made up of plants from both areas. Because of this, only the dominant trees of this habitat are listed below, while for typical grasses of the area, turn to the next section.

Some animals like the combination of the shelter of the oak trees and the good feeding of the open grass country. A surprising number of birds, particularly the soaring hawks, prefer this habitat above all others. There is an extensive savanna belt rimming the Central Valley in the foothills of the mountains.

The animals shown in silhouette are: A—Turkey Vulture; B—Mourning Dove; C—Crow; D—Yellow-billed Magpie; E—Badger; F—Common King Snake; G—California Meadow Mouse; H—Western Spadefoot Toad; I—California Ground Squirrel.

Live oaks. Photo by Joseph Muench, courtesty National Aububon Society.

The Valley Grassland

Grassland (foreground), savanna and oak woodland (middleground), and chaparral (hills). Photo by Brooking Tatum.

The grasslands of California range all the way from tall, dense grasses, growing in rich soil, to low, sparse grass on hard-packed ground. This habitat's main characteristic is wide, open country with no trees, except where disturbed by human habitation or cultivation. The Central Valley once supported vast stetches of native grassland, marshes, and extensive streamside woodland, but it is now predominated by agricultural lands. Rainfall in the grassland ranges from 6–20 inches, with most of it falling in the winter and spring to produce the growing season. Usually the grasslands turn brown in summer and form the driest and hottest part of the region. At such times many animals move to other wildlife areas or estivate in holes.

Of all the wildlife habitats in California, the grassland is the most difficult one for which to list typical plants. This is because in some grassland areas one plant may be exceedingly common while it is rare elsewhere. The list below is, therefore, not complete for all parts of the region.

The animals shown in silhouette are: A—Red-tailed Hawk; B—Marsh Hawk; C—Meadow Lark; D—Black-tailed Jackrabbit; E—Tiger Salamander; F—Gopher Snake; G—Red-wing Blackbird; H—Botta Pocket Gopher.

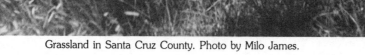

Grassland in Santa Cruz County. Photo by Milo James.

Rocky Areas and Cliffs

This habitat includes rocky outcrops, slopes, and talus in the oak-pine woodland and shrubland. The crevices and caves in rocks form shelter for many creatures and a few animals live practically nowhere else.

Desertlike Areas

In parts of the Central Valley (particularly the southern San Joaquin Valley), in the valleys and hills of the inner Coast Ranges of eastern San Luis Obispo County, and in inland areas of the southern coast counties there are areas of great dryness and alkalinity that appear like extensions of the real desert. These are of two types: alkali flats in valleys and rocky deserts in the surrounding hills.

Common Indicator Plants

Alkali Flats

Rocky Desert

Common Animals

Freshwater Areas

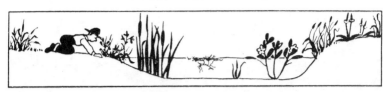

Freshwater areas in the state include creeks, rivers, lakes, ponds, pools, and marshes. Along the coast the freshwater marshes gradually merge into the saltwater marshes, which are considered separately, though many of the same animals are found there. The largest number of animals are found in slow or still water where there is much plant cover for them to hide in.

Clapper rail. Photo by Pat Kirkpatrick, courtesy National Audubon Society.

The Coastal Strand and Salt Marshes

Photo by permission of Redwood Empire Association.

The coastal strand of sandy beaches and dunes, extending up and down the entire coast, has an average annual rainfall of 15–70 inches. Its vegetation is low or prostrate and usually succulent or fleshy. Coastal salt marshes are found most extensively on tidelands along the coast from sea level to 10 feet, and receive an average annual rainfall of 15–40 inches.

In and On Buildings

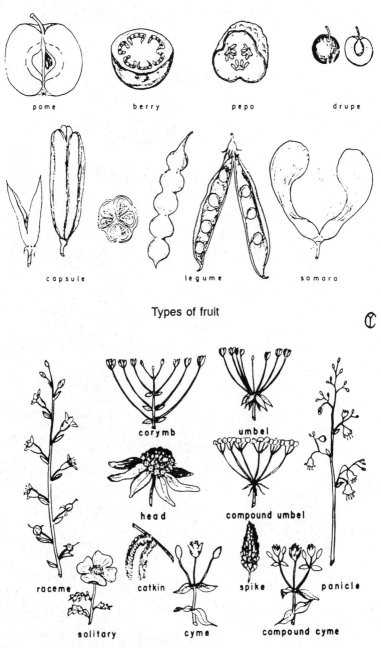

pome   berry   pepo   drupe

capsule   legume   samara

Types of fruit

C

corymb   umbel

head   compound umbel

raceme

solitary   catkin   cyme   spike   compound cyme   panicle

Types of inflorescences

2.

Plant Identification

The illustrations below show different kinds of flowers, flower formations (or inflorescence), and leaves useful in identifying plants. Each picture is numbered. When you see one of these numbers following a term in the *Glossary of Plant Terms*, found in this chapter, you can look here to find a helpful illustration of what the term means. Although we have tried to describe each species in plain language, it was sometimes necessary to use more precise plant terms to give the reader a more accurate description. All of the special plant terms used in this book are defined in the glossary.

When studying a plant to determine its name, examine every part of it: the leaves, the flowers, the fruit, the seeds, the bark, and the way the branches are formed. Also, carefully note its habitat. When you compare this knowledge with the information provided by the plant illustrations and descriptions, you may come up with the correct species name, and if not that, at least the correct genus name. If you get in too big a hurry, however, and do not carefully double-check everything, it is also easy to make a mistake. **Warning:** Although edible plants are indicated in the species descriptions, never attempt to eat a wild plant without first positively identifying it.

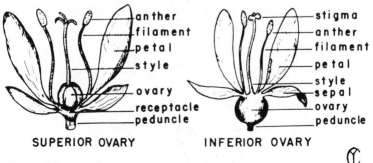

Parts of flowers

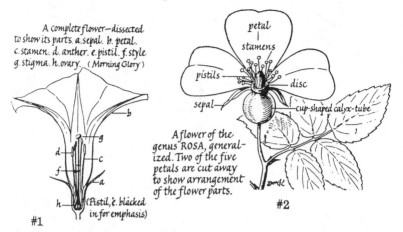

A complete flower—dissected
to show its parts. a. sepal. b. petal.
c. stamen. d. anther. e. pistil. f. style
g. stigma. h. ovary. (Morning Glory)

(Pistil, e. blacked
in for emphasis)
#1

petal
stamens
pistils
disc
sepal
cup-shaped calyx-tube

A flower of the
genus ROSA, general-
ized. Two of the five
petals are cut away
to show arrangement
of the flower parts.

#2

#1 and #2. Two typical flowers, showing the names of their parts.

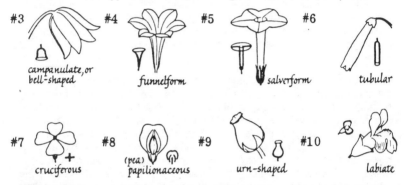

#3 campanulate, or
bell-shaped

#4 funnelform

#5 salverform

#6 tubular

#7 cruciferous

#8 (pea) papilionaceous

#9 urn-shaped

#10 labiate

#3 to #10. Types of flowers: #3 and #4 are **apetalous,** which means
without distinct petals and sepals; #7 and #8 are **choripetalous,** which
means the petals and sepals are each completely free from each other;
#5, #6, #9, and #10 are **sympetalous,** which means the petals and
sepals are all more or less closely joined together.

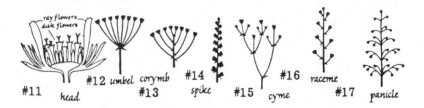

ray flowers
disk flowers

#11 head

#12 umbel

#13 corymb

#14 spike

#15 cyme

#16 raceme

#17 panicle

#11 to #17. Types of flower formations. The daisy and sunflower look
like single flowers, but really are heads of flowers (#11).

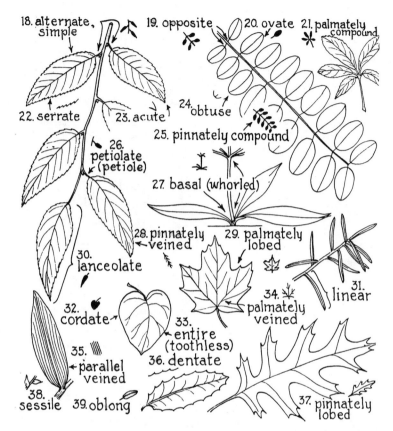

18. alternate, simple
19. opposite
20. ovate
21. palmately compound
22. serrate
23. acute
24. obtuse
25. pinnately compound
26. petiolate (petiole)
27. basal (whorled)
28. pinnately veined
29. palmately lobed
30. lanceolate
31. linear
32. cordate
33. entire (toothless)
34. palmately veined
35. parallel veined
36. dentate
37. pinnately lobed
38. sessile
39. oblong

#18 to #39. Main types of simple and compound leaves. The small figure beside each big one shows the generalized shape from which each leaf form shown takes its name.

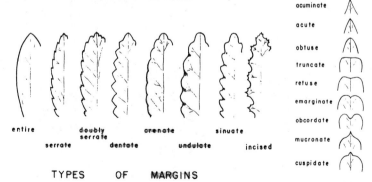

entire
serrate
doubly serrate
dentate
crenate
undulate
sinuate
incised

TYPES   OF   MARGINS

acuminate
acute
obtuse
truncate
retuse
emarginate
obcordate
mucronate
cuspidate

APICES

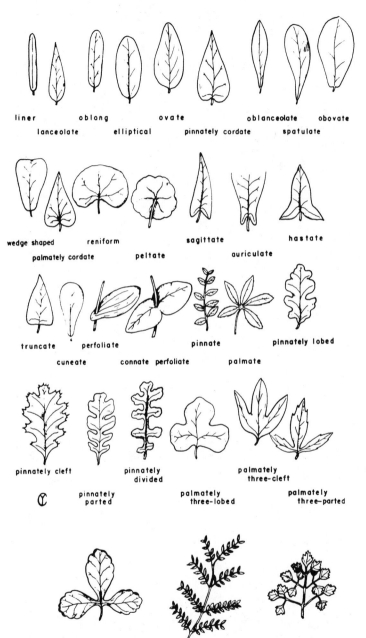

Types of leaves

Glossary of Plant Terms

achene. A dry, hard, one-seeded fruit not splitting at maturity.

acute. (#23) Having a short-tapered, sharp tip.

alternate. (#18) Refers to leaves having a staggered arrangement, not opposite.

annual. Lasting only one season, growing from a seed to maturity and dying in one year.

appressed. Usually said of hairs pressed against or nearly parallel to a stem.

ascending. Curving or angling upward from a base.

awn. A slender bristle, usually stiff, as on the end of a bract on a grass spikelet.

basal. (#27) Located at the base.

beak. A narrow, elongate, stiffened tip, as on an achene.

biennial. Lasting for two years.

blade. The flattened, extended portion of a leaf or petal.

bract. A rudimentary leaf just below a flower or cone.

bractlet. A secondary bract.

calyx. Collective term for the sepals of a flower; the outermost or lowermost whorl of flower parts encircling the flower bud.

compound. Composed of two or more parts; not simple.

cordate. (#32) Heart-shaped.

corolla. Collective term for the petals of a flower.

corymb. (#13) A broad, flat-topped cluster of flowers in which the outer flower stalks are long and those toward the center progressively shorter.

cyme. (#15) A flat-topped or convex flower cluster with primary branches again branching, and the uppermost flowers bloom first.

deciduous. Falling off, especially referring to plants that lose their leaves each fall.

decumbent. Almost lying flat on the ground but with the tips curling up. (see prostrate)

dentate. (#36) Having margins with teeth pointing outward.

elliptic. Having the shape of an ellipse, or flattened circle.

emergent. At least partly above water.

entire. (#33) Means with smooth, unbroken margins; not toothed or lobed.

erect. Perpendicular to the ground.

evergreen. Retaining leaves through the winter.

floret. The individual flower in the grass family; a small flower in a dense head.

flower. The reproductive structure of a large group of plants.

frond. The leaf of a fern.

glandular. Having small, usually spheric bodies that give out a sticky substance.

glaucous. Covered with a whitish or bluish powdery or waxy film.

glume. In grasses, one of usually two sheathing bracts that form the lowest part of a spikelet.

head. (#11) A dense, flattened cluster of sessile (stalkless) flowers attached to a common receptacle.

herb. A plant with non-woody stems that dies to the ground each winter (includes annual, biennial, and perennial plants).

internode. The segment of a stem between two leaves or nodes.

keeled. Having a ridge or crease generally centered on the long axis of a structure.

lanceolate. (#30) Means narrow and tapering like the head of a lance.

leaflet. A leaflike unit of a compound leaf.

linear. (#31) Means that a leaf is much longer than wide (usually over ten times).

node. The joint of a stem where leaves, branches, or flowers arise.

oblanceolate. Inversion of lanceolate, with leaf blade wider instead of narrower above the middle portion.

oblong. (#39) Longer than wide with nearly parallel sides and rounded ends; wider than linear.

obovate. Inversion of ovate, with leaf blade wider above instead of below the middle of the leaf.

obtuse. (#24) Having a short-tapered, blunt tip or base; not acute.

opposite. (#19) Two leaves branch off a stem at the same point.

ovate. (#20) Egg-shaped, widest below the middle of the leaf.

palmate. (#29, and #34) Having lobes or divisions radiating from a central point.

palmately compound. (#21) Having a number of leaflets all arising from a single point.

panicle. (#17) Formation with irregularly-branched secondary stems, like a branched or compound raceme; also refers to the indeterminate seed-bearing tufts on grasses and other flowering plants.

perennial. Living for more than two years and not woody above ground.

petiolate. (#26) Having a short stem or petiole.

pinnate. (#25, #28, and #37) Having a main central axis with two sets of secondary branches or units on opposite sides of the axis.

pistillate. A flower with only a pistil or pistils (the female or seed bearing structure of a flower) and no stamens.

prostrate. Stems lying flat on the ground without the tips curling up. (see decumbent)

raceme. (#16) One central stem along which individual flowers grow on small primary stems at intervals from the base toward the apex (lower flowers bloom first).

rootstock. A horizontal underground stem rooting on its lower side.

rosette. A radiating cluster of leaves usually at the base of a plant.

serrate. (#22) Having margins with teeth pointing tipward.

sessile. (#38) Means a leaf has no stem.

sheath. The lower part of the leaf in grasses, sedges, etc. that wraps around the stem.

shrub. A woody plant with several branches near the base.

simple. (#18) Having a single leaf or stem, not compound.

sorus (pl. **sori**). The cluster of spore cases (sporangia) on the underside of fern fronds.

spike. (#14) An elongated, unbranched flower cluster with flowers attached directly to the central stalk.

spikelet. A secondary spike found in grasses and sedges.

spore. The reproductive unit of ferns and their relatives, similar to a seed.

staminate. A flower with only stamens (the male or pollen-bearing structure of a flower) and no pistils.

subshrub. A plant with lower woody stems, but the upper stems and twigs not woody and dying back each year.

ternate. Split into three small divisions.

umbel. (#12) A cluster of flowers with stalks of nearly equal length which arise from about the same point, like the ribs of an umbrella.

whorled. (#27) Having three or more similar structures (leaves, petals, etc.) encircling a single node.

Abbreviations and Symbols

*	=	edible plants
bldg.	=	buildings
coast.	=	coastal strand (beaches and dunes) and salt marshes
des.	=	desertlike areas
grass.	=	grassland
oak	=	oak woodland, and pine-oak woods
rocks	=	rocky areas in oak-pine woodland and shrubland
sav.	=	savanna
shrub.	=	shrubland (chaparral and coastal sage scrub)
spp.	=	species (plural)
ssp.	=	subspecies
str-wd.	=	streamside woodland
syn.	=	synonym
var.	=	variety
water	=	freshwater areas, marshes, sloughs, ponds, mudflats
n.	=	northern
e.	=	eastern
s.	=	southern
w.	=	western
c.	=	central
sw.	=	southwestern
cw.	=	central western

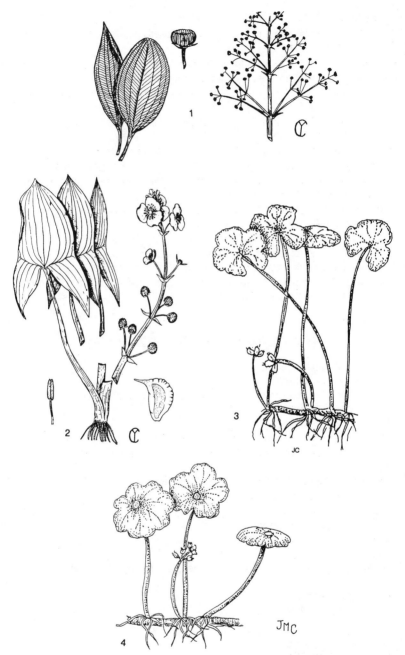

3.

Common Plants

The plant families and genera in this chapter are
listed in alphabetical order for ease of reference.

A. Freshwater Plants

ALISMATACEAE, WATER PLANTAIN FAMILY (leafless stems; flowers
have 3 white or pink petals)

1. ***Common Water Plantain,** *Alisma plantago-aquatica*. **[water]** Flowering
stem 2–4 ft. (6–12 dm) high; flowers generally white in pyramid-shaped
panicle of whorled branches; oblong to ovate leaves reach above the water
surface. Starchy bases of plant edible, but strong-flavored when fresh; best
used after thoroughly drying. Margins of ponds.

2. ***Common Arrowhead** or **Tule Potato,** *Sagittaria latifolia*. **[water]** Plant
8–47 in. (2–12 dm) tall, mostly underwater; leaves arrowhead-shaped on
long stalks; juice milky; flowers white in whorls of 3; seed with strong beak.
Starchy tubers at the end of rootstocks may be baked or boiled like
potatoes. Edge of ponds or slow streams, meadows.

APIACEAE, CARROT FAMILY (commonly with hollow stems and
flowers in umbels)

3. **Buttercup Water Pennywort,** *Hydrocotyle ranunculoides*. **[water]**
Plant floating or creeping on mud with roots in water; leaf blades
generally ¾–2 in. (2–5 cm) wide, rounded to kidney-shaped, with 3–7
round-toothed lobes; 5–10 flowers in umbels. Shallow waters and
shores of ponds and slow streams below 3,000 ft.

4. **Whorled Water Pennywort,** *Hydrocotyle verticillata*. **[water]** Similar
to *H. ranunculoides* but leaf blades 8–13 lobed and more rounded;
seeds on stems resemble a string of beads; erect leaves on long stems;
flowers in whorls or small hemispherical umbels.

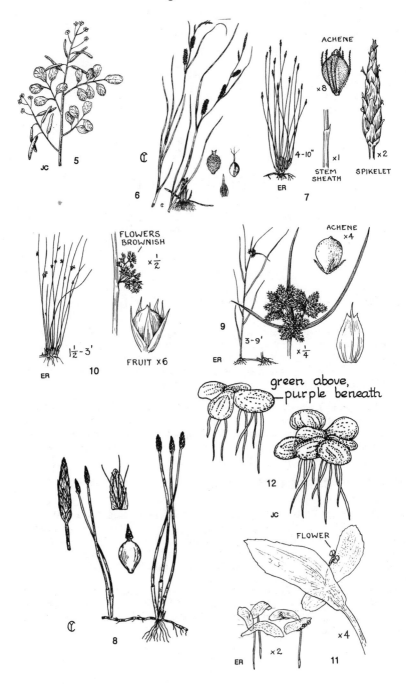

ACHENE

×8

STEM
SHEATH

SPIKELET

4-10"

×1

×2

JC 5

6

7

ER

FLOWERS
BROWNISH

×½

FRUIT ×6

½-3'

ER 10

ACHENE
×4

9

3-9'

ER

×¼

green above,
purple beneath

12

JC

FLOWER

8

×4

×2

ER 11

BRASSICACEAE, MUSTARD FAMILY (plants with pungent watery juice; 4-petaled crosslike flowers)

5. ***Water Cress,** *Rorippa nasturtium-aquaticum* (syn. *Nasturtium officinale*). **[water]** Stems 4–24 in. (1–6 dm) long, forming thick mats, or creeping up banks; tiny white flowers in clusters; generally 3–7 widely oblong to ovate, shiny green leaflets. Widely cultivated for edible greens. Wet banks and quiet water below 8,000 ft.

CYPERACEAE, SEDGE FAMILY (grasslike or rushlike herbs; stems usually solid and triangular)

6. **Woolly Sedge,** *Carex lanuginosa.* **[water, grass.]** Stems 12–39 in. (3–10 dm) high rising from long creeping roots, sharp-angled and rough to the feel; leaf blades 1/16–1/4 in. (2–6 mm) wide, flat, and rough, often exceeding stems in height; scales on flower spikes reddish-brown tinged. Generally in marshy places. (Note: Muntz treats 144 species of *Carex* in California, so this species may be easily confused.)

7. **Parish's Spike-Rush,** *Eleocharis parishii.* **[water]** Long, reddish rootstock; stems round, much grooved, 4–12 in. (1–3 dm) tall, with linear-lanceolate, many-flowered spikelets on top; spikelet much wider than stem; basal stem sheaths purplish brown, becoming straw-colored above; achene shiny, yellowish to light brown, with a well-defined nodule on top. Meadows and wet places.

8. **Common Spike-Rush,** *Eleocharis palustris.* **[water]** Plant 20–39 in. (.5–1 m) tall, pale green to dark green; similar to *E. parishii* but taller and spikelet not much wider than stem; flower bract brown to purplish. Widespread in marshes, pond margins, and ditches.

9. ***Pacific Coast Bulrush** or **Tule,** *Scirpus robustus.* **[water]** Sharply triangular stem 1½–5 ft. (5–15 dm) tall; long linear leaves flat to V-shaped, hairless except for midrib and margin, which are finely scabrous. There are many kinds of bulrushes or tules in California. *Scirpus* is a common genus. The roots of all its species are starchy and may be eaten raw or cooked. Marshes.

JUNCACEAE, RUSH FAMILY (round or two-edged stems)

10. **Spreading Rush,** *Juncus patens.* **[water, str-wd.]** Slender stems 1–3 ft. (3–9 dm) high, round and blue-green, densely tufted with light brown flowers. Moist places, such as stream banks and near springs.

LEMNACEAE, DUCKWEED FAMILY (tiny plants that float free on water)

11. **Star Duckweed,** *Lemna trisulca.* **[water]** Forms dense colonies of partly floating but mostly submerged fronds; tiny fronds are flattened, oblong to almost lanceolate, and 1/4–3/8 in. (6–10 mm) long; flower cluster enclosed by a saclike spathe. Cold springs, pools, and slow streams.

12. **Greater Duckweed** or **Water Flaxseed,** *Spirodela polyrhiza.* **[water]** Fronds solitary or united in groups of 2–5; fronds oblong to round, 3/16–3/8 in. (5–10 mm) long, flat, dark shiny green above, somewhat convex and red-purplish below. Quiet fresh water.

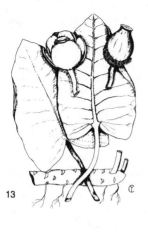

13

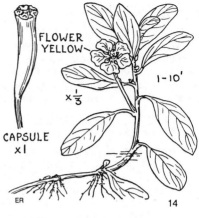

FLOWER YELLOW

CAPSULE x1

$\times \frac{1}{3}$

1-10'

ER

14

15

3 mm.

CY

16

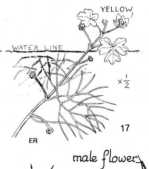

YELLOW

WATER LINE

$\times \frac{1}{2}$

ER

17

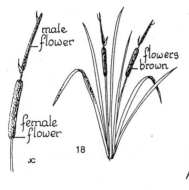

male flower

female flower

flowers brown

JC

18

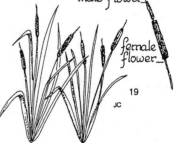

male flower

female flower

JC

19

NYMPHAEACEAE, WATER-LILY FAMILY

13. *Yellow Pond Lily, Nuphar luteum ssp. polysepalum. [water] Large yellow flower, 2¾–4¾ in. (7–12 cm) wide, often tinged red, with green sepals rounded and concave at the end of long stem; floating or emergent leaves long-stemmed, cordate to oval in shape, pinnately veined, 4–16 in. (1–4 dm) across. Core of tubers sweet and rich in starch; seeds can be popped and eaten like popcorn. Ponds and slow streams. Coast Ranges south to San Luis Obispo Co., Sierra Nevada south to Mariposa Co.

ONAGRACEAE, EVENING-PRIMROSE FAMILY

14. Creeping Water Primrose, Ludwigia peploides (syn. Jussiaea repens). [water] Creeping stems 1–10 ft. (3–30 dm) long, often matted or floating; flowers yellow, with 5 petals and 10 stamens; seeds large and tough. Lakeshores, ditches, and stream banks under 3,000 ft.

POTAMOGETONACEAE, PONDWEED FAMILY (stems jointed and leafy; submersed leaves thin)

15. *Long-Leaved Pondweed, Potamogeton nodosus. [water] Stem much branched, 3–6½ ft. (1–2 m) long; greenish flowers in short spike; submerged leaves grasslike; floating leaves thicker, elliptical to ovate, and 2–4 in. (5–9 cm) long. Starchy rootstocks are edible. Ponds and streams north of Orange Co.

16. Fennel-Leaf Pondweed, Potamogeton pectinatus. [water] Many-branched stem less than 31 in. (80 cm) long; threadlike leaves all submerged (no floating leaves); flowers in spike. Often weedy in reservoirs; an important food for waterfowl.

RANUNCULACEAE, BUTTERCUP FAMILY

17. Water Crowfoot Buttercup, Ranunculus aquatilus. [water] Often forms mats on the water. Submersed stems 8–24 in. (2–6 dm) long, rarely reaching 5 ft. (15 dm); submersed leaves disected into linear lobes resembling crow's feet; larger floating leaves, ⅜–¾ in. (1–2 cm) wide; sepals light green and half the length of the petals; 5 white petals, often yellow at bases. Ponds, lake margins, and slow streams.

TYPHACEAE, CATTAIL FAMILY (solid, jointless, and circular stems)

18. *Southern Cattail, Typha domingensis. [water] Plant 6½–13 ft. (2–4 m) tall; 6–9 light yellowish green leaves equaling or slightly exceeding upper spike, sheathing at base; short interval between male and female spikes. Young shoots may be eaten raw; both starchy rootstocks and immature flower spikes can be eaten after cooking them. Marshes.

19. *Broad-Leaved Cattail, Typha latifolia. [water] Plant 5–10 ft. (1.5–3 m) tall; 12–16 light green, swordlike leaves, exceeding stem in height, with sheaths at base; no interval between dark brown female spike and upper, greenish or yellowish male spike. Marshes, lakes, ponds.

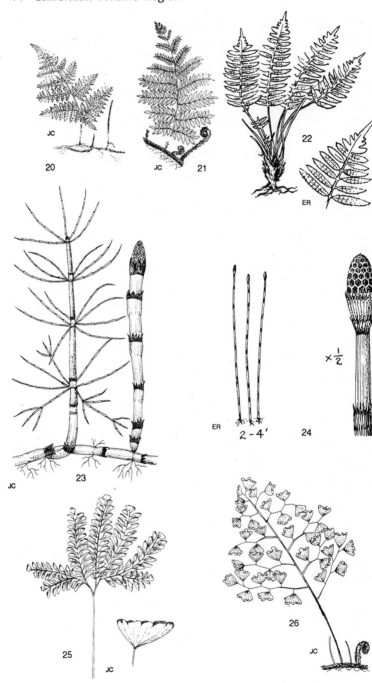

B. Ferns and Their Allies

Plants without seeds or flowers, reproducing by means of spores.

DENNSTAEDTIACEAE, BRACKEN FAMILY

20. Common Bracken Fern, *Pteridium aquilinum* var. *pubescens.* **[oak, shrub.]** Graceful fronds 1–5 ft. (3–15 dm) long; stalks stout, generally solitary; rootstocks black; stems light-colored and covered with tiny hairs underneath. Pastures, woods, meadows, hillsides in partial to full sunlight in many plant communities. Moist places at lower elevations; common groundcover in forests higher up. Not in Central Valley.

DRYOPTERIDACEAE, WOOD FERN FAMILY

21. Lady Fern, *Athyrium felix-femina* var. *cyclosorum.* **[str-wd. oak]** A large, lacy-looking fern, 2–5 ft. (6–15 dm) long; fronds delicate with drooping tips and finely-toothed subleaflets; stem straw-colored, smooth and brittle. Woods, along streams, and in meadows. Not in Central Valley or Peninsular Ranges.

22. Western Sword Fern, *Polystichum munitum).* **[oak, shrub.]** 1½–5 ft. (5–15 dm) long fern with stems covered with papery, needlelike brown scales; single long fronds appear in clumps; frond lobes with earlike protuberances on upperside of base. Wooded hillsides, shaded slopes in many plant communities. Not in the Sierra Nevada foothills or lower s. California.

EQUISETACEAE, HORSETAIL FAMILY (hollow, jointed stems)

23. Common Horsetail, *Equisetum arvense.* **[str-wd. water]** Two kinds of stems: sterile stems 4–24 in. (10–60 cm) tall, green, ridged, with slender branches in dense whorls at joints; separate fertile stems 2–10 in. (5–25 cm) tall, branchless, pink-brown, bear the spores in cones. Wet places in woods and meadows.

24. Common Scouring Rush, *Equisetum hyemale* **ssp.** *affine.* **[str-wd.]** Stems 2–6 ft. (6–18 dm) high, rigid, ridged, and evergreen, unbranched except when injured; each joint has a small ashy-colored sheath with black bands at each end; spores borne in oval cones at top. Can be used to scour eating utensils and pots. Along stream banks, sandy or gravelly areas.

PTERIDACEAE, BRAKE FAMILY

25. Northern Maidenhair or **Five-Finger Fern,** *Adiantum aleuticum.* **[rocks, str-wd.]** Fronds close together, erect, 8–31 in. (2–8 dm) high; stalks stout and reddish brown to blackish; horizontally held, fan-shaped leaflets in 5-finger shape distinctive. Shady, moist banks, streamsides, on serpentine in moist woods and canyons. More common in the north, but as far south as the Transverse Ranges.

26. Southern Maidenhair or **Venus-Hair Fern,** *Adiantum capillus-veneris.* **[rocks, str-wd.]** Fronds 8–27 in. (2–7 dm) long,

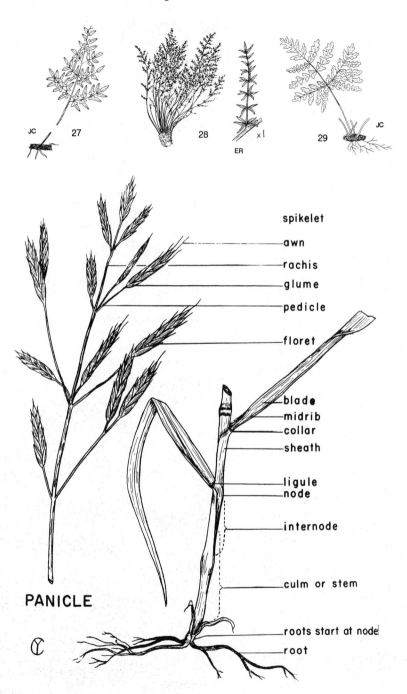

JC   27

28   x l

ER

29   JC

spikelet
awn
rachis
glume
pedicle
floret

blade
midrib
collar
sheath

ligule
node

internode

culm or stem

roots start at node
root

PANICLE

ascending to pendent (hanging), with slender, purplish black stems as long as the blades or a bit shorter. Shady, rocky or moist banks. Coast Ranges, Cascade and n. Sierra Nevada foothills, outer South Coast Ranges, and lower s. California except on the coast.

27. **Coffee Fern**, *Pellaea andromedifolia*. **[rocks, shrub. oak]** Fronds 6–27 in. (1.5–7 dm) long, with straw-colored stems; scales tan to orange-brown. Leaves dull green to red-purple above. Dry rocky areas. Baja, California to Mendicino and Butte counties.

28. **Bird's-foot Fern**, *Pellaea mucronata*. **[rocks, shrub. oak]** Fronds 6–19 in. (1.5–5 dm) long; rigid, erect stems dry, wirelike, and purplish brown; blades 2–3 times pinnate; pinnules (smallest segments of the fronds) usually ternate, resembling a bird's foot. Dry rocky slopes, especially in coastal sage scrub, chaparral, and foothill woodland.

29. **Goldenback Fern**, *Pentagramma triangularis*. **[rocks, oak, shrub.]** Fronds 4–16 in. (1–4 dm) long and clustered; dark brown stems are shiny; blades triangular or generally 5-sided; undersides have a white to yellow, waxy powder that comes off on your hands. Shaded slopes or rocky places.

C. Grasses

Parts of a typical grass *To help identify grasses the illustration to the left shows parts of a complete grass. The illustration below shows parts of a floret.*

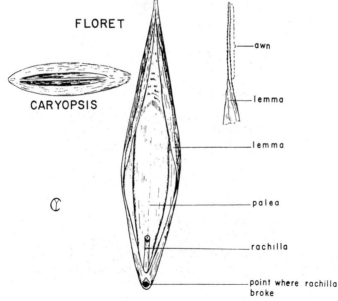

FLORET

CARYOPSIS

awn

lemma

lemma

palea

rachilla

point where rachilla broke

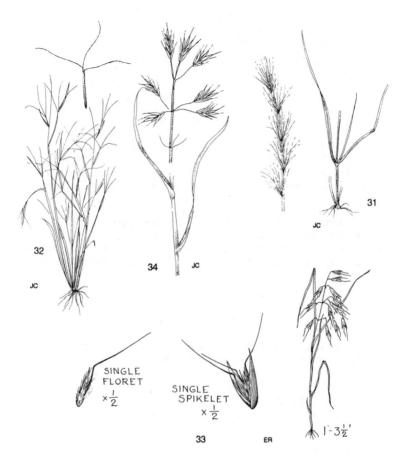

32
JC

34 JC

31
JC

SINGLE
FLORET
×½

SINGLE
SPIKELET
×½

33   ER

1'-3½'

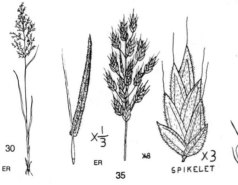

30
ER

×⅓

ER

35   ×8

×3
SPIKELET

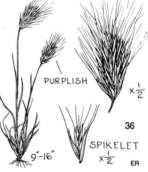

PURPLISH

×½

36

9"-16"

SPIKELET
×½   ER

POACEAE, GRASS FAMILY (stems usually round and hollow; flowers with no visible petals)

30. **Redtop,** *Agrostis gigantea.* **[grass. oak, shrub.]** Perennial, 8–39 in. (2–10 dm) tall, usually erect, but sometimes bent over; 1 or more stems rise from numerous creeping rootstocks; panicle purplish to green, 4–12 in. (1–3 dm) long, pyramid-shaped, with rather dense whorls of branches. An important meadow grass, also used in lawn seed mixtures. Roadsides, fields, disturbed areas. Introduced from Europe.

31. **Six-Weeks Three-Awn,** *Aristida adscensionis.* **[des. rocks, shrub. grass.]** Annual, 2–28 in. (5–70 cm), stems branching at base; panicle narrow and rather dense; awns about ½ in. (1–1.5 cm) long. Dry, open places, rocky sites, shrubland. E. San Luis Obispo Co. to deserts, South Coast, Transverse, and Peninsular ranges.

32. **Oldfield Three-Awn,** *Aristida oligantha.* **[grass. oak, shrub.]** Wiry, almost leafless plants. Annual, much branched stem 12–28 in. (3–7 dm) long; panicle open 4–10 in. (1–2.5 dm) long; spikelets without stems spreading; each floret with 3 nearly equal awns 1½–2¾ in. (4–7 cm) long. The sharp-pointed, barbed callus of the floret easily penetrates hair or clothing. Dry slopes, fields, grassland, shrubland, foothill woodland.

33. ***Wild Oats,** *Avena fatua.* **[grass. oak, shrub.]** Annual, 1–4 ft. (3–12 dm) tall; panicle open and loosely arranged; spikelets usually 3-flowered; each floret is protected by two bracts with a stout, bent awn extending from each one. The sheaths of the joints of young wild oats are edible as are the seeds. Waste and cultivated areas. Introduced from Europe.

34. **California Brome,** *Bromus carinatus.* **[grass. oak, shrub.]** Perennial, 20–59 in. (5–15 dm) tall; stems and leaf blades scaley or partially covered with soft hairs; blades flat and 8–12 in. (2–3 dm) long; sheaths rough to touch; panicle 6–12 in. (1.5–3 dm) long with spreading or drooping branches. Many plant communities in dry open places (not common in Central Valley).

35. **Soft Chess,** *Bromus hordeaceus.* **[grass. oak, shrub.]** Annual, soft-hairy all over; stems 8–31 in. (2–8 dm) high; sheaths bent backward; panicle erect, 2–4 in. (5–10 cm) long; lowest glume (or bract) of each spikelet floret has an awn, or bristle. Open, often disturbed places.

36. **Foxtail Chess,** *Bromus madritensis* ssp. *rubens.* **[grass. oak, shrub.]** Annual, stems 6–18 in. (1.5–4 dm) high, with dense, erect, bristly, reddish panicle, ¾–2¾ in. (2–7 cm) long, at top; leaf sheaths and blades covered with dense, soft hairs; spikelets have 7–11 florets (tiny flowers). In waste and cultivated areas at low elevations.

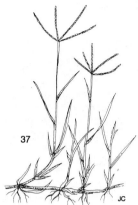

37

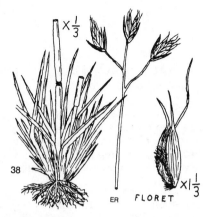

$\times \frac{1}{3}$

38

ER FLORET $\times 1\frac{1}{3}$

39

JC

40

JC

41

ER

42

ER $\times \frac{1}{2}$

leafless stems

43

JC papery flower cluster

44

14"-30" ER

37. Bermuda Grass, *Cynodon dactylon.* **[grass. oak, shrub. des.]** Stems 4–16 in. (1–4 dm) long, flattened, wiry, rising from rough, woody rootstocks. A perennial that spreads over the ground in rootstalks and trailing stems, showing 4–5 slender spikes at top of each stem; glumes purplish. Forms very tough sod in fields, lawns, orchards, etc. Introduced from Africa.

38. California Oatgrass, *Danthonia californica.* **[grass. oak, shrub.]** Perennial, 4–39 in. (1–10 dm) tall; panicle small with 1–5 large spikelets on spreading stems; leaf blades usually flat, hairless to densely hairy; the basal sheathing bracts (or glumes) of the spikelets may be swollen and contain thin, distorted spikelets. Generally moist, open sites, meadows, open woods.

39. Saltgrass, *Distichlis spicata.* **[coast.]** Perennial, erect stems, 4–20 in. (1–5 dm) long, rise from stout, yellowish rootstocks. Forms tough patches of stiff grass, spreading scaly runners over the ground to form new plants; upper leaf blades often exceed panicle, which is green or purplish and club-shaped with 8–35 crowded spikelets. Salt marshes, moist, alkaline areas.

40. Stinkgrass, *Eragrostis cilianensis.* **[grass. oak, shrub. des.]** Annual, 8–20 in. (2–5 dm) tall, with spreading to ascending stems; strong, musty odor when fresh; panicles pyramidal or ovoid in shape, dense, 2–8 in. (5–20 cm) long, gray-green; leaf blades have wartlike glands on the margins. Cultivated and waste areas. Introduced from Europe.

41. Common Velvetgrass, *Holcus lanatus.* **[grass. oak, shrub.]** Perennial, 24–78 in. (6–20 dm) tall; shade loving; whole plant grayish green and covered with soft, velvety hairs; panicle about 3–6 in. (8–15 cm) long, closely flowered, pale, and purplish-tinged; each spikelet has two florets, one of which has no awn; awn on other floret bent. Likes moist ground of cultivated fields, meadows, roadsides. Introduced from Europe.

42. Mouse Barley, *Hordeum murinum* s s p. *glaucum.* **[grass. oak, shrub.]** Summer annual, 4–24 in. (1–6 dm) tall, with dense, bristly spikes similar to Foxtail Chess but flatter; sheaths hairless; most of the basal bracts on the spikelets are bordered with hairs; awns at ends of bracts about 1 in. (2–3 cm) long. Moist, generally disturbed places, fields. Introduced from Europe.

43. Junegrass, *Koeleria macrantha.* **[grass. oak, shrub.]** Perennial, stems 8–28 in. (2–7 dm) tall; plants in clumps; slender, erect stems end in dense spikes of yellowish or silvery green spikelets; leafy at base, blades slender and stiffly upright; lower leaf sheaths covered with soft hairs. Dry, open places, clay to rocky soil, shrubland, woodland.

44. Italian Ryegrass, *Lolium multiflorum.* **[grass. oak, shrub.]** Annual, 16–32 in. (4–8 dm) tall, usually erect but sometimes partly lying on the ground, pale or yellowish at base; spike sometimes as much as a foot

45   $1'-3\frac{1}{3}'$ ER

48   $1\frac{1}{2}'-3\frac{1}{3}'$ ×2 SPIKELET   ER

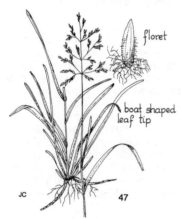

floret

boat shaped leaf tip

JC   47

46   CY

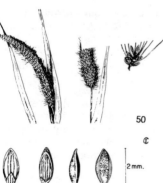

50

2 mm.

51   JC

49   JC

(3 dm) long and nodding; spikelets with 10–20 tiny flowers. Common lawn grass but prevalent elsewhere, especially in the Coast Ranges. Introduced from Europe.

45. Purple Needlegrass, *Nassella pulchra.* **[grass. oak, shrub.]** Perennial, stems 12–39 in. (3–10 dm) tall; leaf blades deep green, flat or rolled inward at the margins; panicle nodding, loose, 7–24 in. (1.8–6 dm) long, with slender, spreading branches; awn or bristle of each floret rough, usually bent twice, and 2⅜–3½ in. (6–9 cm) long; lower bracts purplish. Oak woodland, chapparral, grassland.

46. Hood Canary Grass, *Phalaris paradoxa.* **[grass. shrub.]** Annual, 1–2 ft. (3–6 dm) tall, usually spreading at the base; leaf blades flat; 5–6 sterile spikelets surround single fertile one; short awn only on bract of fertile spikelet. Grain fields, waste areas. Central Valley, sw. California. Introduced from Europe.

47. Kentucky Bluegrass, *Poa pratensis* ssp. *pratensis.* **[grass. oak, shrub. str-wd.]** Perennial, generally 8–28 in. (2–7 dm) tall; ribbonlike leaves green or blue-green, soft and smooth, scattered on stem, the basal leaves up to 1 ft. (3 dm) long; panicle open and pyramid-shaped; tiny spikelets green or purplish; plants form dense sod. Meadows, fields, stream banks, open woods. Turns brown during hot summer months.

48. One-Sided Bluegrass, *Poa secunda* ssp. *secunda.* (syn. *Poa scabrella*) **[grass. oak, shrub.]** Perennial, 6–39 in. (1.5–10 dm) tall; slender, erect, smooth or scaley stems; basal leaves soft and slender; panicle linear to lanceolate, generally dense and more or less 1-sided, with branches appressed to ascending (spreading only in flowering); the basal bracts of spikelets feel rough. Good soils on open or protected hillsides.

49. Rabbitfoot Grass or **Annual Beard Grass,** *Polypogon monspeliensis.* **[str-wd. grass. oak, shrub.]** Stems 8–39 in. (2–10 dm) tall; panicle thick, ¾–6 in. (2–15 cm) long, not more than ¾ in. (2 cm) wide, densely covered with soft, silky, yellowish awns. Waste places at low elevations; frequent on damp ground around springs or stream banks. Introduced from Europe.

50. Green Foxtail, *Setaria viridis.* **[grass. oak, shrub.]** Annual, 8–39 in. (2–10 dm) tall, much branched at base; leaf blades narrow, hairless; panicle soft, ¾–6 in. (2–15 cm) long, green or rarely purplish, densely flowered, slightly nodding near tip. Cultivated and waste areas, roadsides. Introduced from Eurasia.

51. California Cord Grass, *Spartina foliosa.* **[coast.]** Course perennial from a strong, creeping rootstock; stem thick, solitary or in clumps, 24–59 in. (6–15 dm) tall; leaf blades wide at base, flat or inrolled at tip; panicle dense, cylindrical. Salt marshes, mudflats, and shores along the entire coast.

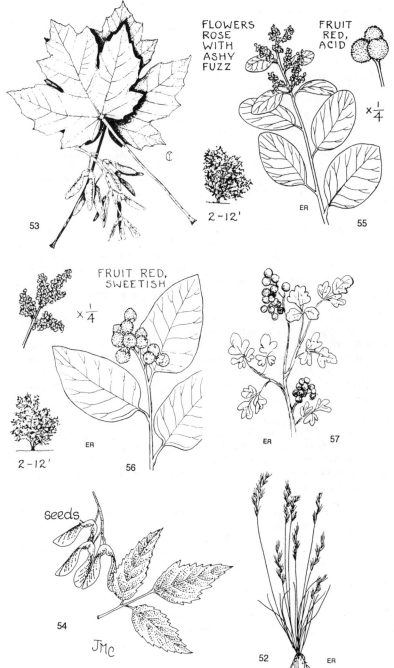

FLOWERS
ROSE
WITH
ASHY
FUZZ

FRUIT
RED,
ACID

$\times \frac{1}{4}$

2-12'

53

55

ER

FRUIT RED,
SWEETISH

$\times \frac{1}{4}$

2-12'

56

ER

57

ER

seeds

54

JMC

52

ER

52. **Six-weeks Fescue**, *Vulpia octoflora*. **[grass. oak, shrub.]** Annual, slender grass, stems 2–16 in. (5–40 cm) tall, hairless or with tiny soft hairs; tiny spikelets about ¼ in. (5–10 mm) long in a raceme. Grows quickly after rain, then dies, leaving seeds. Open area, sandy to rocky soil.

D. Trees, Shrubs, Subshrubs, and Vines

ACERACEAE, MAPLE FAMILY (fruits in ribbed, 2-winged pairs)

53. **Big Leaf Maple**, *Acer macrophyllum*. **[str-wd. oak]** Wide-topped tree 16–98 ft. (5–30 m) tall; twigs course, greenish to brownish; large, deciduous leaves palmately lobed; tiny flowers in drooping racemes; 2-winged fruits brown-hairy. Not in Central Valley.

54. **Box Elder**, *Acer negundo* var. *californicum*. **[str-wd. grass. oak]** Round-topped tree, 20–65 ft. (6–20 m) tall; branchlets slender, hairy, greenish; leaves have 3–5 pinnately compound leaflets (usually 3); leaflets 2–4¾ in. (5–12 cm) long, toothed, central leaflet largest; small flowers yellowish green hang on drooping, slender stalks; 2-winged fruits have less than 45 degree spread between wings. Streamsides, bottomlands in many plant communities. Common ornamental tree.

ANACARDIACEAE, SUMAC FAMILY (generally aromatic trees or shrubs, sometimes with milky resin)

55. ***Lemonade Berry**, *Rhus integrifolia*. **[shrub. oak]** Forms dense thickets; rounded aromatic shrub or small tree 3–26 ft. (1–8 m) high. Branchlets finely hairy, stout, reddish; evergreen leaves 1–2⅜ in. (2.5–6 cm) long, oblong-ovate, nearly flat, tip more or less obtuse, margin entire to toothed; flowers white to pinkish in dense, stout panicles; berries reddish, flattened, glandular-hairy. A lemonade-like drink can be made with the berries. Canyons, usually north-facing slopes, ocean bluffs, in coastal sage scrub, chaparral, and s. oak woodland. Santa Barbara Co. to n. Baja, inland to Riverside Co.

56. ***Sugar Bush**, *Rhus ovata*. **[shrub. oak]** Evergreen shrub or small tree 6½–33 ft. (2–10 m) tall; branchlets hairless, stout, reddish; leaves widely ovate, leathery, 1½–3 in. (4–8 cm) long, folded along the mid-rib, tip more or less acute, margin entire; flowers in stout-branched panicle; sepals red with hair on margins; petals white to pinkish; fruit reddish, glandular-hairy, edible. Canyons, usually south-facing slopes in chaparral and s. oak woodland, usually not on coast. Santa Barbara Co. south to n. Baja.

57. ***Skunkbrush** or **Squaw Bush**, *Rhus trilobata*. **[shrub. oak]** Diffusely branched shrub, 20–98 in. (5–25 dm) high; branches spreading, often turned down at tips, strongly aromatic when crushed; outer branchlets hairy; leaves deciduous, thin, flat, generally 3-lobed or with 3 leaflets; yellowish flowers in clustered spikes appear before leaves in spring; edible fruit generally bright orange, covered with soft,

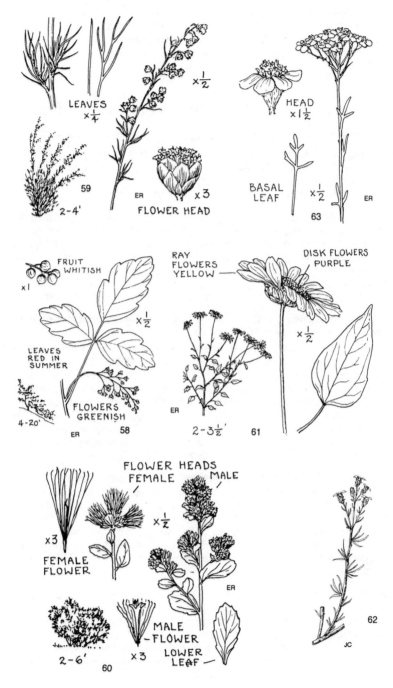

LEAVES
×¼

59

2-4'

×½

ER ×3

FLOWER HEAD

HEAD
×1½

BASAL
LEAF

×½

ER

63

FRUIT
WHITISH

×1

×½

LEAVES
RED IN
SUMMER

FLOWERS
GREENISH

4-20'

ER

58

RAY
FLOWERS
YELLOW

DISK FLOWERS
PURPLE

×½

ER

2-3½'

61

FLOWER HEADS
FEMALE   MALE

×½

×3

FEMALE
FLOWER

MALE
FLOWER

LOWER
LEAF

ER

2-6'

60

×3

62

JC

sticky hairs. Slopes, canyons, washes, especially in the interior valleys, in chaparral, foothill woodland, and coastal sage scrub.

58. **Western Poison Oak**, *Toxicodendron diversilobum*. **[oak, shrub. sav.]** Erect bushy shrub, 2–13 ft. (6-40 dm) high, sometimes a vine up to 82 ft. (25 m) long; twigs gray-brown to red-brown; leaflets in 3s (the third usually larger than the lower two), ¾–2¾ in. (2–7 cm) long, bright shiny green above, usually turning bright red in early fall, margins entire, wavy or slightly lobed; tiny whitish fruits spherical; can cause severe dermatitis when touched. Oak woodlands and chaparral but in many plant communities, usually shaded.

ASTERACEAE, SUNFLOWER OR DAISY FAMILY (most sunflowers have heads consisting of outer ray flowers and central, tubular disk flowers)

59. **California Sagebrush**, *Artemisia californica*. **[shrub. coast.]** Shrub 2–8 ft. (6–25 dm) tall, often broader than high, branched from base; leaves light green to gray, pinnately divided into threadlike lobes, more or less hairy, margins curled under; many tiny flower heads in long, leafy racemelike panicles. Coastal strand, coastal sage scrub, chaparral, dry foothills, esp. near coast. Central w. and sw. California to n. Baja.

60. **Chaparral Broom** or **Coyote Brush**, *Baccharis pilularis*. **[shrub. coast. oak]** Shrub under 10 ft. (3 m) tall, sticky; stems prostrate to erect; branches spreading or ascending; leaves oblanceolate to obovate, toothed to entire; flower heads numerous, small, yellowish white; white, feathery seeds appear in fall. Coastal strand, coastal sage scrub, northern coastal scrub, and oak woodland in most of region.

61. **California Encelia**, *Encelia californica*. **[shrub.]** Much-branched, broadly rounded shrub, 20–59 in. (5"15 dm) tall; green leaves scattered along stems, diamond-shaped or narrowly ovate, acute; solitary heads with yellow ray flowers and brown-purple disk flowers. Coastal sage scrub and chaparral near the coast from Santa Barbara Co. to n. Baja; also in w. Transverse and w. Peninsular ranges.

62. **Coastal Goldenbush** or **Mock Heather**, *Ericameria ericoides*. **[coast. shrub.]** Broad, compact shrub less than 39 in. (1 m) tall, with clustered, parallel branches; herbage somewhat resinous; leaves very numerous, threadlike; flowering heads in paniclelike clusters; bracts fringed with long, soft hairs; ray flowers 2–6, yellow; disk flowers 8–14, yellow. Sand dunes and sandy soil in the hills near the coast. Marin Co. south to Los Angeles Co. There are numerous species and varieties of goldenbush in California.

63. **Golden Yarrow**, *Eriophyllum confertiflorum*. **[oak, shrub. grass.]** Subshrub or shrub, usually 8–27½ in. (2–7 dm) tall, with many erect stems; very leafy below, less so above; leaves and stems soft-hairy; leaves deeply 3–5 lobed, segments linear; many heads with deep yellow ray flowers in small terminal clusters. Dry habitats in many plant communities. Not in Central Valley.

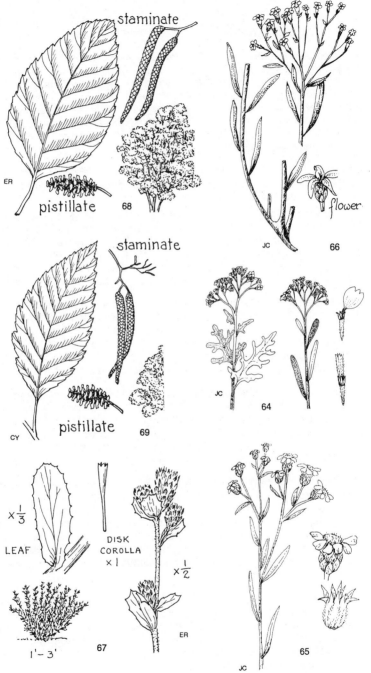

staminate

pistillate 68

ER

staminate

pistillate 69

CY

flower

JC 66

JC 64

×⅓

LEAF

DISK
COROLLA
×1

×½

ER

1'–3' 67

65

JC

64. Seaside Woolly Sunflower, *Eriophyllum staechadifolium.* **[shrub.]** Much-branched subshrub, 12–59 in. (3–15 dm) high; stems decumbent to erect; leaves linear to linear-oblanceolate, entire or pinnately compound, with rolled-under margins; yellow flower heads in dense corymbs. Sand dunes and coastal scrub under 300 ft. Central coast from Santa Barbara Co. northward.

65. California Snakeweed or **Matchweed,** *Gutierrezia californica.* **[oak, shrub. grass]** Erect or spreading subshrub, 8–24 in. (2–6 dm) high, with many stiff, rough-feeling branches; stems sometimes reddish; leaves linear; yellow flower heads in corymbs, heads somewhat match-shaped (hence the common name); bracts green-tipped. Grassland, woodland, outcrops, shrubland under 1,000 ft. Not in the Sierra Nevada or Cascade foothills and not in the Sacramento Valley.

66. Broom Snakeweed or **Matchweed,** *Gutierrezia sarothrae.* **[shrub. grass. des.]** Many green or tan, erect or spreading stems form a round shrublet, 4–24 in. (1–6 dm) tall, with hundreds of tiny yellow flower heads in loose clusters; heads somewhat match-shaped; leaves resinous, lance-linear if solitary, threadlike if clustered. Bundles of dried stems were used to make brooms. Grassland, desert, scrub. South coast from Point Conception to Baja and in the Transverse and Peninsular ranges.

67. Saw-Toothed Goldenbush, *Hazardia squarrosa.* **[shrub.]** Shrub 12–90 in. (3–23 dm) tall, usually resinous, many stemmed, woody at base; leaves many, sessile, leathery, oblong to obovate, sharply saw-toothed; flower heads with 9–30 red-tinged disk flowers only; pappus, or fluffy end of the achene, yellow-tawny. Coastal sage scrub and chaparral (inland as far as s. San Joaquin Valley) from Marin Co. to n. Baja. Another common goldenbush, *Isocoma menziesii*, forms mats of rounded or open bushes.

BETULACEAE, BIRCH FAMILY (thin, smooth bark; leaves alternate and simple)

68. White Alder, *Alnus rhombifolia.* **[str-wd.]** Generally 33–70 ft. (10–21 m) tall, maximum height 115 ft. (35 m), straight trunk and open, rounded crown; bark whitish or gray-brown; green leaves thick, ovate or elliptical with a double row of serrate (fine or course) edges, 2–4⅜ in. (5–11 cm) long; flowers appear in winter and early spring before the leaves: male yellowish in elongate, drooping catkins; female reddish in cones ⅜–¾ in. (1–2 cm) long. Many plant communities along permanent streams; not in Central Valley.

69. Red Alder, *Alnus rubra.* **[str-wd. shrub.]** 40–82 ft. (12–25 m) tall, straight trunk and pointed or rounded crown; bark thin, smooth, mottled, light gray to whitish; inner bark red-brown; branchlets light green when young, turning bright, deep red with age; leaves ovate to elliptical and acute with a double row of serrate edges, dark yellowish green above, paler and rusty-hairy below. Streamsides and marshy places below 3,000 ft. Coastal California from Santa Barbara north.

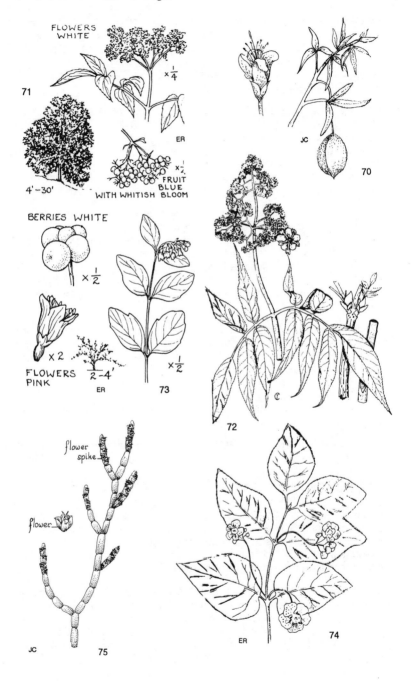

FLOWERS
WHITE

71

$\times \frac{1}{4}$

ER

4'–30'

$\times \frac{1}{2}$
FRUIT
BLUE
WITH WHITISH BLOOM

JC

70

BERRIES WHITE

$\times \frac{1}{2}$

$\times 2$

FLOWERS
PINK

2–4'

ER

$\times \frac{1}{2}$

73

72

flower
spike

flower

JC   75

ER   74

CAPPARACEAE, CAPER FAMILY

70. **Bladderpod,** *Isomeris arborea.* **[shrub. des. coast.]** Rounded shrub, generally 20–78 in. (5–20 dm) tall, profusely branched, minutely hairy, ill-smelling with watery sap; leaves generally consist of 3 oblong-elliptic leaflets; yellow flowers in terminal racemes; large, light brown bladderlike capsules on stalks; large, smooth seeds. Desert flats and washes; numerous in subalkaline hills, bluffs, and stable dunes in coastal sage scrub from San Luis Obispo Co. to Baja; San Joaquin Valley, s. Sierra Nevada foothills and Tehachapi Mountains into desert.

CAPRIFOLIACEAE, HONEYSUCKLE FAMILY

71. ***Blue Elderberry,** *Sambucus mexicana.* **[str-wd. oak]** Shrub, 6½–26 ft. (2–8 m) tall, generally as wide as tall and lacking a main trunk; leaves often fall off in dry season, pinnately compound of 3–9 leaflets; leaflets hairy or not, serrate; white flowers in flat-topped panicles; round berries nearly black but densely white-glaucous so as to appear blue. The fruit is sweet and juicy, and makes good pies and jellies. Stream banks, open places in woods.

72. **Red Elderberry,** *Sambucus racemosa.* **[str-wd. oak, shrub.]** Shrub 6½–19 ft. (2–6 m) tall; leaves deciduous to almost evergreen, 5–7 leaflets; leaflets 2–6 in. (5–16 cm) long, lanceolate to oblong-ovate, sharply serrate, hairy along veins below; white flowers in more or less dome-shaped panicles; berries bright red, not glaucous. Red elderberries have been reported toxic from some localities, edible in others. Moist places in many plant communities.

73. **Common Snowberry,** *Symphoricarpos albus* var. *laevigatus.* **[str-wd. oak]** Plant 2–6 ft. (6–18 dm) tall with stiff, spreading, graceful branches; deciduous leaves ¾–2 in. (2–5 cm) long, dark green, oval, smooth above; flowers bell-shaped, pink, 5-lobed with hairy throats, in short-stemmed racemes; berries pulpy, white, may be toxic to humans. Stream banks, north slopes, shady woods in mixed evergreen forests, foothill woodland, and yellow pine forest. Coast Ranges and coast, sw. California, n. Sierra Nevada foothills, w. edge of the Cascades.

CELASTRACEAE, STAFF-TREE FAMILY

74. **Western Burning Bush,** *Euonymus occidentalis.* **[str-wd. shrub.]** Deciduous shrub or small tree, 6½–19 ft. (2–6 m) tall; branches slender, smooth, often climbing; leaves thin, opposite, ovate to obovate, 1⅛–5½ in. 3–14 cm) long, fine-toothed; hanging flowers have 5 brown-purple, round, speckled petals; fruit a smooth, deeply 3-lobed capsule. Shaded stream banks, canyons, mixed evergreen woods, yellow and closed cone pine forests. Peninsular Ranges, Santa Barbara Co. north in Coast Ranges and near coast.

CHENOPODIACEAE, GOOSEFOOT FAMILY (usually grayish to whitish, scaly or glaucous, i. e. having a powdery or waxy film)

75. **Iodine Bush,** *Allenrolfea occidentalis.* **[des.]** Shrub, 20–79 in. (5–20 dm) tall, woody, somewhat glaucous; stems much branched, jointed;

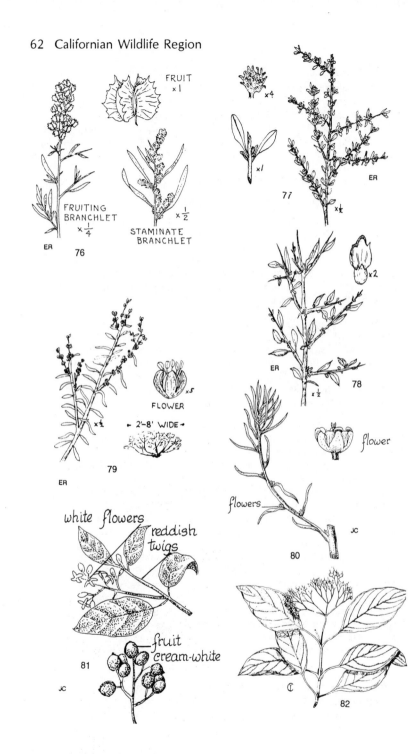

FRUIT
×1

×4

×1

ER

77

FRUITING
BRANCHLET
×¼

STAMINATE
BRANCHLET

ER   76

×½

×2

ER

78

×½

×5

FLOWER

← 2'–8' WIDE →

79

ER

flower

flowers

80

JC

white flowers

reddish
twigs

fruit
cream-white

81

JC

82

℃

leaves triangular, scalelike, clasped to the stems. Alkaline places such as San Joaquin Valley flats; deserts.

76. **Four-Wing Saltbush** or **Shadscale**, *Atriplex canescens.* **[des.]** Shrub, 16–79 in. (4–20 dm) tall, much-branched, round in shape; leaves linear to oblanceolate, 3/8–2 in. (1–5 cm) long, densely white-scaly; flowers in long, spikelike panicles; fruiting bracts topped with 2 teeth, 4-winged on sides. Salt flats, semideserts, arid foothills from San Benito and San Luis Obispo cos. south to San Diego Co.

77. **Many-Fruited Saltbush**, *Atriplex polycarpa.* **[des.]** Shrub, 20–79 in. (5–20 dm) high, intricately-branched; leaves light gray, crowded on young twigs, oblong to narrowly oblanceolate, lost in hot weather; main branches stiff, small branches spinelike; fruiting bracts broad and shallowly to deeply toothed at top and sides. Alkaline soils below 5,000 ft. in creosote, shadscale, sagebrush scrubs. San Joaquin and adjacent interior valleys, etc.

78. **Spinescale**, *Atriplex spinifera.* **[des.]** Shrub, 1–6 1/2 ft. (3–20 dm) high, taller than broad, with many ascending to erect branches; twigs become rigid, divergent spines; leaves light gray, dropping off in summer; fruiting bracts strongly convex below. S. San Joaquin Valley, inner South Coast Ranges, nw. Transverse Ranges.

79. ***Bush Seepweed**, *Suaeda moquinii.* **[des.]** Shrub 8–59 in. (2–15 dm) tall; annual stems shiny yellow-brown, spreading or erect, glaucuous; leaves yellow-green or red, linear to narrowly lanceolate; sepals of flowers deeply cleft, green; stems die after flowering. Young plants of this genus are edible as greens and have a salty flavor; seeds can be eaten raw or parched. Alkaline places below 5,250 ft. San Joaquin Valley to San Diego Co., Inyo Co., Lassen Co. into Wyomming, etc.

80. ***Woolly Sea-Blite**, *Suaeda taxifolia.* **[coast.]** Shrub less than 59 in. (15 dm) long, usually densely hairy and glaucuous; stems spreading or erect, dull gray-brown; leaves crowded on branches, lanceolate to linear, 1/2–1 in. (1.5–3 cm) long; flowers in clusters throughout plant, 1–3 per cluster. Coastal bluffs, edges of salt marshes below 50 ft. elevation. South coast, Santa Barbara Co. to n. Baja.

CORNACEAE, DOGWOOD FAMILY

81. **Brown Dogwood**, *Cornus glabrata.* **[str-wd. oak, shrub.]** Thicket-forming shrub or small tree, 6 1/2–20 ft. (2–6 m) tall; smooth, slender branches brownish to reddish purple; leaves gray-green, lanceolate to elliptic, almost smooth above, 3/4–2 in. (2–5 cm) long; tiny flowers appear in many-flowered, round to nearly flat-topped clusters; fruit white to bluish. Many plant communities, usually in moist places; not as common in s. California.

82. **American Dogwood**, *Cornus sericea.* **[str-wd. oak, shrub.]** Shrub generally 5–13 ft. (1.5–4 m) tall. Very hard-wooded shrub; branches smooth, reddish to purplish, older stems grayish green; leaves 2–4 in.

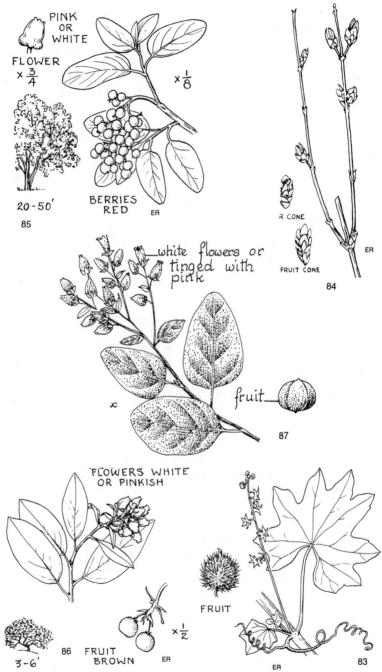

PINK
OR
WHITE

FLOWER
× 3/4

× 1/8

20-50'

85

BERRIES
RED

ER

R CONE

FRUIT CONE

ER

84

_white flowers or
tinged with
pink

fruit

JC

87

FLOWERS WHITE
OR PINKISH

86 FRUIT
BROWN

3-6'

× 1/2

ER

FRUIT

ER

83

(5–10 cm) long, ovate to lanceolate, dark green and smooth above in maturity, covered with soft white hairs when young; flowers 4-petaled, white, in cymes; fruit white to cream. Highly variable species with many local forms. Many plant communities, usually in moist places.

CUCURBITACEAE, GOURD FAMILY

83. **Common Wild Cucumber** or **Man-Root**, *Marah fabaceus*. **[str-wd. oak, coast. shrub. sav.]** Perennial with vinelike stems, generally 10–23 ft. (3–7 m) long, often tangled, with branching tendrils; leaves thin, 2–4 in. (5–10 cm) broad, palmately 5–7 lobed, more or less cordate; tiny flowers numerous, yellowish green, cream, or white, in racemes; fruit spiny, round and green. Stream banks, washes, shrubby and open areas in foothill woods, chaparral, coastal strand; many plant communities.

EPHEDRACEAE, EPHEDRA FAMILY

84. **Desert Tea**, or **Mormon Tea**, *Ephedra californica*. **[des. shrub. grass.]** Erect or spreading shrub, generally 1–3 ft. (3–9 dm) high, with light greenish stems and scalelike leaves; scales and fruiting bracts (equivalent to cones in pines) arranged in 3's; bracts light yellow to reddish brown. Scattered in dry grassland and chaparral in the s. Sierra Nevada foothills, Tehachapi Mtns., w. San Joaquin Valley, South Coast Ranges, and sw. California to Baja.

ERICACEAE, HEATH FAMILY

85. ***Pacific Madrone**, *Arbutus menziesii*. **[oak]** Wide-branched tree, 16–130 ft. (5–40 m) tall. Reddish brown bark peels into papery strips, showing yellowish green, smooth new bark; old trunks are fissured and dark; evergreen leaves 3–4¾ in. (8–12 cm) long, ovate to oblong, bright green above, pale below; flowers white or pink, urn-shaped corollas; round, orange-red berries edible. In oak woods and coniferous forests. Coast Ranges, Transverse and Peninsular ranges to Baja, Sierra Nevada to Mariposa Co.

86. ***Hoary Manzanita**, *Arctostaphylos canescens*. **[shrub. oak]** Shrub 1–6½ ft. (3–20 dm) tall; trunk dark red-brown; leaves and branchlets densely covered with fine, white hairs; leaves pale green, ¾–2 in. (2–5 cm) long, round-ovate to elliptic, glaucous; base of flower densely white-hairy. Rocky, dry slopes, mostly above 650 ft. in chaparral and coniferous forests. Santa Cruz and Santa Clara cos., Marin Co. north in North Coast Ranges.
(Note: There are many species of red-barked manzanitas in the chaparral. The acidic berries of all manzanitas are edible and make good pies, cider, and jelly.)

87. ***Bigberry Manzanita**, *Arctostaphylos glauca*. **[shrub. oak]** Large, erect shrub, treelike, 6½–26 ft. (2–8 m) tall; bark smooth, red-brown; leaves smooth, ¾–2 in. (2–5 cm) long, oblong-ovate to round, entire to toothed, white-glaucous; flowers white to pinkish urn-shaped corollas in short, dense clusters; berries brownish, sticky. Dry, rocky slopes in

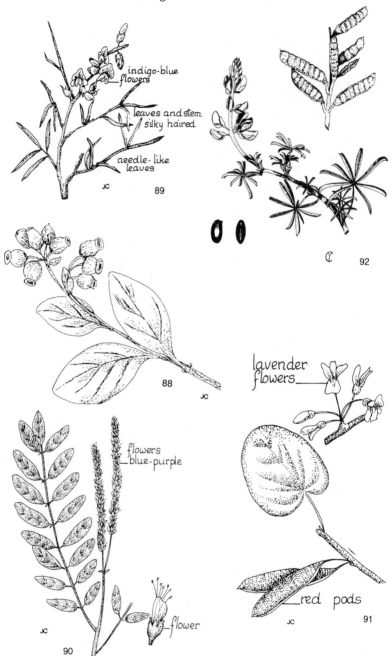

indigo-blue
flowers

leaves and stem
silky haired

needle-like
leaves

89

92

88

lavender
flowers

flowers
blue-purple

flower

red pods

90

91

chaparral and woodland. Inner South Coast Ranges from Mt. Diablo south, Transverse and Peninsular ranges to Baja.

88. *Parry Manzanita, *Arctostaphylos manzanita*. [shrub. oak] Shrub or small tree, 6½–26 ft. (2–8 m) tall, with long crooked branches and smooth, dark red-brown bark; branchlets often densely soft-hairy; leaves smooth, shiny bright green, ¾–2 in. (2–5 cm) long, widely ovate to obovate, entire; flowers white or pink urn-shaped corollas in open clusters; berries white at first, turning deep red. Dry slopes, rocky soils in chaparral, foothill woodland, northern oak woodland, and yellow pine forest under 4,500 ft. Inner North Coast Ranges to Contra Costa Co., s. Cascade and Sierra Nevada foothills to Mariposa Co.

FABACEAE, LEGUME FAMILY (legumes usually in 2-valved seed pod)

89. California False Indigo, *Amorpha californica*. [shrub. oak] Shrub 5–10 ft. (1.5–3 m) high. Similar to *A. fruticosa* below, but taller and main axis of leaves with pricklelike glands; banner of flowers red-purple; racemes generally scattered. Dry shrubby or wooded slopes. Foothills of Cascade and n. Sierra Nevada, Coast Ranges, Transverse and Peninsular ranges to n. Baja.

90. False Indigo, *Amorpha fruticosa*. [str-wd. shrub.] Shrub 3–8 ft. (1–2.5 m) high; stems more or less densely covered with short hairs; main axis of leaves without pricklelike glands; leaves 4–8 in. (10–20 cm) long with 11–25 pinnate leaflets, gland-dotted, heavily scented; flowers generally in dense spikelike racemes; only 1 petal present; calyx covered with hair. Along stream banks, canyons in coastal sage scrub and chaparral near coast. Also San Bernadino Mountains and Peninsular Ranges.

91. *Western Redbud or Judas Tree, *Cercis occidentalis*. [oak, shrub. str-wd.] Spreading or rounded shrub or small tree under 23 ft. (7 m) tall; deciduous leaves 1¼–3½ in. (3–9 cm) broad, cordate to kidney-shaped, almost leathery; flowers 2–5, reddish purple to pink, in umbel-like clusters attached nearly stemlessly to the branches; pods oblong, flat, 2–3 in. (5–8 cm) long. Buds, flowers, and young pods edible raw or cooked. Dry, shrubby slopes, canyons, stream banks in foothill woodland and chaparral. Inner Coast Ranges from Humboldt Co. to Solano Co., Sierra Nevada foothills to Tulare Co., San Joaquin Valley, Peninsular Ranges.

92. Yellow Bush Lupine, *Lupinus arboreus*. [coast. shrub.] Erect shrub with numerous short branches, 39–79 in. (10–20 dm), green and hairless to silver-hairy; leaves with 5–12 oblanceolate, palmately compound leaflets; raceme 4–12 in. (10–30 cm) long, flowers mostly spread-out, whorled or not; petals generally yellow; pods brown to black, hairy. Coastal strand and coastal sage scrub from Ventura Co. north.

POD
×½

FLOWERS
MANY
COLORED

×½

94

ER

FLOWERS
PURPLE-
RED

POD

×½

3 - 8'

95

ER

JC

93

yellow flowers.

96

JC

97

98

ER

93. Long-Bracted Bush Lupine, *Lupinus chamissonis.* **[coast.]** Erect, branching shrub, 20–79 in. (5–20 dm) high, with tiny, silver, densely appressed hairs; branches short, leafy; leaves with 5–9, oblanceolate, palmately compound leaflets; racemes 2–6 in. (5–15 cm) long with flowers in whorls surrounded by lance-shaped bracts; petals lavender to blue, the banner petal short-hairy on neck and with a yellow spot. Dunes and sandy beaches. Pacific Coast from Marin Co. south to Los Angeles Co.

94. Particolor Lupine, *Lupinus variicolor.* **[shrub. coast.]** Low-lying subshrub, 8–20 in. (2–5 dm) long, with slender stems lying flat to decumbent; leaves with 6–9 palmately compound, dark green, oblanceolate leaflets. The only lupine with many-colored blossoms often on the same plant, ranging from white, yellow, pink, or purple; pods dark mottled. Grassy fields, sand dunes, slopes on coastal strand and northern coastal scrub. San Luis Obispo Co. north along coast. There are many kinds of lupines in California.

95. Chaparral Pea, *Pickeringia montana.* **[shrub. oak]** Shrub, 3–9½ ft. (1–3 m) tall, densely and irregularly branched; branchlets have spines; bark smooth and green; evergreen leaves palmate, 1–3 leaflets; leaflets elliptic or ovate, ⅜–¾ in. (1–2 cm) long; flowers in racemes showy purple-red. Dry hillsides and ridges in chaparral and open woodlands. Coast Ranges from Mendocino Co. south, Transverse and Peninsular ranges to Baja, n. Sierra Nevada foothills.

96. *Honey Mesquite, *Prosopis glandulosa* var. *torreyana.* **[des. grass.]** Shrub or tree, generally 10–20 ft. (3–6 m) tall, usually with crooked, spiny branches; crown often wider than tall; leaves 7–17 pairs of linear to oblong leaflets; leaflets ⅜–1 in. (1–2.5 cm) long, opposite; flowers greenish yellow in spikelike racemes. Long pods, minus the hard seeds, can be eaten raw or cooked. Creosote bush scrub, grasslands, alkali flats, washes, sandy alluvial flats, mesas. In San Joaquin Valley and south to Mexico.

FAGACEAE, OAK FAMILY (nuts have a scaly cup; edible after leeching)

97. Tanbark Oak, *Lithocarpus densiflorus.* **[oak]** 65–148 ft. (20–45 m) tall, narrow conical crown (in forest); bark thick, grayish brown, deeply fissured; branchlets thickly covered with rust-colored hairs at first, becoming smooth and reddish brown with age; evergreen leaves leathery, light green and hairy above, turning smooth and shiny with age, prominent parallel veins end in sharp teeth; catkins stout, erect to spreading, 2½–4 in. (6–10 cm) long; acorns light yellow-brown, cups hairy, covered with long, recurved scales. Mixed evergreen and moist woods below 6,000 ft.; Santa Barbara and Ventura cos. near coast north to sw. Oregon; some isolated groves in the Sierra Nevada.

98. Coast Live Oak, *Quercus agrifolia.* **[oak, sav. shrub.]** 32–82 ft. (10–25 m) tall, branches wide-spreading and twisting; leaves evergreen, 1–3½ in. (2.5–9 cm) long, usually broad with a smooth or spiny-toothed

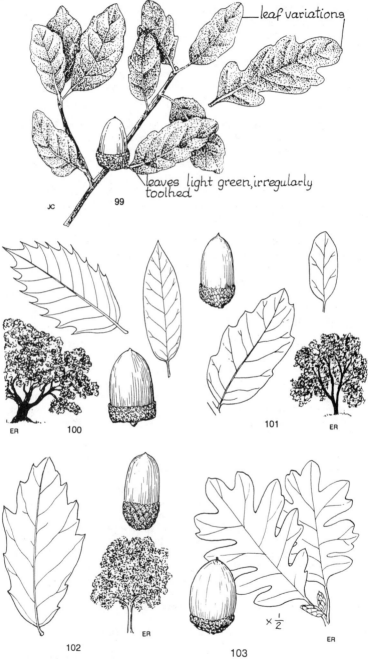

leaf variations

leaves light green, irregularly toothed

JC

99

ER 100

101 ER

102 ER

103 ×$\frac{1}{2}$ ER

margin turned downward, dark green; acorns with narrow cones and tapering to a pointed tip. The acorns of this and other oaks were leached, ground into meal, and cooked as mush or bread by the Indians. Lower slopes and valleys of the Coast Ranges from Sonoma Co. south to n. Baja.

99. **Scrub Oak**, *Quercus berberidifolia*. **[shrub. oak]** 3–10 ft. (1–3 m) tall, occasionally much taller, with a round and spreading crown; a very dense shrub or small tree with rigid, short branchlets at right angles to the branches; leaves evergreen, irregularly spiny to toothed, varying from deeply-lobed to shallow-scalloped or entire, ½–1 in. (1.5–2.5 cm) long; acorns ovoid, broad at base, rounded or acute at apex. Chaparral, foothill woods from Tehama Co. south.

100. **Canyon Live Oak** or **Golden Cup Oak**, *Quercus crysolepis*. **[oak, shrub.]** 20–65 ft. (6–20 m) tall, with large, spreading, horizontal branches (in open areas where branches begin to grow near the ground, the crown may extend 130 ft. (40 m) across); grows as a shrub on exposed mountain slopes above 4,000 ft.; bark light gray; leaves elliptical to oblong, 1–3 in. (3–8 cm) long, tip pointed, edges turned under, often with spiny teeth, dark green above, golden minutely hairy below; acorns usually egg-shaped; cups have thick scales densely covered with golden hairs. Prefers cool, moist canyons, but also grows on slopes and ridges. Coast Ranges and the Sierra Nevada south to n. Baja.

101. **Blue Oak**, *Quercus douglasii*. **[oak, sav.]** 20–65 ft. (6–20 m) tall, with a broad, rounded crown; bark thin, scaly, light gray; leaves deciduous, 1¼–3 in. (3–8 cm) long, oblong to ovate, smooth-edged to shallowly and irregularly lobed, thin but firm, blue-green above, paler and finely hairy beneath; acorns usually broadest near the base and rounded at the tip; cups shallow, enclosing only the base of the acorn, the scales slightly bumpy. Dry slopes in foothill woods on both sides of the Central Valley, w. Transverse Ranges.

102. **Mesa** or **Engelmann Oak**, *Quercus engelmannii*. **[oak, sav.]** 16–60 ft. (5–18 m) tall; young twigs densely matted with fine, woolly hairs; bark gray-brown, deeply fissured; leaves evergreen, ¾–2⅜ in. (2–6 cm) long, dull bluish green and smooth above, soft-hairy below, entire to slightly serrate; acorns oblong-cylindric to ovoid, blunt-tipped. Uncommon. Dry rolling mesas and foothills in sw. California (not north of L.A. Co.) away from the coast.

103. **Oregon Oak**, *Quercus garryana*. **[oak]** 25–66 ft. (8–20 m) tall, rounded crown; bark grayish and thin with square-shaped scales; leaves deciduous, 2–6 in. (5–15 cm) long, deeply 5–7 lobed, lobes entire or 2-toothed, surface shiny dark green above, dull light green below; twigs reddish brown (hairy the first year). Hillside woods, mixed evergreen and northern oak woods up to 4,500 ft. San Francisco Bay area and North Coast Ranges north to British Columbia, Cascade and Sierra Nevada foothills, Tehachapi Mtns.

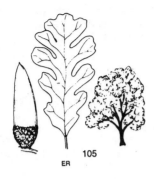

105

ER

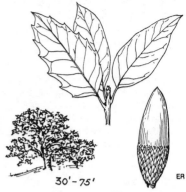

30'-75'

106

ER

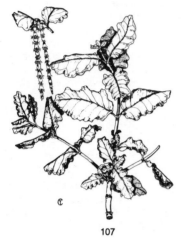

107

104

BERRY
BLUE-
BLACK

ROSE

× ½

× ½

4-9'

109

LEAVES
FUZZY BELOW

ER

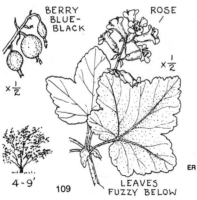

ER

108

104. **California Black Oak**, *Quercus kelloggii*. **[oak]** 32–82 ft. (10–25 m) tall, trunk straight, broad rounded crown; bark dark, smooth when young, getting thicker and developing deep ridges with age; deciduous leaves alternate, 4–8 in. (10–20 cm) long, usually 6-lobed with spiny tips, bright green and smooth above; acorns oblong-ovoid tapering to generally rounded tips. Valleys, slopes, and woodland in the whole region except Central Valley and southern coast.

105. **Valley Oak** or **Roble Oak**, *Quercus lobata*. **[oak, grass.]** 40–100 ft. (12–30 m) tall, rarely taller, crown open, broadly rounded; bark light gray, thick, developing deep fissures with age; leaves deciduous, 2–4¾ in. (5–12 cm) long, shiny dark green, with 6–10 rounded, deep lobes, yellowish veins on pale undersurface; acorns narrower than most oaks and cone-shaped; scales of cup conspicuously warty. Uncommon. Valleys and slopes in rich soil, usually below 2,000 ft. Inner and middle Coast Ranges, Cascade and Sierra Nevada foothills, Central Valley, Transverse Ranges, from Shasta Co. to Los Angeles Co.

106. **Interior Live Oak**, *Quercus wislizenii*. **[oak, sav. shrub.]** Similar to the Coast Live Oak, but generally smaller; 30–70 ft. (9–21 m) tall, with a very broad, dome-shaped crown; leaves evergreen, 1–2 in. (2.5–5 cm) long, oblong to lanceolate with smooth or spiny-toothed margins, shiny dark green; acorns with minute hairs at tips; cups usually covering ½ or more of acorn, maturing second year. Interior valleys, canyons, and slopes of foothill woodland and chaparral in most of the region; not in Central Valley.

GARRYACEAE, SILK TASSEL FAMILY

107. **Wavyleaf Silk Tassel**, *Garrya elliptica*. **[shrub. oak, coast.]** Shrub or small tree, under 26 ft. (8 m) tall; rounded crown with a short trunk branching close to the ground; evergreen leaves simple, opposite, 2–4 in. (5–10 cm) long, elliptic, wavy margins, leathery and dark green, densely hairy below; male and female flowers on separate trees; male flowers in catkinlike, drooping tassels; flower has 4-lobed calyx and no petals; fruits white-hairy. Ocean bluffs, sand dunes, dry hillsides in coastal scrub, chaparral, foothill pine woodland. Outer Coast Ranges from Ventura Co. north, central coast, n. Sierra Nevada foothills, Sacramento Valley.

108. **Yellowleaf Silk Tassel**, *Garrya flavescens*. **[shrub. oak]** Erect shrub 5–10 ft. (1.5–3 m) tall; young twigs gray-hairy; leaves yellow-green or gray-green, elliptic to obovate, margin flat to wavy; fruiting catkins 1⅛–2 in. (3–5 cm) long, covered with dense, silky hair. Dry slopes in chaparral and pine-oak woodland above 2,000 ft. Not in Central Valley.

GROSSULARIACEAE, GOOSEBERRY FAMILY

109. ***Chaparral Currant**, *Ribes malvaceum*. **[shrub. oak]** A graceful, drooping bush, 4–7 ft. (1–2 m) tall, with slender branches; leaves deciduous, grayish green, 3–5 lobed, obtuse and double-toothed, densely hairy; early spring flowers in racemes, sepals pink to purple,

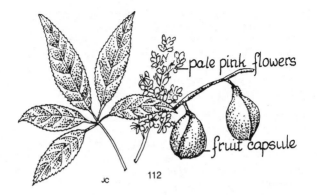

pale pink flowers

fruit capsule

JC   112

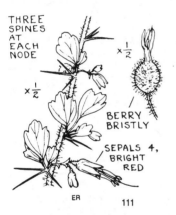

THREE
SPINES
AT
EACH
NODE

×½

×½

BERRY
BRISTLY

SEPALS 4,
BRIGHT
RED

ER   111

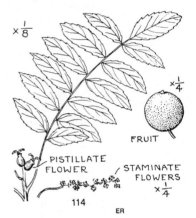

×⅛

×¼

FRUIT

PISTILLATE
FLOWER

STAMINATE
FLOWERS
×¼

114   ER

PALE BLUE OR
WHITE

FRUIT
×1

2-8'

LEAF ×½
UNDER SIDE
STRONG VEINED,
FELTY

JC   113

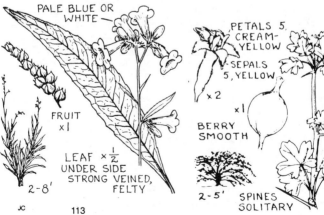

PETALS 5,
CREAM-
YELLOW

SEPALS
5, YELLOW

×2

×1

BERRY
SMOOTH

×⅔

2-5'   SPINES
SOLITARY

110

ER

petals pink to white; berries edible, purple-black. Chaparral, dry open or wooded slopes. Whole region except Central Valley.

110. ***Oak Gooseberry**, *Ribes quercetorum*. **[oak, shrub.]** A scraggly bush, 2–5 ft. (6–15 dm) tall, with arched, spreading branches covered with usually solitary spines; leaves light green, generally hairy, 3–5 cleft, toothed lobes; edible berries black, hairless; sepals yellow; petals cream color, a little longer than the stamens. Oak woodlands, chaparral; Sierra Nevada foothills from Tuolumne Co. to Kern Co. and inner Coast Ranges from Alameda Co. to n. Baja.

111. ***Fuchsia-Flowered Gooseberry**, *Ribes speciosum*. **[shrub.]** 4–7 ft. (1–2 m) tall; leaves evergreen, leathery, shiny dark green, somewhat 3-lobed, usually less than 1 in. (2.5 cm) long; 4 bright red sepals on each flower; 3 stout spines at each node of stem; berries dry and bristly, edible. Shaded canyons in coastal sage scrub and chaparral below 1,500 ft. near coast from Santa Clara Co. to n. Baja.

HIPPOCASTANACEAE, BUCKEYE FAMILY

112. **California Buckeye**, *Aesculus californica*. **[oak, str-wd.]** Large bush or tree, 13–39 ft. (4–12 m) tall with broad, rounded crown; winter buds quite sticky; leaves palmately compound with 5–7 leaflets; leaflets 2–6 in. (5–15 cm) long, oblong-lanceolate, finely serrate; flowers white or pale rose, 5–8 stamens with orange anthers; fruit spherical, leathery, 2–3 in (5–8 cm) diameter, usually with 1 glossy brown seed. All parts toxic. Dry slopes, canyons, stream banks, mostly in foothill woodlands. Siskiyou and Shasta cos. south to Los Angeles Co. on both sides of the Central Valley.

HYDROPHYLLACEAE, WATERLEAF FAMILY

113. ***Yerba Santa**, *Eriodictyon californicum*. **[oak, shrub.]** Erect shrub, 3–9½ ft. (1–3 m) tall, bark shredding and twigs sticky; evergreen leaves 2–6 in. (5–15 cm) long, often sticky with varnished appearance, leathery, lanceolate to oblong, entire to toothed, hairy and veiny below; flowers funnel-shaped, white to purple, sparsely hairy, in open, terminal panicles. Dried leaves can be used to make a bitter tea. Slopes, fields, roadsides in foothill woodland, northern oak woodland, chaparral, and mixed evergreen forests. Coast Ranges and coast, Central Valley, Cascade and Sierra Nevada mountains.

JUGLANDACEAE, WALNUT FAMILY

114. ***California Black Walnut**, *Juglans californica*. **[oak, str-wd.]** Small tree with short trunk soon branching, generally 10–33 ft. (3–10 m) tall, rarely up to 60 ft. (18 m); bark smooth and grayish white when young, becoming dark and deeply fissured with age; branchlets reddish brown; leaves in featherlike arrangement with 11–19 leaflets; leaflets 1–4 in. (3–10 cm) long, ovate to lanceolate, finely serrate, often curved; nut (including husk) small, ¾–1⅜ in. (2–3.5 cm) wide, sweet, edible. Dry or moist stream banks, slopes, canyons, and valleys. Southern inner North Coast Ranges, s. Sacramento Valley to n. San Joaquin

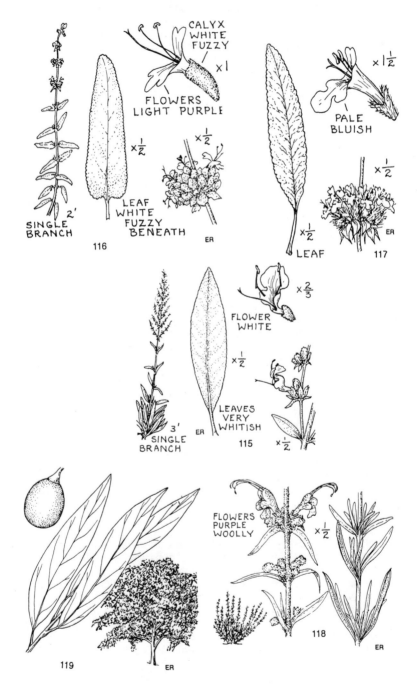

CALYX WHITE FUZZY

×1

FLOWERS LIGHT PURPLE

×½

×½

LEAF WHITE FUZZY BENEATH

2'

SINGLE BRANCH

116

ER

×1½

PALE BLUISH

×½

×½

LEAF

117

ER

×⅔

FLOWER WHITE

×½

3'

SINGLE BRANCH

LEAVES VERY WHITISH

115

×½

ER

FLOWERS PURPLE WOOLLY

×½

118

119

ER

ER

Valley, San Francisco Bay area and outer South Coast Ranges to sw. California.

LAMIACEA, MINT FAMILY

115. ***White Sage**, *Salvia apiana*. **[shrub.]** Herb to subshrub, stem under 39 in. (1 m) tall; leaves crowded at base of plant, 1½–3 in. (4–8 cm) long, widely lanceolate, covered with tiny, white, appressed hairs, minutely toothed; flowers few in spikelike clusters, these in racemelike panicles; corolla white with lavender; nutlets shiny light brown, keeled. All *Salvia* spp. attract bees and have edible seeds. Dry slopes in coastal sage scrub, chaparral, and yellow pine forest. Santa Barbara Co. to Baja near coast, Transverse and Peninsular ranges, w. edge of desert.

116. ***Purple Sage**, *Salvia leucophylla*. **[shrub.]** Prostrate to erect shrub, 3–5 ft. (1–1.5 m) tall, much branched, densely grayish white hairy; flowers rose-lavender in dense headlike whorls; whorls 3–5, crowded or scattered; nutlets brown or dark gray. Dry, open slopes in coastal sage scrub. Outer South Coast Ranges, south coast, western Transverse Ranges, San Gabriel Mtns., and Baja.

117. ***Black Sage**, *Salvia mellifera*. **[shrub.]** Openly branched shrub, 3–6½ ft. (1–2 m) tall, with leafy twigs covered with numerous tiny, stiff, sharp, appressed hairs, sometimes glandular; leaves ¾–2¾ in. (2–7 cm) long, oblong-elliptic to obovate, hairy below; flowers numerous in compact, headlike clusters surrounded by short, spine-tipped bracts; corolla white to pale blue or lavender; nutlet generally brown. In coastal sage scrub, lower chaparral. Central western and sw. California from Contra Costa Co. to n. Baja.

118. **Woolly Bluecurls**, *Trichostema lanatum*. **[shrub.]** Many-branched, rounded shrub, under 59 in. (15 dm) tall; pleasant scent; stem with short, appressed hairs near base, sometimes woolly near the top; leaves linear with margins rolled under, green above, gray-hairy below; blue flowers in dense, nearly stemless cymes off main stem, covered with blue, pink, or white wool. Coastal scrub and chaparral in the South Coast Ranges, the Transverse and Peninsular ranges, and the south coast to Baja.

LAURACEAE, LAUREL FAMILY

119. ***California Bay** or **Laurel**, *Umbellularia californica*. **[str-wd. oak, shrub.]** Generally 23–98 ft. (7–30 m) tall, trunk forked into several large, spreading branches; leaves evergreen, 1⅛–4 in. (3–10 cm) long, slender and lanceolate, dark green and shiny above, with a pungent and spicy fragrance when crushed; flowers pale yellow, formed in flat-topped clusters on stem at leaf bases, late winter or early spring; fruits greenish, turning purplish when ripe, olivelike, producing a thin-shelled brown nut that is edible when cooked. Mountain slopes, canyons, valleys, mixed woods at lower elevations; prefers moist soil.

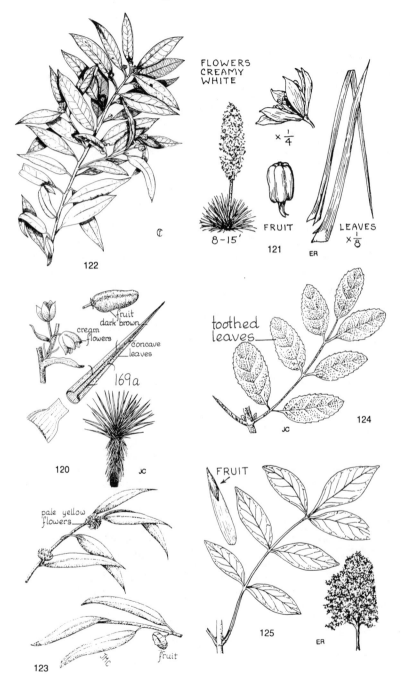

FLOWERS
CREAMY
WHITE

× 1/4

FRUIT

8-15'

121

LEAVES
× 1/8

ER

122

fruit
dark brown

cream
flowers

concave
leaves

169a

toothed
leaves

124

JC

120   JC

pale yellow
flowers

FRUIT

125

ER

123

fruit

JMC

LILIACEAE, LILY FAMILY

120. *Mohave Yucca or Spanish Dagger, *Yucca schidigera*. [des. shrub.] Trunk simple or branched, 3–15 ft. (1–4.5 m) tall (rarely with no trunk), with a large head of daggerlike, spine-tipped leaves on top; leaves 1–5 ft. (3–15 dm) long, yellowish green, sickle-shaped in cross-section; flowers cream colored or with purplish tinge. Creosote scrub, chaparral, coastal and desert areas from Riverside and San Bernadino cos. south.

121. *Our Lord's Candle or Whipple's Yucca, *Yucca whipplei*. [shrub. des.] A single flowering stalk, 5–11½ ft. (1.5–3.5 m) tall, rises from a thick basal rosette of narrow, gray-green, spine-tipped leaves in spring; plant dies after fruiting; creamy white blossoms in a long compact panicle, looking somewhat like a candle's flame. Fruits edible raw or cooked. Dry, often stony slopes, mostly in chaparral, and costal or desert scrub from the southern South Coast Ranges south.

MYRICACEAE, WAX MYRTLE FAMILY

122. Wax Myrtle or Bayberry, *Myrica californica*. [shrub. str-wd. coast.] Shrub or small tree to 30 ft. (9 m) tall, with many slender, ascending branches; branchlets green and covered with tiny hairs when young, turning smooth then rough and gray to brown with age; evergreen leaves alternate, 2–4 in. (5–10 cm) long, oblanceolate, shiny dark green; female catkins reddish green, shorter than yellowish male catkins; fruits globe-shaped, warty, dark purple when ripe, in crowded clusters. Near the coast in coastal sage scrub, along streams, moist sand dunes, hillsides, canyons of coastal California.

MYRTACEAE, MYRTLE FAMILY

123. Blue Gum Eucalyptus, *Eucalyptus globulus*. [shrub. grass.] Tree 33–262 ft. (10–80 m) tall; narrow, rounded crown; bark smooth, bluish gray, shreds in long, thin strips, exposing greenish tan beneath; leaves leathery, evergreen, hanging, 4–7¾ in. (10–20 cm) long, narrowly lanceolate or sickle-shaped, aromatic. Often used as a windbreak; introduced from Australia. Disturbed areas under 1,000 ft. Outer Coast Ranges, western Transverse Ranges, Peninsular Ranges, and south coast to San Diego Co., San Francisco Bay area and Central Valley.

OLEACEAE, OLIVE FAMILY

124. California Ash, *Fraxinus dipetala*. [shrub. oak] Shrub or small tree, 6½–23 ft. (2–7 m) tall, with slender branchlets; deciduous leaves have 3–7 (rarely 9) leaflets, each ¾–2¾ in. (2–7 cm) long, ovate to obovate, generally serrate; panicles have many tiny, white flowers, each flower with 2 white petals; winged fruits are dry, flattened, in short clusters. Canyons and slopes in chaparral and foothill woodland. Coast Ranges, Transverse and Peninsular ranges, Cascade and Sierra Nevada foothills.

125. Oregon Ash, *Fraxinus latifolia*. [str-wd. oak] Tree 32–82 ft. (10–25 m) tall; deciduous leaves consist of 5–7 leaflets, each ¾–4 in. (2–10 cm) long, widely elliptic to narrowly ovate, entire to shallowly

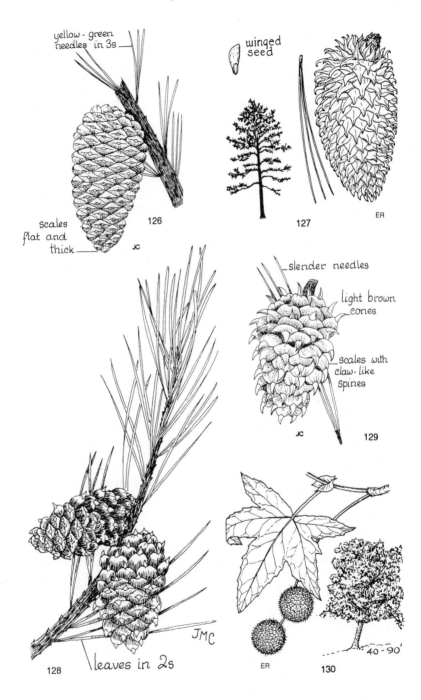

yellow-green needles in 3s

scales flat and thick

126

JC

winged seed

127

ER

slender needles

light brown cones

scales with claw-like spines

JC

129

128

JMC

leaves in 2s

ER

130

40-90'

toothed, dark green above, pale and sparsely hairy below; 2 tiny stamens with calyx, no petals; fruit in dense clusters. In canyons, woodlands, and near streams. Coast Ranges from Santa Clara Co. north, Sierra Nevada, Central Valley.

PINACEAE, PINE FAMILY

126. Knobcone Pine, *Pinus attenuata.* **[oak, shrub.]** Generally 9–50 ft. (3–15 m) tall, rarely taller; narrow, pointed crown of slender, nearly horizontal branches curled upward at ends, becoming irregular with age; needles in 3's, yellowish green, 3–7 in. (8–18 cm) long; cones stalkless, shiny yellow-brown, 2½–7 in (6–18 cm) long, abundant, clustered in rings or whorls; cones often remain closed unless burned and are formed much more massively on one side; cone scales knoblike and topped with a short, stout spine. Foothill woods, chaparral, rocky ground.

127. *Coulter Pine, *Pinus coulteri.* **[oak, shrub.]** Generally 40–80 ft. (12–24 m) tall, sometimes taller; straight trunked with rows of nearly horizontal branches; needles in 3's, dark blue-green, 6–12 in. (15–30 cm) long, stiff and sharp pointed; bark dark brownish gray, irregularly furrowed, forming yellowish plates when mature; cones 8–14 in. (20–35 cm) long, egg-shaped, very heavy (up to 5 pounds), slightly shiny, bent down on stout stalks, clawlike spines; seeds edible. Chaparral to lower mixed conifer or hardwood forests in cw. and sw. California from Contra Costa Co. to n. Baja.

128. Bishop Pine, *Pinus muricata.* **[shrub. oak]** Generally 40–80 ft. (12–24 m) tall, sometimes taller; needles in 2's in crowded clusters, dark yellow-green to dull green, stiff, blunt-pointed, 2–6 in. (5–15 cm) long; cones stalkless, 2–3½ in. (5–9 cm) long, shiny yellow-brown; many cones cluster together in rings or whorls, remaining closed for many years; cone scales knoblike and topped with a stout spine. Low coastal hills, mainly between Humboldt and Santa Barbara cos., also n. Baja.

129. *Foothill Pine (formerly Digger Pine), *Pinus sabiniana.* **[oak, shrub.]** Generally 40–98 ft. (12–30 m) tall, sometimes taller; crooked, forking trunk and branches; needles in 3's, gray-green, 4–15 in. (10–38 cm) long; bark dark gray, irregularly furrowed, forming yellow plates when very old; cones 4–10 in. (10–25 cm) long, ovate-oblong, bent down on long stalks, clawlike spines. Seeds edible. Foothill woodland, n. oak woodland, chaparral, and mixed conifer and hardwood forests below 4,500 ft.

PLANTANACEAE, SYCAMORE FAMILY

130. Western Sycamore, *Platanus racemosa.* **[str-wd. oak, shrub.]** Large, stout tree, 32–115 ft. (10–35 m) tall, often branched near base; bark smooth, pale, old bark flakes away in thin plates, usually from upper trunk and branches, exposing whitish inner bark; leaves deciduous, 5–10 in. (12–25 cm) wide and long, palmately and deeply lobed, large-toothed, light green and hairy on both surfaces when

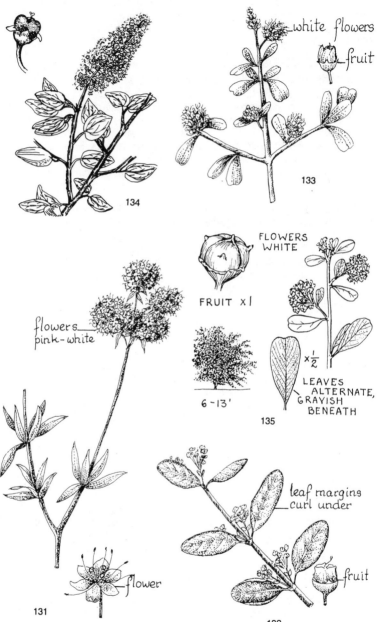

white flowers

fruit

133

134

FLOWERS
WHITE

FRUIT x1

flowers
pink-white

6~13'

135

LEAVES
ALTERNATE,
GRAYISH
BENEATH

x½

leaf margins
curl under

fruit

flower

131

132

young; male and female flowers tiny, forming 2–7 dense clusters on hanging stalks with new leaves in spring; fruit dry, fuzzy-looking balls maturing in autumn. Many plant communities along streams or nearby in woods; Central Valley and bordering mountains, cw. and sw. California to Baja.

POLYGONACEAE, BUCKWHEAT FAMILY (achene mostly 3-angled, sometimes lens-shaped)

131. California Buckwheat, *Eriogonum fasciculatum.* **[des. shrub.]** Low spreading shrub, usually 2–4 ft. (6–12 dm) tall, some stems lying down, but with tips rising; branchlets very leafy, softly hairy to smooth, ending in leafless stalks bearing open cymes; flowers pinkish white in dense, nearly spherical clusters; leaves linear to oblanceolate green above, white-woolly beneath, strongly rolled inward on edges. Dry slopes, washes, and canyons in scrub on both sides of the Central Valley from Santa Clara Co. south.

RHAMNACEAE, BUCKTHORN FAMILY

132. Hoaryleaf Ceanothus, *Ceanothus crassifolius.* **[shrub.]** Stiffly and openly branched shrub, 6½–11 ft. (2–3.5 m) tall; branchlets white- to rusty-hairy, becoming brown or gray; evergreen leaves leathery, opposite, ¾–1⅛ in. (2–3 cm) long, more or less ovate, olive-green and minutely rough above, woolly below; flowers white with globelike caps in umbel-like clusters; seeds shiny black. Dry ridges and slopes in chaparral. Outer South Coast Ranges, Transverse and Peninsular ranges, from Santa Barbara Co. to n. Baja.

133. *Buck Brush or **Wild Lilac,** *Ceanothus cuneatus* var. *cuneatus.* **[shrub. oak]** Shrub 3–10 ft. (1–3 m) tall, rigidly branched with gray bark; small evergreen leaves dull green above, minutely gray-hairy below, oblanceolate to obovate, entire; flowers in umbels, white or pale blue to lavender, often turning whole hillsides into fragrant, blossoming slopes in the spring; the fruit capsules show 3 little horns on top. Leaves and flowers can be boiled for 5 minutes or so to make a good tea. Dry hillsides, ridges, and fans in chaparral, sagebrush scrub, and foothill woodlands. Not in Central Valley.

134. Chaparral Whitethorn, *Ceanothus leucodermis.* **[shrub. oak]** Shrub, 6½–13 ft. (2–4 m) tall, with thorns; branches rigid, widely spreading; bark smooth, pale green; evergreen leaves alternate, 3-ribbed, entire to finely serrate, both surfaces gray-glaucuous; flowers blue to whitish in raceme-like clusters under 4¼ in. (11 cm) long; seeds shiny, dark olive-brown. Dry, rocky or sandy slopes in foothill woods and chaparral. Sierra Nevada foothills, South Coast Ranges, Transverse and Peninsular ranges, from Marin Co. to n. Baja.

135. Bigpod Ceanothus, *Ceanothus megacarpus* var. *megacarpus.* **[shrub.]** Shrub 3–13 ft. (1–4 m) tall, ascending or erect; young bark covered with fine hairs, gray to red-brown, becoming smooth and gray with age; evergreen leaves alternate, ⅜–1 in. (1–2.5 cm) long, elliptic to obovate, entire, smooth and dull green above, finely gray-hairy below;

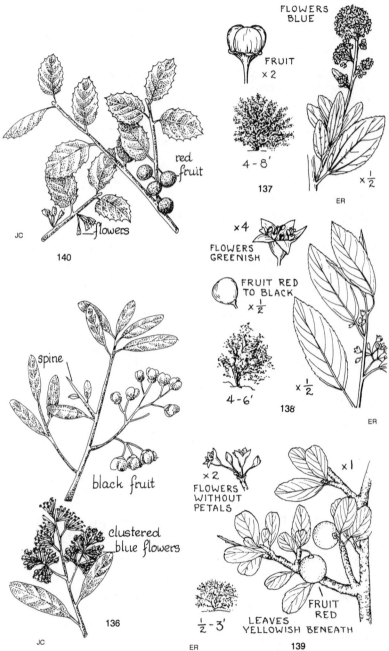

FLOWERS
BLUE

FRUIT
×2

4 - 8'

137

×½

ER

red
fruit

flowers

JC

140

×4

FLOWERS
GREENISH

FRUIT RED
TO BLACK
×½

4 - 6'

138

×½

ER

spine

black fruit

clustered
blue flowers

136

JC

×2
FLOWERS
WITHOUT
PETALS

×1

FRUIT
RED

LEAVES
YELLOWISH BENEATH

½ - 3'

ER

139

flowers white or pale lavendar; horns prominent. Dry slopes and canyons below 2,450 ft in chaparral and coastal sage scrub. Outer South Coast Ranges, central coast from Marin Co. to Santa Barbara Co., Catalina Island.

136. Greenbark Ceanothus, *Ceanothus spinosus.* **[shrub.]** Erect shrub, more or less treelike, 6½–19 ft. (2–6 m) tall; bark smooth olive-green; branchlets ascending, stiff, and spine-tipped; evergreen leaves alternate, ⅜–1½ in. (1–4 cm) long, entire, oblong to elliptic; flowers pale blue to nearly white. Dry slopes in coastal sage scrub and chaparral. Outer South Coast Ranges, w. Transverse Ranges, and Peninsular Ranges from Monterey Co. to n. Baja.

137. Blue-Blossom Ceanothus, *Ceanothus thyriflorus.* **[shrub.]** Shrub, 3–19 ft. (1–6 m) tall, prostrate to erect; twigs green, angled; trunk and branches usually straight; evergreen leaves ¾–2 in. (2–5 cm) long, dark green above, paler below, oblong-ovate to widely elliptic, 3-ribbed; aromatic flowers light to deep blue, rarely almost white, in dense panicles at end of long, leafy stems; fruit dark and sticky at ripening. Wooded slopes and canyons below 2,000 ft. in chaparral and mixed evergreen forests. Outer Coast Ranges from Santa Barbara Co. north.

138. *California Coffeeberry or **Buckthorn,** *Rhamnus californica.* **[shrub. oak]** Low, spreading or upright, rounded shrub, 3–16 ft. (1–5 m) high; bark bright gray or brown; young twigs usually have reddish bark; 5-petaled flowers in umbels with 6-50 flowers; evergreen leaves ¾–3 in. (2–8 cm) long, shiny, ovate to elliptic, margin serrate to entire, sometimes rolled under; berries green, turning red to black when ripe. Known to be an effective laxative. Sandy and rocky places near coast, hillsides and ravines in coastal sage scrub, chaparral, and woods in Coast Ranges from Siskiyou Co. south and throughout cw. and sw. California.

139. *Spiny Redberry or **Buckthorn,** *Rhamnus crocea.* **[shrub. oak]** Shrub 1–6½ ft. (1–2 m) tall, gray-green with much-branched, rigid, often spine-tipped branches; evergreen leaves ⅜–⅝ in. (10–15 mm) long, obovate, thick, sharply toothed or entire; 1–6 flowers in umbel, no petals; red berries are nutritious and can be eaten raw or cooked. Dry washes and canyons in coastal sage scrub, chaparral, oak woodland. Coast Ranges from Lake Co. south and throughout cw. and sw. California.

140. *Holly-Leaf Redberry or **Buckthorn,** *Rhamnus ilicifolia.* **[shrub. oak]** Shrub 5–13 ft. (1.5–4 m) tall; branches stiff, ascending; twigs hairless to densely hairy; evergreen leaves ovate to round, ¾–1½ in. (2–4 cm) long, thick, spiny toothed; edible berries red. Dry slopes in chaparral, northern oak woodland, foothill woodland, etc.

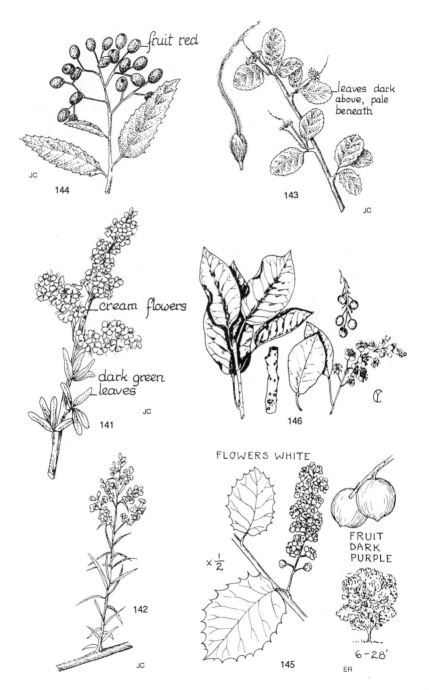

fruit red

144

leaves dark
above, pale
beneath

143

cream flowers

dark green
leaves

141

146

FLOWERS WHITE

142

× ½

145

FRUIT
DARK
PURPLE

6-28'

ROSACEAE, ROSE FAMILY

141. Chamise or **Greasewood,** *Adenostoma fasciculatum.* **[shrub.]** Much-branched shrub 2–12 ft. (0.6–3.6 m) tall; well-developed woody burl at base; bark gray-brown on trunk, reddish, nearly smooth on twigs, turning shreddy with age; leaves evergreen, stiff, more or less linear, in alternate clusters; flowers white, 5-petaled, in dense terminal panicles. Dominant plant of the middle and southern chaparral; dry slopes and ridges. Coast Ranges from Mendocino Co. to n. Baja, foothills of Sierra Nevada.

142. Red Shank or **Ribbon Bush,** *Adenostoma sparsifolium.* **[shrub.]** Erect, almost treelike shrub, 6½–20 ft. (2–6 m) tall. Red-brown trunk; leaves as in *A. fasciculatum,* except not clustered, resemble tiny ribbons; flowers white in open panicles, less than 6 in. (15 cm) long. Dry slopes, flats, chaparral. Southern outer South Coast Ranges and coast, Transverse and Peninsular ranges to Baja.

143. Birchleaf Mountain Mahogany, *Cercocarpus betuloides* var. *betuloides.* **[shrub.]** Widespreading bush or tree 5–20 ft. (1.5–6 m) tall; evergreen leaves obovate to round, ⅜–1½ in. (1–4 cm) long, dark green above, pale green and sparsely hairy below, finely toothed to serrate, lateral featherlike veins; bark smooth becoming scaly; flowers 1–3, yellow with 5 sepals; seed capsules have feathery tail. Indians used the hard wood for digging sticks, the bark for dyeing leather. Dry, rocky slopes and washes in chaparral.

144. *Christmas Berry or **Toyon,** *Heteromeles arbutifolia.* **[shrub. oak]** Shrub or small tree, generally 6–16 ft. (2–5 m) tall; bark light gray, smooth; twigs dark red, slender, hairy when young; leaves evergreen, alternate, 2–4 in. (5–10 cm) long, thick and leathery, sharp-toothed, shiny dark green on top; flowers 5-petaled, white; fruit red, rarely yellow, edible. In canyons and on slopes in chaparral and foothill woods.

145. *Holly-Leaved Cherry, *Prunus ilicifolia.* **[shrub. oak]** Dense evergreen shrub or tree 3–49 ft. (1–15 m) tall; bark turns gray or reddish brown; leaves shiny green, ¾–4½ in. (2–12 cm) long, ovate to rounded, spiny-serrate or entire, leathery; flowers white and 5-petaled, clustered in dense racemes in early spring; fruit somewhat sweet and edible but mostly pit. Dry slopes, canyons of chaparral and foothill woods; s. North Coast Ranges (Napa Co.) and throughout cw. and sw. California to Baja.

146. *Western Chokecherry, *Prunus virginiana* var. *demissa.* **[shrub. oak]** Shrub or small tree up to 20 ft. (6 m) tall, often forming dense thickets; bark brownish gray, smooth becoming scaly; leaves deciduous, shiny dark green on top, alternate, 2–4 in. (5–10 cm) long, elliptical, finely serrate, turning yellow in autumn; flowers in spring grow in dense, elongated racemes; fruits dark red to black, juicy. Moist places in oak-pine woodland, shrubland, rocky slopes, canyons; not in Central Valley.

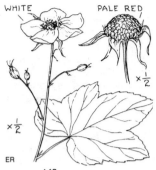

WHITE

PALE RED

$\times \frac{1}{2}$

$\times \frac{1}{2}$

ER

148

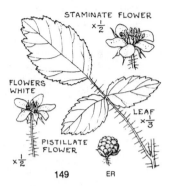

STAMINATE FLOWER $\times \frac{1}{2}$

FLOWERS WHITE

LEAF $\times \frac{1}{3}$

PISTILLATE FLOWER

$\times \frac{1}{2}$

149   ER

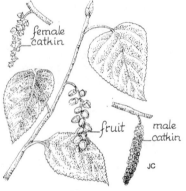

female catkin

fruit

male catkin

JC

150

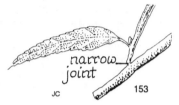

narrow joint

JC   153

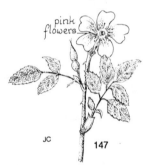

pink flowers

JC   147

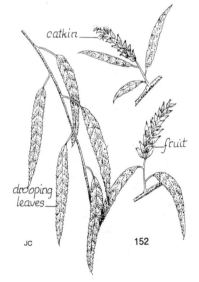

catkin

fruit

drooping leaves

JC   152

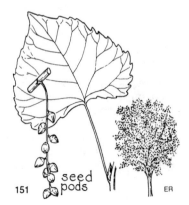

seed pods

151   ER

147. *California Wild Rose, *Rosa californica*. [str-wd. oak, shrub.] Erect, branching bush, 31–98 in. (8–25 dm) tall, with stout, recurved prickles; leaves consisting of 5–7 oval leaflets, each ⅜–1⅜ in. (1–3.5 cm) long, singly or doubly serrate, softly hairy and often glandular beneath; flowers white or pink in corymbs; rose hips (fruit) globular to ovoid, often with a distinct neck, edible raw or cooked (sugar improves flavor). Moist places, canyons, near streams in many plant communities.

148. *Thimbleberry, *Rubus parviflorus*. [str-wd. oak, shrub.] Deciduous shrub, 3–6 ft. (1–2 m) tall, no prickles; leaves palmately 5-lobed, cordate at base, 4–6 in. (10–15 cm) long and wide, finely toothed; 4–7 white to pink flowers in open terminal cluster; ripe berries red, raspberry-like, sweet. Usually in moist shady places in open woods and canyons; not in Central Valley.

149. *California Blackberry, *Rubus ursinus*. [str-wd. oak, shrub.] Erect as a bush or stems climbing or trailing, covered with slender, straight thorns; leaves evergreen, pinnately compound or palmately lobed, irregularly toothed, generally ovate; flowers white; ripe berries black, delicious. Woods, meadows, roadsides, usually near water.

SALICACEAE, WILLOW FAMILY (leaves simple and alternate; bitter inner bark can be eaten as an emergency food)

150. Black Cottonwood, *Populus balsamifera* ssp. *trichocarpa*. [str-wd.] 65–164 ft. (20–50 m) tall with a broad, open crown; bark grayish, deeply creviced in old trunks; leaves ovate, almost heart shaped at base, tapering to acute ends, thick and leathery, dark green above, paler below often with spots of brown resin, 1½–3 in. (4–8 cm) long, margins finely toothed; leaf stems long, about ⅓ to ½ blade length; male catkins densely flowered, female catkins loosely flowered. Along streams, alluvial bottomlands.

151. *Fremont Cottonwood, *Populus fremontii* ssp. *fremontii*. [str-wd.] 40–98 ft. (12–30 m) tall with a broad, open crown and whitish, roughly cracked bark (smooth on young trunks); leaves lustrous, yellowish green, thick and firm, 1½–3½ in. (4–9 cm) wide, nearly cordate; twigs yellow, becoming gray; catkins edible; seed pods bear light brown, silky-haired seeds. Moist places, mainly near streams, alluvial bottomlands.

152. Weeping Willow, *Salix babylonica*. [str-wd.] Generally 30–40 ft. (10–13 m) tall, maximum height 65 ft. (20 m), wide-spreading with long, drooping or hanging branches; leaves bright green, 3–6 in. (8–15 cm) long, narrowly lanceolate, finely serrate; twigs gray-brown to yellow-brown. Imported from China. Moist places, usually near or in towns.

153. Goodding's Black Willow, *Salix gooddingii*. [str-wd.] Generally 20–65 ft. (6–20 m) tall, sometimes taller; dark bark rough; yellowish branchlets brittle; leaves grayish green, 1¼–5½ in. (3–14 cm) long, narrowly lanceolate, finely serrate; staminate catkins yellow, 1½–3 in.

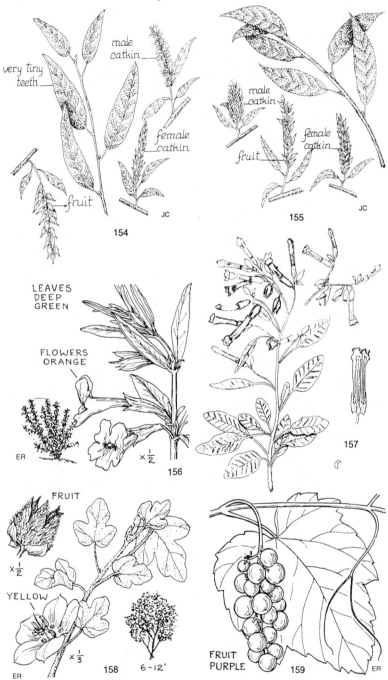

very tiny teeth

male catkin

female catkin

fruit

JC

154

male catkin

fruit

female catkin

JC

155

LEAVES DEEP GREEN

FLOWERS ORANGE

ER

×½

156

157

FRUIT

×½

YELLOW

×⅓

ER

158

6-12'

FRUIT PURPLE

159

ER

(4–8 cm) long; pistillate catkins shorter. The slender branchlets of this willow are still collected by southwestern Indians for weaving watertight baskets. Many plant communities on stream banks and wet places below 2,000 ft.

154. **Red Willow,** *Salix laevigata*. **[str-wd.]** Maximum height 50 ft. (15 m) tall; bark rough, dark, reddish brown; twigs red-brown to yellowish; slender branchlets light to dark orange-brown; leaves 2–5 in. (5–12 cm) long, lanceolate to oblong-lanceolate, light green above, paler beneath; male flowers with 4–6 stamens; female fruit catkins with cone-shaped capsules. Many plant communities near streams, wet places.

155. **Pacific Willow,** *Salix lucida* ssp. *lasiandra*. **[str-wd.]** Generally 20–50 ft. (6–15 m) tall; branchlets dark colored and stout; twigs shiny reddish to brownish; leaves 2–5 in. (5–13 cm) long, lanceolate to broadly lanceolate, finely-serrate margins, shining dark green above, whitish below; flowers yellow to brown: male catkin with 5–9 stamens, female catkin matures in early summer and bears light reddish brown, ¼ in. (6 mm) long, fruit. Many plant communities on stream banks and wet places.

SCROPHULARIACEAE, FIGWORT FAMILY

156. **Bush Monkeyflower,** *Mimulus aurantiacus*. **[rocks, oak, shrub.]** Shrub, 39–59 in. (10–15 dm) tall, hairless to hairy, stems and leaves sticky; leaves deep green, fuzzy below, linear to obovate, edges generally rolled under; flowers white to buff, yellow, orange, or red, the throat shaped like a funnel. This is a highly complex species with many local forms. Cliffs, rocky hillsides, canyons, disturbed areas, coastal scrub, borders of chaparral, open woods in many plant communities.

SOLANACEAE, NIGHTSHADE FAMILY

157. **Tree Tobacco,** *Nicotiana glauca*. **[sav. oak, shrub. str-wd.]** Shrub or small tree, 6½–26 ft. (2–8 m) tall; evergreen leaves soft, dull green, entire, more or less ovate, 2–8 in. (5–21 cm) long; flowers yellow, tubular, somewhat contracted at throat, in loose-branching, open panicles. This plant is poisonous to livestock and humans. Open, disturbed places; native of South America. Not in Cascade and n. Sierra Nevada foothills.

STERCULIACEAE, CACAO FAMILY

158. **California Fremontia** or **Flannelbush,** *Fremontodendron californicum* ssp. *californicum*. **[shrub. oak]** Erect shrub, 6½–16 ft. (2–5 m) tall, twigs densely stellate-hairy; evergreen leaves ⅜–2 in. (1–5 cm) long, dull green, generally 3 main lobes, rarely entire, undersurface with tawny hairs appearing starlike; showy yellow flowers bloom in May and June. Dry, rocky soils in chaparral and oak-pine woodland.

VITACEAE, GRAPE FAMILY

159. ***California Wild Grape,** *Vitis californica*. **[str-wd. oak]** Vines generally 6½–49 ft. (2–15 m) long with shreddy bark, usually climbing up trees or trailing down banks or cliffs; distinctive large, shallowly

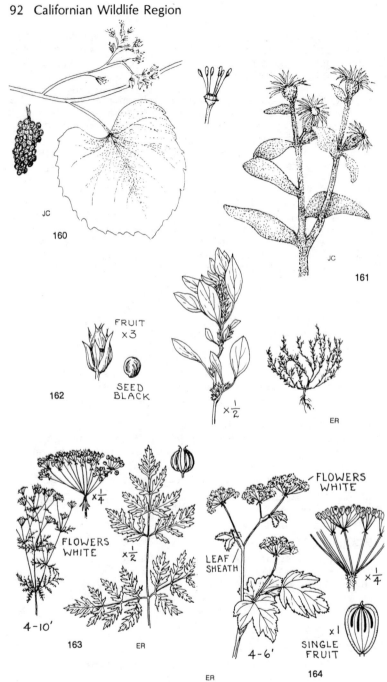

JC

160

161
JC

162

FRUIT
x3

SEED
BLACK

×½

ER

163

FLOWERS
WHITE

×¼

×½

4-10'

ER

164

FLOWERS
WHITE

LEAF
SHEATH

×¼

×1
SINGLE
FRUIT

4-6'

ER

lobed, heart-shaped leaves, 2¾–5½ in. (7–14 cm) wide; tiny flowers greenish yellow, fragrant; purple grapes have a waxy or powdery film. Canyons, stream banks below 3,000 ft. in northern oak woodland, foothill woodland, and mixed evergreen forests. Siskiyou Co. to San Luis Obispo in Coast Ranges and along coast, Central Valley, Cascade and Sierra Nevada foothills.

160. *Desert Wild Grape, Vitis girdiana. [str-wd. oak, shrub.] Vines generally 3–19 ft. (1–6 m) long. Similar to V. californica but smaller with black grapes and stems and undersurfaces of leaves more densely matted-hairy. Stream banks, canyon bottoms in s. oak woodland and coastal sage scrub. Southern California from Santa Barbara Co. to Baja.

E. Herbs

AIZOACEAE, ICE PLANT FAMILY

161. *Common Ice Plant, Mesembryanthemum crystallinum. [coast. scrub.] A succulent annual or biennial with forked, trailing stems under 39 in. (1 m) long; plant covered with glistening, round, colorless, bladderlike bumps; leaves flat with wavy margins, ovate to spoon-shaped; flowers white becoming reddish with age. Fruit, leaves, and stems edible. Coastal strand and coastal sage scrub from Monterey Co. south to Baja.

AMARANTHACEAE, AMARANTH FAMILY

162. *Tumbleweed Amaranth or Pigweed, Amaranthus albus. [grass.] Annual, 4–27 in. (1–7 dm) tall; stems ascending to erect with bushy branches; leaves elliptic to obovate or spatulate; flowers greenish in small clusters in axils of stems throughout plant; bracts green and spined, much longer than sepals; seeds dark red-brown, edible. The young leaves of any Amaranthus species can be eaten after boiling. Becomes a dry tumbleweed in summer. Cultivated fields, along roadsides, etc.

APIACEAE, CARROT FAMILY

163. Poison Hemlock, Conium maculatum. [str-wd. oak, grass. shrub.] Biennial, 2–10 ft. (.6–3 m) tall, musty smelling; stems purple-spotted; leaves fernlike, pinnately compound; flowers in terminal compound umbels. Children have been fatally poisoned by blowing whistles made from the hollow stems of this highly toxic plant. Moist, especially disturbed places. Native to Europe.

164. *Cow Parsnip, Heracleum lanatum. [str-wd. oak, grass. shrub.] Perennial, 3¼–10 ft. (1–3 m) tall, strong-scented; stem stout, covered with densely matted, soft hairs; leaf blades round to kidney shaped, 8–20 in. (2–5 dm) wide and long, divided into 3 rough-toothed leaflets; large umbels of tiny white flowers at top of plant. The cooked root tastes like rutabaga, but this plant should be positively identified before

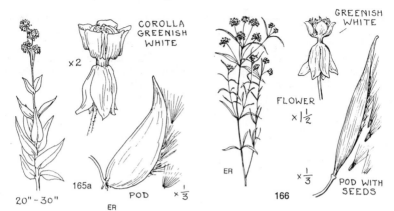

COROLLA GREENISH WHITE

×2

165a

20"-30"

POD ×⅓

ER

GREENISH WHITE

FLOWER ×1½

×⅓

POD WITH SEEDS

166

ER

167

168

JC

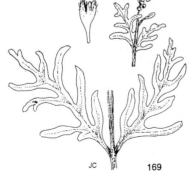

JC 169

170

eating as similar-appearing species are deadly poisonous. Likes moist places, wooded or open.

ASCLEPIADACEAE, MILKWEED FAMILY (herbs or shrubs with milky sap)

165. Kotolo or **Indian Milkweed,** *Asclepias eriocarpa.* **[oak, shrub. grass.]** Perennial with simple, erect stems, 16–35 in. (4–9 dm) tall, covered with short densely-matted hairs; leaves opposite or in whorls of 3–4, blade lanceolate, elliptic, or ovate; corolla reflexed to ascending, cream, sometimes tinged pink; hoods slightly raised above corolla base; seeds whitish. Dry, barren areas in many plant communities. **165a. Desert Milkweed,** *A. erosa.* In dry washes of southern California.

166. Narrow-Leaf Milkweed, *Asclepias fascicularis.* **[oak, shrub. grass.]** Perennial with leafy stems, 20–35 in. (5–9 dm) tall, generally hairless; leaves in whorls of 3–5, narrowly lanceolate; corolla reflexed, greenish white, sometimes tinged purple, with hoods bearing horns surrounding the stamens. Dry places in valleys and foothills; not on the coast.

ASTERACEAE, SUNFLOWER OR DAISY FAMILY

167. *Yarrow or **Milfoil,** *Achillea millefolium.* **[oak, shrub. grass.]** A strongly scented perennial, generally 12–39 in. (3–10 dm) tall; leaves feathery, fernlike; small white to pink flower heads in flat-topped, corymbiform clusters at top of a tough, fibrous stem. The plant can be brewed and ingested to coagulate blood. Open areas in many habitats.

168. Beach Bur, *Ambrosia chamissonis.* **[coast.]** Perennial with branching stems sprawling from taproot; forms loose mats less than 13 ft. (4 m) across; stems brown to gray, course-hairy; leaves under 2 in. (5 cm) long, variable, toothed to 3-pinnately lobed, silky hairy; yellow or translucent staminate flower heads in dense terminal spikes; bur with straight, sharp spines. Beaches, dunes along the entire coast.

169. Western Ragweed, *Ambrosia psilostachya.* **[oak, shrub. grass.]** Perennial 20–78 in. (5–20 dm) tall, little branched, with running rootstocks; stems more or less straw colored, soft-hairy to bristly; herbage glandular-aromatic when rubbed; leaves lanceolate to ovate, simple or 1–2 pinnately divided into leaflets; staminate flowers yellow or translucent in nodding spikes or racemes; pistils clustered below; bur greenish brown with 0–7 spines. Roadsides, dry fields.

170. Pearly Everlasting, *Anaphalis margaritacea.* **[oak, shrub.]** A white-woolly, fragrant perennial, 4–47 in. (2–12 dm) tall; several evenly leafy stems rise from a slender rootstock; leaves sessile, 1¼–4 in. (3–10 cm) long, entire, linear to lanceolate, gray or green above, white-hairy below; small flower heads disclike, in crowded clusters; bracts ovate, pearly white. In openings in woods, hillsides, roadsides, disturbed places. Throughout the Coast Ranges, n. and c. coast, the San Bernardino mts., and the Sierra Nevada.

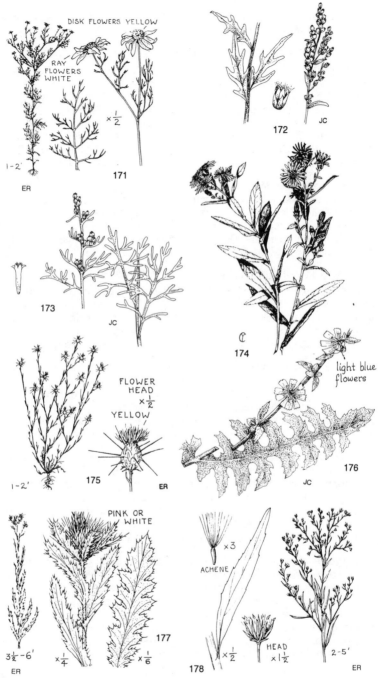

DISK FLOWERS YELLOW

RAY FLOWERS WHITE

$\times \frac{1}{2}$

1-2'

ER

171

172

JC

173

JC

174

FLOWER HEAD $\times \frac{1}{2}$ YELLOW

1-2'

175

ER

light blue flowers

176

JC

PINK OR WHITE

$3\frac{1}{2}-6'$

ER

$\times \frac{1}{4}$

$\times \frac{1}{6}$

177

$\times 3$

ACHENE

$\times \frac{1}{2}$

HEAD $\times 1\frac{1}{2}$

178

2-5'

ER

171. **Mayweed** or **Chamomile,** *Anthemis cotula.* **[oak, shrub. grass. coast.]** Annual, 4–20 in. (1–5 dm) tall, with pinnately divided leaves consisting of linear segments; yellow disk flowers and white ray flowers; bracts green with pale brown margins; ill-smelling. Disturbed areas, fields, roadsides, coastal dunes, chaparral, oak woodland.

172. *****Silver Wormwood,** *Artemisia ludoviciana.* **[oak, shrub.]** Perennial, 12–39 in. (3–10 dm) tall, from a rootstalk bearing many slender, simple, gray to white-hairy stems; leaves entire to deeply lobed, densely white-hairy; foliage aromatic (like turpentine) when crushed; tiny flower heads in narrow, open to dense, nodding panicles. Dry, sandy to rocky soils in the Sierra Nevada foothills, the San Joaquin Valley, and sw. California.

173. *****Coastal Sagewort,** *Artemisia pycnocephala.* **[coast.]** Perennial with decumbent stems, densely leafy and white to gray silky-hairy throughout; forms mounds 12–28 in. (3–7 dm) tall; leaves pinnately divided into linear lobes; sessile flower heads densely clustered on narrow, spikelike panicle. Rocky or sandy soil in the coastal strand. From Santa Barbara Co. north.

174. **Pacific Aster,** *Aster chilensis.* **[coast. shrub.]** Perennial with elongate rootstocks, 16–39 in. (4–10 dm) tall; one to several erect stems, branching and hairy above, ending in narrow or broad cymes; bracts green-tipped, the outer ones green more or less to the base; ray flowers violet. Grassy areas, salt marshes, disturbed areas under 1,500 ft. Ventura Co. north on coast and in outer Coast Ranges.

175. **Yellow Star-Thistle,** *Centaurea solstitialis.* **[oak, shrub. grass.]** Annual, 4–39 in. (1–10 dm) tall, with many spiny branches rising from the base and covered with gray cottony hair; flower heads are bright yellow. This weed spreads very rapidly and is destructive to pastureland. Fields, roadsides, disturbed areas. (One of 11 species of star thistle in the Californian wildlife region.)

176. *****Chicory,** *Cichorium intybus.* **[oak, shrub. grass.]** Perennial under 39 in. (1 m), rising from a deep, woody taproot; stems wiry, branched, with a few small leaves on the upper part; basal leaves 4–8 in. (1–2 dm) long, pinnately lobed, edged with sharp teeth; showy heads of pale blue ray flowers profusely scattered along stems, rarely pink or white. Leaves makes a good spinach substitute; root, best eaten boiled or roasted, can be used in place of coffee. Roadsides, disturbed places.

177. *****Indian Thistle,** *Cirsium brevistylum.* **[shrub.]** Annual or biennial, 1–6 ft. (3–19 dm) tall, with stout but tender stem, very hairy, leafy, and sharp-spiny throughout; leaves gray-hairy beneath; flowers white to purple. Roots and peeled stems edible raw or cooked. Moist places in coastal scrub and woods along the whole coast.

178. **Horseweed,** *Conyza canadensis.* **[oak, shrub. grass.]** Annual, 4–78 in. (1–20 dm) tall; stem leafy, generally simple below, many-branched above, usually with stiff hairs (rairly hairless); lower

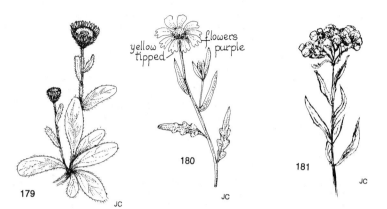

179   JC

180   JC

yellow tipped

flowers purple

181   JC

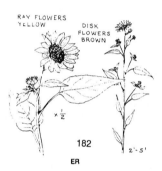

RAY FLOWERS YELLOW

DISK FLOWERS BROWN

x ½

182

ER

2'- 5'

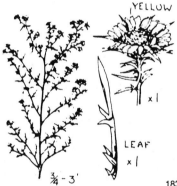

YELLOW

x 1

LEAF x 1

¾ - 3'

183

YELLOW

x 1

x 1

x 1

2-9'

ER

184

RAYS YELLOW WITH WHITE TIPS

x ¼

4 -16"

ER

185

leaves entire or toothed with stems, the upper leaves sessile and entire, narrower; small flower heads form a dense panicle; ray flowers small, white, 2-toothed. Common weed in waste places.

179. **Seaside Daisy,** *Erigeron glaucus.* **[shrub. coast.]** Perennial, under 16 in. (4 dm) tall; bristly, sticky, leafy stems rise from a decumbent base; leaves thick, widely obovate to spoon-shaped, entire or with 2–4 pairs of shallow teeth; flower heads at end of stems with numerous pale violet to lavender ray flowers surrounding a yellowish disk. Coastal scrub, old dunes, and beaches from Santa Barbara Co. north.

180. **Indian Blanket** or **Firewheel,** *Gaillardia pulchella.* **[oak, shrub.]** Leafy-stemmed annual, 8–16 in. (2–4 dm) tall, with branching stems covered with tiny rough hairs; upper leaves entire, lanceolate; lower leaves oblong, pinnately toothed to entire; disk reddish maroon, domelike, with bristly scales; ray flowers light red or purple, often yellow-tipped or multi-colored. Disturbed, urban places throughout sw California and in San Francisco Bay area.

181. **Cudweed,** *Gnaphalium palustre.* **[str-wd. grass. shrub. oak]** Annual, usually branched at base, leafy, under 12 in. (3 dm) tall; foliage tufted loosely with long wool, which usually falls from leaves; most leaves spoon-shaped, a few near heads oblong or lanceolate; heads in small clusters surrounded by wool; bracts about each head brown with whitish tips. Moist places, stream banks.

182. ***Common Sunflower,*** *Helianthus annuus.* **[oak, shrub. grass.]** Annual under 9½ ft. (3 m) tall; stem usually stout, very hairy, and branching in the upper half; leaves long-stemmed, 4–16 in. (1–4 dm) long, usually toothed, widely lanceolate to ovate; flower heads large, somewhat convex, usually with maroon disk and bright yellow rays; ovate bracts rough-hairy, narrowing abruptly. Seeds delicious raw or roasted. Roadsides, fields, many habitats.

183. **Common Spikeweed,** *Hemizonia pungens.* **[grass.]** Annual, 4–47 in. (1–12 dm) long, with many rigid, bristly branches; herbage yellowish green with a honeylike scent; lower leaves linear-lanceolate, deeply 2-divided, the upper leaves linear, spine-tipped; flower heads sometimes densely clustered; bracts keeled, spine-tipped. Grassland and marshes in valleys and foothills below 1,500 ft. Cascade Range foothills, Central Valley, and South Coast Ranges.

184. **Branchy Goldfields,** *Lasthenia californica.* **[grass. oak, shrub. coast.]** Slender annual, under 16 in. (4 dm) tall, simple or freely branched, covered with tiny hairs; leaves linear to oblanceolate, entire, more or less succulent in coastal habitat; heads with bright, golden yellow ray flowers. Abundant on open grassland and in many habitats.

185. **Tidy Tips,** *Layia platyglossa.* **[oak, shrub. grass.]** Annual, 1½–27 in. (4–70 cm) tall, decumbent to erect, glandular, not aromatic; leaves linear to lanceolate or oblanceolate, sometimes fleshy; lower leaves

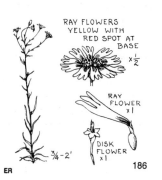

RAY FLOWERS
YELLOW WITH
RED SPOT AT
BASE   x½

RAY
FLOWER
x1

DISK
FLOWER
x1

¾-2'

ER   186

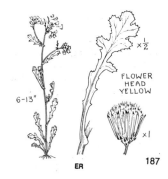

6-13"

FLOWER
HEAD
YELLOW

x½

x1

ER   187

yellow
flowers

188

JC

CY

191

flowers
yellow-orange

189

JC

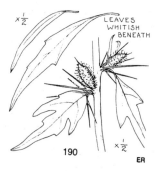

x½

LEAVES
WHITISH
BENEATH

x½

190

ER

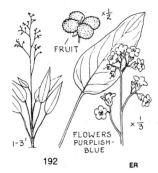

x½

FRUIT

1-3'

FLOWERS
PURPLISH-
BLUE

x⅓

192

ER

lobed; yellow ray flowers white-tipped; seeds with 15–30 bristles. Many habitats throughout region but not in the Sierra or Cascade mts.

186. **Common Madia**, *Madia elegans*. [grass. oak, shrub.] Slender annual, 4–98 in. (1–25 dm) tall, with erect, simple to branched, leafy stems, soft-hairy below, slightly to heavily glandular above; leaves linear to broadly lanceolate, soft-hairy to bristly; flower heads in open cymes; yellow ray flowers maroon-spotted at base; seeds brown or black, flat, rough feeling. Dry areas, grassland, open woods, roadsides.

187. **Common Groundsel**, *Senecio vulgaris*. [oak, shrub. grass.] Annual, 4–24 in. (1–6 dm) tall, simple or branched, very leafy; leaves 1¼–4 in. (3–10 cm) long, oblanceolate to obovate, deeply and unevenly lobed; flower heads with yellow central disk flowers only; bracts about 21 and black-tipped; tiny, hairy achenes. Weed in gardens and disturbed places.

188. **California Goldenrod**, *Solidago californica*. [oak, shrub. grass.] Stout perennial with stems 8–59 in. (2–15 dm) tall rising from short rootstocks, usually densely soft-hairy; leaves oblanceolate to obovate, serrate; flower heads in long, 1-sided panicles; ray flowers 6–11, yellow; disk flowers 6–17, yellow. Margins of woods, grassland, disturbed places.

189. **Golden Crownbeard** or **Cowpen Daisy**, *Verbesina encelioides* ssp. *exauriculata*. [grass. shrub.] Many-branched, erect annual, 8–51 in. (2–13 dm) tall, unpleasant smelling; stems covered with fine hairs; leaves dull green, 1½–4 in. (4–10 cm) long, nearly triangular, conspicuously toothed, rough-hairy; achenes in yellow flower heads turn from black to white-olive when mature. Fields, disturbed areas, roadsides. San Joaquin and Salinas valleys south to Ventura and Riverside counties, and along the south coast.

190. **Spiny Cocklebur**, *Xanthium spinosum*. [grass. oak, shrub.] Annual, under 39 in. (1 m) tall; tough, slender stems with 3-pronged, golden spines by the side of each leaf; leaves linear to elliptic, nearly entire to pinnately lobed, white-hairy below, gray-green above; fruit a cylindrical, spine-tipped bur. Disturbed areas.

BORAGINACEAE, BORAGE FAMILY

191. **Orange Fiddleneck**, *Amsinckia menziesii*. [oak, grass. shrub.] Annual weed or wildflower, 12–35 in. (3–9 dm) tall; flowers orange-yellow, clustered on coiled, very bristly stems; leaves long and narrowly to broadly lanceolate. Abundant in open, generally disturbed places, such as roadsides and fields.

192. **Hound's Tongue**, *Cynoglossum grande*. [oak, shrub.] Perennial, 12–35 in. (3–9 dm) tall; leaves 3–8 in. (8–20 cm) long on long basal stalks, ovate shaped resembling a dog's tongue; loose-clustered flowers each have 5 deep blue petals with 5 white, two-lobed tiny pads around the center tube. Shaded or open places in oak or mixed woodland and

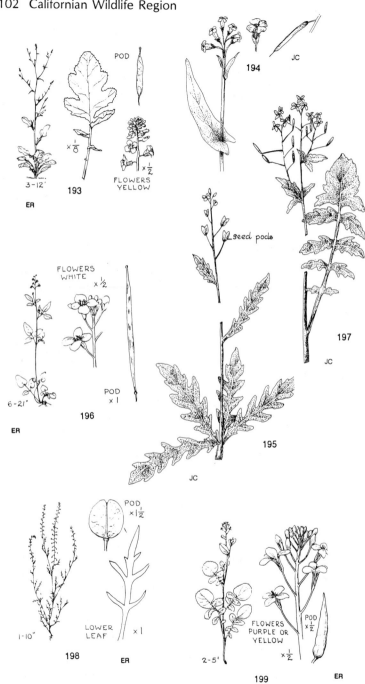

POD

×⅛

193

3-12'

ER

FLOWERS
YELLOW

×½

194

JC

seed pods

197

JC

FLOWERS
WHITE   ×½

POD
× I

196

6-21"

ER

195

JC

POD
×1½

LOWER
LEAF   ×1

198

1-10"

ER

FLOWERS
PURPLE OR
YELLOW

POD
×½

×½

199

2-5'

ER

chaparral. Santa Barbara Co. n. in Coast Ranges, Sierra foothills, Tulare Co. n. to British Columbia.

BRASSICACEAE, MUSTARD FAMILY

193. *Black Mustard, *Brassica nigra.* [grass. oak, shrub.] Annual, stem erect, 16–78 in. (4–20 dm) tall, generally branched above; hairs sparse to dense; basal leaves pinnately lobed (with large terminal lobe), toothed; upper leaves sessile and smaller; flowers bright yellow; pod with long beak; seeds dark red-brown. The source of most table mustard. Abundant in fields and disturbed areas.

194. *Field Mustard or Turnip, *Brassica rapa.* [grass. oak, shrub.] Annual, stem erect, simple to freely branched, 8–39 in. (2–10 dm) tall; small cruciferous yellow flowers in long racemes; large lower leaves wavy-toothed, more or less pinnately-lobed, with earlike lobes at their bases; middle and upper leaves sessile and clasping the stem; flowering Jan. to May. Young greens are edible. Fields, meadows, orchards, disturbed places.

195. **Shepherd's Purse**, *Capsella bursa-pastoris.* [grass. oak, shrub.] Annual, erect stem 4–20 in. (1–5 dm) tall, branched or almost simple; basal leaves in rosette; tiny flowers white, distinctly clawed, and clustered at the tops of the stems; flattened seed pods look like tiny purses. Common on sheep trails, grazing areas, and disturbed places.

196. **California Toothwort** or **Milk Maids**, *Cardamine californica.* [grass. oak, shrub.] Perennial, usually has one stem 8–27½ in. (2–7 dm) long, rising from tuberlike rhizome; upper leaves 3–5, widely ovate to oblong, entire to wavy or toothed; rhizome leaflets generally 3, ovate to cordate; flowers small, white to pale rose, in a single raceme, sometimes in 2. Usually shady banks and slopes in canyons and woods; many plant communities.

197. *Tansy Mustard, *Descurainia sophia.* [grass. shrub. des. oak] Annual or biennial; stem 12–27 in. (3–7 dm) high, short branched above, leafy, with minute sparse to dense hairs; leaves very deeply 2-3 pinnately lobed to compound; leaflets generally linear; flowers yellow; seed pods ascending, linear with one row of seeds. Disturbed areas, fields, roadsides, canyon bottoms, desert. Introduced from Eurasia.

198. **Tongue Peppergrass**, *Lepidium nitidum.* [grass. oak, shrub.] Annual, stem erect to spreading, 4–16 in. (1–4 dm) high, with 0 to many branches; basal leaves linear, 1–4 in. (3–10 cm) long, deeply pinnately divided; upper leaves are less divided to simple and entire; flowers tiny, with white petals, 6 stamens (the 2 shorter only filaments); pods ovate to round, smooth, shiny. Open flats and slopes in alkaline soils in scrub, valley grassland, chaparral, etc.

199. *Wild Radish, *Raphanus sativus.* [grass. oak, shrub.] Annual or biennial, 1–4 ft. (3–12 dm) tall, freely branched; lower leaves pinnately lobed with terminal lobe or leaflet widely ovate to round; upper leaves

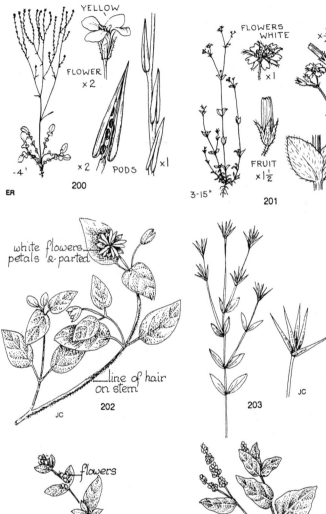

YELLOW

FLOWER ×2

-4'

×2   PODS   ×1

200

ER

FLOWERS WHITE

×1

×¾

FRUIT ×1½

×1

3-15"

201

ER

white flowers petals 2-parted

line of hair on stem

202

JC

203

JC

flowers

204   JC

205   JC

toothed; flowers white with purplish veins, or yellowish or purplish. The root is edible but hot! Fields, disturbed places, roadsides.

200. *Hedge Mustard, *Sisymbrium officinale*. [grass. oak, shrub.] Annual, stiffly erect, 12–39 in. (3–10 dm) tall, with few widely divergent branches; covered with sharp hairs, especially near base; leaves in basal rosette, oblanceolate, and deeply pinnately or irregularly lobed; small pale yellow flowers in long and narrow racemes; seed pods appressed or not, narrowly awl-shaped containing dark brown seeds. Disturbed places and roadsides.

CARYOPHYLLACEAE, PINK FAMILY (leaves opposite and entire)

201. Mouse-Ear Chickweed, *Cerastium glomeratum*. [grass. oak, shrub.] Annual, 3–15 in. (8–38 cm) high, covered with long, soft hairs, somewhat sticky; flowering stems ascending to erect; flowers white in cymes; leaves on stems hairy, lanceolate or oblanceolate to ovate, thus resembling "mouse ears." Dry hillsides, grasslands, chaparral, disturbed areas.

202. *Common Chickweed or Starwort, *Stellaria media*. [grass. oak, shrub.] Annual with delicate stems up to 19½ in. (5 dm) long, mostly lying on the ground, but sometimes erect; stems with a line of hair between each joint; leaves more or less evenly spaced, ⅜–1½ in. (1–4 cm) long, ovate, shiny; flowers white in cymes; bracts leafy. Shaded places in oak woodland, meadows, disturbed areas. Not in s. Coast Ranges, but on the coast and most of our region. Boiled, it tastes like spinach.

203. Shining Chickweed, *Stellaria nitens*. [str-wd. oak, grass. shrub.] Annual, ascending to erect, 1½–9½ in., (4–24 cm) tall; stems bright green, forked, very slender, lacking the line of internodal hair characterizing *S. media*; leaves crowded near base, shiny: lower spoonlike, upper linear-lanceolate; tiny flowers. Sand dunes, stream banks, open woodlands, valley grasslands, and open chaparral.

CHENOPODIACEAE, GOOSEFOOT FAMILY

204. *Beach Saltbush, *Atriplex leucophylla*. [coast.] Perennial under 12 in. (3 dm) tall, somewhat woody at base, densely covered with whitish scales; stems 12–39 in. (3–10 dm) long, prostrate to decumbent, but with ascending to erect branchlets; leaves sessile, crowded, mostly alternate, elliptic to widely ovate; male flowers in dense terminal spikes; female in few-flowered axillary clusters; fruiting bracts have wartlike projections; seeds dark red-brown, edible; young leaves and shoots also edible. Sandy soils and dunes up and down the coast.

205. *Redscale Saltbush or Tumbling Oracle, *Atriplex rosea*. [grass. shrub. oak] Erect annual, 16–59 in. (4–15 dm) tall, with ascending branches; leaves firm, densely scaly underneath, greenish above but becoming red, with wavy-toothed margins; flowers in dense, headlike cymes or interrupted terminal spikes; fruiting bracts often warty. Open, disturbed areas in many plant communities.

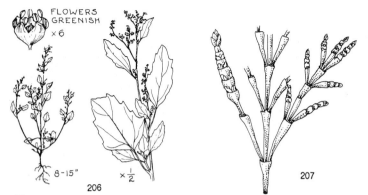

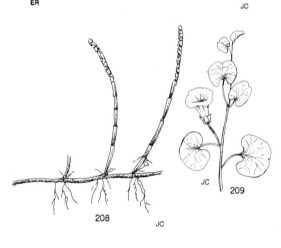

FLOWERS
GREENISH
×6

8-15"

206

ER

207

JC

208

JC

JC 209

211

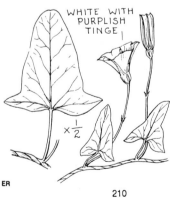

WHITE WITH
PURPLISH
TINGE

×½

ER

210

212

JC

206. ***Dark Green Goosefoot** or **Pigweed**, *Chenopodium murale*. **[grass. oak, shrub.]** Annual with loosely spreading, stout, and watery stems, the branches often lying on the ground; stems 8–24 in. (2–6 dm) long; leaves and stems shiny dark green, feeling mealy when rubbed; flowers in terminal short panicles; sepals partially enclosing fruit; flowers in winter. In cultivated or disturbed areas. Other common species include *C. album*, which is dull green above, and *C. berlandieri*, whose sepals enclose the fruit. All are edible; the seeds can be eaten raw.

207. ***Subterminal Pickleweed**, *Salicornia subterminalis*. **[coast. des. shrub.]** Perennial 2¾–12 in. (7–30 cm) long; stem spreading to erect; branches ascending, ending in a spike, final 5–14 nodes of spike lack flowers. Salt marshes, alkaline flats, coastal sage scrub below 2,600 ft. Central and s. coast; San Joaquin Valley.

208. ***Creeping Pickleweed**, *Salicornia virginica*. **[coast. des.]** Forms extensive colonies; perennial 8–28 in. (20–70 cm) long with stem creeping, rooting at nodes; branches decumbent to erect, ending in dense, cylindrical spikes, generally 3 flowers per node; leaves opposite, clasped to stem. Edible as a salad green, or shoots and branches can be pickled. Salt marshes, alkaline flats below 325 ft. Along entire coast; also San Joaquin Valley.

CONVOLVULACEAE, MORNING-GLORY FAMILY (gen. twining or trailing stems)

209. **Beach Morning-Glory**, *Calystegia soldanella*. **[coast.]** Perennial growing from deep roots; stems trailing, hairless; leaves kidney-shaped, blunt, and slightly fleshy; flowers pink or rose, funnel-shaped on short stalks, remaining open most of the day. Pacific beaches in sand.

210. **Bindweed** or **Orchard Morning Glory**, *Convolvulus arvensis*. **[grass. oak, shrub.]** Rising from deep persistent roots with long trailing or twining stems makes this a troublesome weed; leaves oblong to ovate with arrowhead-shaped base; flowers funnel-shaped, white or pinkish, with 2 narrow bracts on stalk well below the calyx. Cultivated areas, fields, roadsides. Native to Europe.

CRASSULACEAE, STONECROP FAMILY

211. **Canyon Dudleya**, *Dudleya cymosa*. **[rocks, oak, shrub.]** Perennial with stout, reddish flower stems rising 4–8 in. (1–2 dm) high from basal rosette of thick, succulent leaves; leaves grayish green, generally oblanceolate to spoon-shaped, with acute tips; flowers in flat-topped cyme, yellow to red. Rocky outcrops, slopes, talus in pine-oak woodland, chaparral, etc. Whole region except the Central Valley.

212. **Lance-Leaved Dudleya**, *Dudleya lanceolata*. **[rocks, oak, shrub.]** Perennial with stout, reddish flower stems rising 8–24 in. (2–6 dm) tall from basal rosette of lance-shaped, succulent leaves; flowers yellow to red. Dry, rocky slopes in chaparral, coastal sage scrub of South Coast Ranges and Transverse and Peninsular ranges.

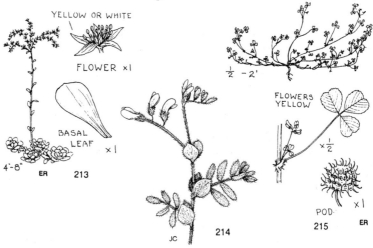

YELLOW OR WHITE

FLOWER ×1

BASAL LEAF ×1

4"-8"   ER   213

½ - 2'

FLOWERS YELLOW

×½

POD ×1

215   ER

JC   214

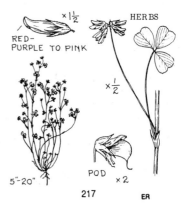

×3

FLOWERS YELLOW

×1

PODS ×2½

ER   216

×1½

RED-PURPLE TO PINK

HERBS

×½

POD ×2

5"-20"

POD ×2

217   ER

flowers pink

seed

JC   218

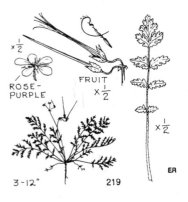

×½

ROSE-PURPLE

FRUIT ×½

×½

3-12"   219   ER

213. *Pacific Stonecrop, *Sedum spathulifolium*. [rocks, oak, shrub.] Perennial 4–8 in. (1–2 dm) tall; leaves spoon-shaped, succulent, in several loose basal rosettes, usually whitish in appearance, sometimes green; cyme flat-topped; petals lanceolate, yellow, rarely orange or white. The young stems and leaves make a good salad or potherb. Rocky outcrops, often in shade. Coast Ranges from Ventura Co. north, Cascade and Sierra foothills; not in Central Valley.

FABACEAE, LEGUME FAMILY

214. Silky Beach Pea, *Lathyrus littoralis*. [coast.] A densely, silky gray-hairy perennial with prostrate or ascending stems; leaves pinnately compound consisting of 4–8, obovate to short-oblong leaflets; pink and white flowers in dense racemes; forms dense, colorful patches, often among yellow or red sand verbenas and beach morning glories. Open, coastal sand dunes from Monterey Co. north.

215. California Burclover, *Medicago polymorpha*. [grass. oak, shrub.] Annual with creeping, mat-forming or ascending stems, 4–16 in. (1–4 dm) long; 3 cloverlike, dark green leaflets, often finely toothed; flowers lipped, usually 2–6 in a group; corolla yellow; pods spiral, 2–3 turns. Disturbed areas; common spring pasture.

216. Sourclover, *Melilotus indica*. [str-wd. grass. oak, shrub.] Annual, erect, leafy plant, 4–23 in. (1–6 dm) high. Several branches spread from near the base; leaves divided into 3 leaflets, ⅜–1 in. (1–2.5 cm) long, oblanceolate to wedge-shaped, generally sharply toothed; flowers yellow in slender racemes, compact; pods ovoid with wrinkled coats. Along roadsides, stream banks, in open disturbed places. Introduced from Eurasia. *Melilotus* is potentially toxic to livestock.

217. *Pinpoint Clover, *Trifolium gracilentum*. [oak, grass. shrub.] Stems 4–16 in. (1–4 dm) long, erect to prostrate; leaflets generally 3, obovate, notched at tip; flowers in umbel, pink to red-purple. Open, disturbed areas in foothill woods, valley grassland, chaparral, etc. Many similar *Trifolium* species are found in the Calif. region; all are edible.

FRANKENIACEAE, FRANKENIA FAMILY

218. Alkali Heath, *Frankenia salina*. [des. coast.] Bushy shrub or herb forming mats with smooth to densely hairy twigs and leaves; stems more or less prostrate, 4–24 in. (1–6 dm) long; lower leaves obovate, margins often rolled downward, united in pairs by a membranous base; upper leaves narrower; petals white to dark pink. Salt marshes along the central and southern coast; alkali flats in the Central Valley.

GERANIACEAE, GERANIUM FAMILY

219. Red-Stem Storksbill or Filaree, *Erodium cicutarium*. [oak, shrub. grass. des.] Annual with fleshy, reddish, decumbent to ascending stems, 4–20 in. (1–5 dm) long; forms a flat rosette of leaves on ground at first; leaves fernlike; flowers in loose umbel, red-lavender; fruit beaks stick straight up, curling when picked. Open, disturbed areas, grassland, shrubland. Native to Eurasia.

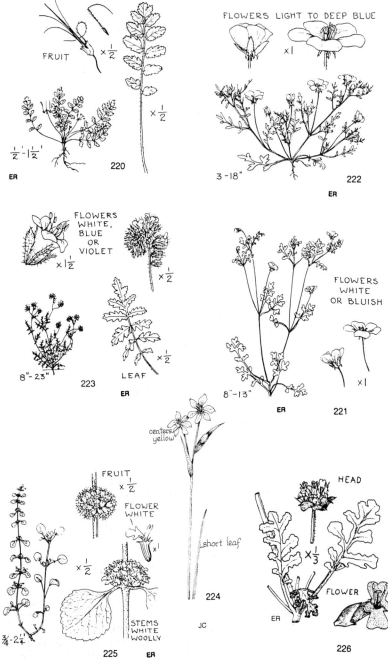

FRUIT ×½

×½

½'-1½'

ER

220

FLOWERS LIGHT TO DEEP BLUE

×1

3-18"

ER

222

FLOWERS
WHITE,
BLUE
OR
VIOLET

×1½

×½

×½

8"-23"   LEAF   ×½

223

ER

FLOWERS
WHITE
OR BLUISH

×1

8"-13"

ER   221

centers
yellow

short leaf

224

JC

FRUIT
×½

FLOWER
WHITE

×1

×½

STEMS
WHITE
WOOLLY

¾-2¼"

225   ER

HEAD

×⅓

ER

FLOWER

226

220. **White-Stem Storksbill** or **Filaree**, *Erodium moschatum*. **[oak, grass. shrub.]** Annual or biennial; fleshy, decumbent to ascending stems whitish, 4–24 in. (1–6 dm) long, short hairy; leaves pinnate; leaflets toothed, ⅜–1⅛ in. (1–3 cm) long; plant forms a flat circle on the ground at first, with flower stems arising later; flowers in loose umbel, red-lavender; fruits have long beaks that curl in circles. Open, disturbed areas, especially in rich soil. Native to Europe.

HYDROPHYLLACEAE, WATERLEAF FAMILY

221. **Variable-Leaved Nemophila**, *Nemophila heterophylla*. **[oak, shrub. str-wd. rocks]** Annual, more or less erect, 4–12 in. (1–3 dm) long, with lightly hairy, slender stems; lower leaves opposite, divided into 5–7 lobes; upper leaves alternate; flowers bowl-shaped, white or bluish. Likes light shade in chaparral, foothill woods, roadsides, stream banks, and talus. Sierra Nevada foothills from Kern Co. north, Coast Ranges from Santa Barbara Co. north.

222. **Baby Blue Eyes**, *Nemophila menziesii*. **[oak, shrub. grass.]** Annual with slender, branched, low-lying stems 4–12 in. (1–3 dm) long, more or less succulent; leaves ¾–2 in. (2–5 cm) long, opposite, pinnately lobed; flowers bowl-shaped and generally bright blue with a white center, often blue-veined and black dotted. In valley grassland, foothill woods, meadows, roadsides, and canyons.

223. **Wild Heliotrope** or **Common Phacelia**, *Phacelia distans*. **[oak, shrub. grass.]** Annual, 6–31 in. (1.5–8 dm) tall, decumbent to erect, simple to branched at base, finely haired, glandular above; leaves fern-shaped; flowers funnel- to bell-shaped, blue, in coiled clusters. Clay to rocky soils in fields and brushy slopes.

IRIDACEAE, IRIS FAMILY

224. **Blue-Eyed Grass**, *Sisyrinchium bellum*. **[grass. oak, shrub.]** Stems 4–24 in. (1–6 dm) high, generally tufted, almost always with leaf-bearing nodes; leaves mostly basal, grasslike, shorter than or extending to near ends of stems; flowers umbel-like, violet, blue, lilac, or rarely white, tips truncate to notched with a small point; two sheathing bracts, often purplish, partly cover flowers. Open, generally moist, grassy places or open woods. Whole region except desert.

LAMIACEAE, MINT FAMILY

225. ***Horehound**, *Marrubium vulgare*. **[oak, grass. shrub.]** Perennial, 4–24 in. (1–6 dm) high; stems erect to ascending, covered with densely matted hairs; leaves ovate to round with toothed margins; hooks on calyx lobes of white flowers cling to clothing. Its tea makes a nutritious tonic. Dry, open ground, especially disturbed areas.

226. ***Chia**, *Salvia columbariae*. **[oak, shrub.]** Annual, 4–20 in. (1–5 dm) tall; stems branched or simple below, generally covered with sparse short hairs; leaves mainly basal, irregularly pinnately lobed, ¾–4 in. (2–10 cm) long; flowers in dense, round clusters are pale to deep blue above purplish, spine-tipped bracts; edible seeds highly nutritious. Dry,

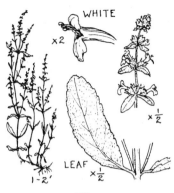

WHITE

×2

×½

LEAF ×½

1-2'

ER   227

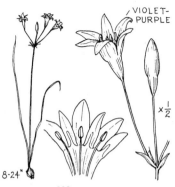

VIOLET-
PURPLE

×½

8-24"

228

ER

JC   229

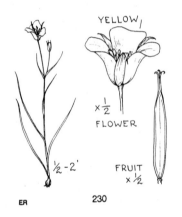

YELLOW

×½
FLOWER

FRUIT
×½

½-2'

ER   230

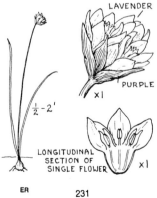

LAVENDER

PURPLE

×1

½-2'

LONGITUDINAL
SECTION OF
SINGLE FLOWER   ×1

ER   231

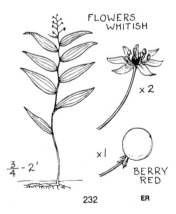

FLOWERS
WHITISH

×2

×1

BERRY
RED

¾-2'

232   ER

disturbed areas in coastal sage scrub, chaparral, and foothill woods. Not in the Cascades or n. Sierra Nevada.

227. **Bugle Hedge Nettle**, *Stachys ajugoides* var. *ajugoides*. **[str-wd. shrub. oak]** Stems often decumbent, 12–24 in. (3–6 dm) long, covered with soft hairs; leaves ¾–2¾ in. (2–7 cm), generally oblong, long silky hairs irritating to skin; flowers generally in 3–6 flowered clusters; corolla white to pale pink. Moist, open places in foothill woods and shrubland. Not in Central Valley or Sierra Nevada or Cascade foothills. *S. ajugoides* is very similar but less hairy, has a pink to purple corolla, and is found in the whole region.

LILIACEAE, LILY FAMILY

228. *****Harvest Brodiaea**, *Brodiaea elegans*. **[grass. oak]** 4–19 in. (1–5 dm), rising from edible bulb; flowers in umbels, blue-purple to violet, funnel-shaped with recurved tips. All *Brodiaea* and similar species have long, narrow basal leaves, usually withered by flowering-time, and 6-lobed flowers. In heavy soils on grassy and open wooded slopes, meadows, valley grassland. Monterey and Tulare cos. to sw. Oregon.

229. *****Fairy Lantern** or **White Globe Lily**, *Calochortus albus*. **[oak, shrub.]** Branched stem 8–31 in. (2–8 dm) tall; basal leaves 12–27 in. (3–7 dm) long; flowers nodding, white to pink, egg-shaped, 2-many. Shaded, often rocky places, in foothill woodland and chaparral. Northern and c. Sierra Nevada foothills, San Francisco Bay area and South Coast Ranges, w. Transverse Ranges. (There are many *Calochortus* species. Those with egg-shaped flowers are generally called globe lilies; those with more open flowers are called Mariposa lilies.)

230. *****Yellow Mariposa Lily**, *Calochortus luteus*. **[grass. oak.]** Slender, erect stems 8–20 in. (2–5 dm) high, bearing a few narrow leaves at top; bulb edible; flowers 1–4, in umbel-like clusters, deep yellow, bell-shaped, usually red-brown lined inside and with central red-brown blotch; gland near base of petals crescent-shaped and hairy matted. Heavy soil in grassland, foothill woods, mixed evergreen forest. Coast Ranges, Sierra Nevada foothills, Sacramento Valley.

231. *****Blue Dicks** or **Wild Hyacinth**, *Dichelostemma capitatum*. **[oak, shrub. grass.]** Stems usually 12–24 in. (3–6 dm) tall; basal leaves narrowly lanceolate, barely keeled; flowers blue-purple to violet, rarely white; bracts whitish to dark purple; bulb edible. Open woods, scrubland, grassland.

232. *****False Solomon's Seal**, *Smilacina stellata*. **[str-wd. oak, shrub.]** Perennial; simple erect stem, 12–28 in. (3–7 dm) high, scaly below, leafy above, rising from a slender, creeping rootstock; small white flowers in a simple, terminal raceme of 5–15 flowers; leaves sessile, oblong-lanceolate to elliptic, bright green; berries round, reddish purple to black. *Smilacina racemosa* is similar but has a thick rootstock, panicle, and red berries dotted with purple. The berries of both species are edible, but purgative if eaten in too large a quantity. Moist woods,

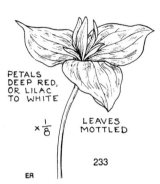

PETALS
DEEP RED,
OR LILAC
TO WHITE

$\times \frac{1}{8}$

LEAVES
MOTTLED

233

ER

234   CY

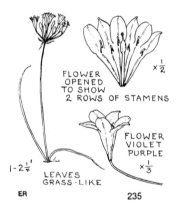

FLOWER
OPENED
TO SHOW
2 ROWS OF STAMENS

$\times \frac{1}{2}$

FLOWER
VIOLET
PURPLE

$\times \frac{1}{3}$

$1-2\frac{1}{4}'$

LEAVES
GRASS-LIKE

ER

235

white flowers

JC

236

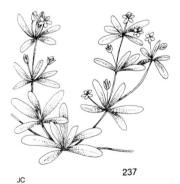

JC

237

238

open hillsides, stream banks in oak woodland, chaparral, and mixed evergreen forest.

233. *Common Trillium, *Trillium albidum*. [shrub. oak, str-wd.] Similar to *T. chloropetalum* except petals white to pinkish, sometimes purplish near base. Edges of redwood and mixed evergreen forests, northern coastal scrub and chaparral, moist canyon slopes and ravine banks. Northwestern California, Cascades and n. Sierra Nevada, San Francisco Bay area to Santa Cruz Co.

234. *Giant Trillium, *Trillium chloropetalum*. [shrub. oak, str-wd.] Erect stem 8–27½ in. (2–7 dm) tall; leaves 3 in a single whorl, sessile, 2¾–8 in. (7–21 cm) long, nearly as broad as long; flower petals fragrant, yellow to dark purple (sometimes white), often brown-spotted, rise out of center of 3 leaves. Brushy or wooded hillsides, usually in moist soil at edges of redwood forests and chaparral. Inner North Coast Ranges and San Francisco Bay area to Santa Cruz Co.

235. *Grass Nut or Ithuriel's Spear, *Triteleia laxa*. [oak, shrub. grass.] Stalk stout, rigid, 4–27 in. (1–7 dm) high. Each umbel with numerous flowers, each flower on a 1–3½ in. (3–9 cm) long stalk, which is only a little longer than the flower; flowers blue or blue-purple to white; basal leaves narrowly lanceolate, keeled; bulb edible. In clay soils in chaparral, mixed evergreen forest, foothill woods, grassland. Coast Ranges and Transverse Ranges, Sierra Nevada foothills from Kern Co. to sw. Oregon.

236. Star Lily, *Zigadenus fremontii*. [grass. shrub. oak] Stems 12–39 in. (3–10 dm) tall, smooth; basal leaves 8–23½ in. (2–6 dm) long, arched and folded with rough margins; starlike flowers yellowish white in panicle or raceme, the petals clawed; bulb 1¼–2⅜ in. (3–6 cm) long; *poisonous*. Dry grassy or wooded slopes, valley grassland. Coast Ranges from Oregon to n. Baja and in Sacramento Valley.

MOLLUGINACEAE, CARPETWEED FAMILY

237. *Carpetweed or Indian Chickweed, *Mollugo verticillata*. [oak, shrub. grass.] Annual with creeping, unequally forked stems forming mats up to 20 in. (5 dm) wide; leaves in whorls of 3–6 more or less oblanceolate blades; flowers in sessile clusters; sepals 5, white inside. Edible as a potherb. Moist, exposed edges of wetlands, roadsides, fields.

NYCTAGINACEAE, FOUR-O'CLOCK FAMILY

238. Yellow Sand Verbena, *Abronia latifolia*. [coast. shrub.] Perennial with succulent, finely glandular-hairy, creeping stems rising from a thick, deep root; stems under 6½ ft. (2 m) long, with short branches, forming a dense mat; leaves thick, fleshy, opposite, rounded; many trumpet-shaped, yellow flowers in hemispherical heads on erect flower stalks; fruit "top"-shaped, 3–5 winged. Beaches, sand dunes, and coastal scrub from Santa Barbara Co. north to British Columbia. The similar *A. maritima* of southern California has wine-red flowers.

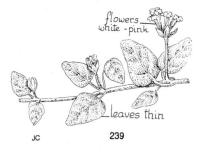

flowers
white-pink

leaves thin

JC   239

yellow flowers
red spot
at petal base

leaves
silver-gray

JC   240

241

242

flowers
yellow to orange

JC

243

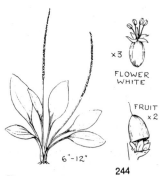

×3

FLOWER
WHITE

FRUIT
×2

6"-12"

244

ER

JC   245

239. **Red-Branched Sand Verbena,** *Abronia umbellata.* **[coast. shrub.]** Annual with slender, succulent, creeping, frequently reddish stems less than 39 in. (1 m) long; leaves ovate to diamond-shaped; flowers tubes more or less green or red, light to bright magenta above. Disturbed sandy areas, dunes, and coastal scrub.

ONAGRACEAE, EVENING PRIMROSE FAMILY (flowers open at dawn and dusk)

240. **Beach Evening Primrose,** *Camissonia cheiranthifolia.* **[coast.]** Perennial with wiry stems prostrate to ascending radiating from a central rosette; stems 4–24 in. (1–6 dm) long, peeling; rosette leaves oblanceolate; upper leaves generally narrowly ovate to obovate, finely toothed; petals bright yellow, fading reddish, bases with 0–2 red dots. Sandy dunes, flats in coastal strand along whole coast.

241. **Foothill Sun Cup,** *Camissonia lacustris.* **[oak, grass. shrub.]** Annual with decumbent or erect stem less than 20 in. (5 dm) long, wiry, peeling; flowers nodding, cup-shaped; yellow petals fading reddish, bases with 0–2 red dots; leaves linear to narrowly elliptic, finely toothed; fruit cylindrical, more or less swollen by seeds, straight or wavy. Open grassland on serpentine, s. inner North Coast Ranges, Sierra Nevada foothills. Very similar *C. strigulosa* is found in cw. and sw. California. More widespread is *C. graciliflora*, which has longer leaves and leathery 4-winged fruit.

242. **Farewell-To-Spring,** *Clarkia amoena.* **[shrub. oak]** A late spring flowering annual with pink to lavender petals with a darker red blotch in the center; leaves 3/4–2½ in. (2–6 cm) long, linear to lanceolate. Dry grassy slopes and openings in brush and woods in northern coastal scrub and outer North Coast Ranges from Monterey Co. north.

PAPAVERACEAE, POPPY FAMILY

243. **California Poppy,** *Eschscholtzia californica.* **[grass. oak, shrub. coast.]** Annual or perennial with smooth, bluish green stems 8–24 in. (2–6 dm) long, falling down in age; leaves fernlike; petals 4, deep orange or yellow-orange, fan-shaped. Grassy, open areas in many plant communities.

PLANTAGINACEAE, PLANTAIN FAMILY

244. **Common Plantain,** *Plantago major.* **[str-wd. oak, shrub. grass.]** Mostly perennial, 6–12 in. (15–30 cm) tall; a few smooth, leafless stems end in slender spikes of tiny, 4-stamened flowers; leaves basal, widely elliptic to cordate-ovate, narrowing more or less abruptly into stems. Young plants edible as potherbs or greens; seeds also edible. Moist, disturbed places. Not in the Sierra Nevada.

PLUMBAGINACEAE, LEADWORT FAMILY

245. **Western Marsh-Rosemary** or **Sea-Lavender,** *Limonium californicum.* **[coast.]** Perennial with heavy, woody, reddish base from which rise leathery, obovate to oblong basal leaves tapering into stout leaf-stalks; leafless stem, 8–20 in. (2–5 dm) tall, branches into densely

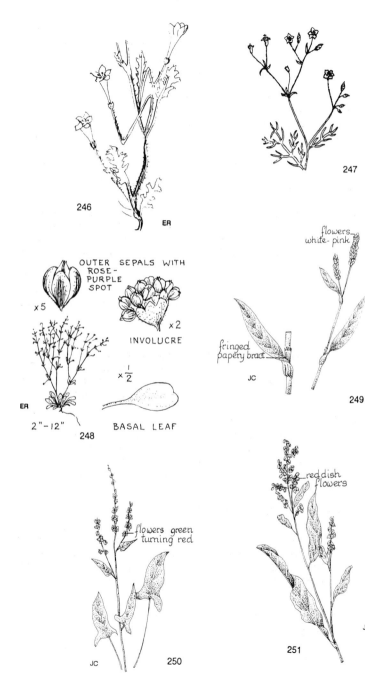

246

ER

247

OUTER SEPALS WITH
ROSE-
PURPLE
SPOT

×5

×2

INVOLUCRE

×½

ER

2"–12"

248

BASAL LEAF

flowers
white-pink

fringed
papery bract

JC

249

flowers green
turning red

JC

250

reddish
flowers

JC

251

flowered, loose panicle; petals oblong, pale violet or blue. Coastal beaches and salt marshes along the whole coast.

POLEMONIACEAE, PHLOX

246. Splendid Gilia, *Gilia splendens.* **[oak, shrub.]** Robust annual herb, 4–31 in. (1–8 dm) tall; usually 1 stem with several branches; fernlike leaves in semi-erect, basal rosette; flowers in loose cyme; funnel-form corollas with slender red to purple tube and white to pale violet throat. Rocky soil in openings in chaparral and foothill woods. South Coast Ranges, Transverse Ranges, and San Jacinto Mts.

247. Bird's Eye Gilia, *Gilia tricolor.* **[oak, shrub. grass.]** Annual with many slender, widely divergent branches, 4–16 in. (1–4 dm) tall, leafy and hairless or white-hairy below; flower formation sticky; basal leaves loose-clustered, 1–2 pinnate; upper leaves palmate, linear lobed; flowers 3-colored with petals light blue, blue-violet at tip, throat of funnel yellow and bearing purple spots. Open, grassy hillsides, valleys, and flatlands in the Coast Ranges, San Joaquin Valley, and Sierra Nevada foothills.

POLYGONACEAE, BUCKWHEAT FAMILY

248. *Wild Buckwheat, *Eriogonum angulosum.* **[oak, shrub. grass.]** One of the more common of 133 species of wild buckwheat found in California. Erect annual, 4–35 in. (1–9 dm) tall, with spreading, more or less angled, forking stems; leaves generally lanceolate with rolled back margins, ⅜–1½ in. (1–4 cm) long, densely matted-hairy, esp. underneath; tiny flowers white to rose. Dry open places in the c. and s. Sierra Nevada foothills, Tehachapi Mts., San Joaquin Valley, South Coast Ranges and coast from Santa Barbara Co. to San Francisco Bay, the Transverse Ranges, and the s. Peninsular Ranges.

249. *Lady's Thumb, *Polygonum persicaria.* **[oak, shrub. grass.]** Annual, ascending to erect, less than 39 in. (1 m) tall; leaves 2–6 in. (5–15 cm) long, alternate, narrowly lanceolate, usually with a dark central spot and gland-dotted beneath; flowers in dense, short spikes are deep pink or occasionally white; jointed stems sometimes swollen above nodes. Moist disturbed areas.

250. *Sheep Sorrel, *Rumex acetosella.* **[grass. oak, shrub.]** Low perennial plants, less than 16 in. (4 dm) tall. Spreads by slender, running rootstocks; flowers nodding in open panicle, yellowish turning reddish with age; leaves arrowhead shaped with two basal lobes more or less pronounced. Leaves and leaf-stems edible when boiled. In moist, more-or-less disturbed places.

251. *Curly Dock, *Rumex crispus.* **[grass. oak, shrub.]** Perennial with smooth, erect stem less than 59 in. (15 dm) tall, arising from stout taproot; tiny green flowers in dense, narrow panicle; distinctive large, lanceolate leaves with curled edges. The whole plant turns reddish brown when the fruit appears. Leaves and leaf-stems edible when boiled. Roadsides, ditches, fields, waste places.

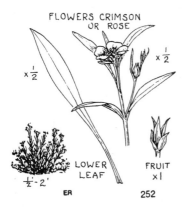

FLOWERS CRIMSON OR ROSE

x ½

x ½

LOWER LEAF

½ - 2'

ER

FRUIT x 1

252

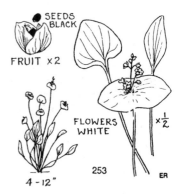

SEEDS BLACK

FRUIT x 2

FLOWERS WHITE

x ½

4 - 12"

253

ER

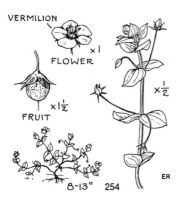

VERMILION

FLOWER

x 1

x 1½

FRUIT

x ½

8-13"   254

ER

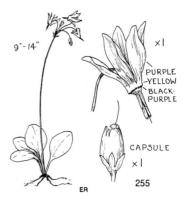

9" - 14"

x 1

PURPLE
-YELLOW
BLACK-
PURPLE

CAPSULE
x 1

ER

255

256

ER

flowers blue

JC

257

PORTULACACEAE, PURSLANE FAMILY

252. *Red Maids, *Calandrinia ciliata*. [grass. oak] Annual with one to many stems spreading from the base; stems 4–16 in. (1–4 dm) long; leaves linear to oblanceolate, flat; flowers in elongated raceme; petals 5, rose-red; seeds shiny black. All species edible raw or cooked. Especially common in cultivated fields and grassy areas in valley grassland and foothill woods, less common elsewhere.

253. *Miner's Lettuce, *Claytonia perfoliata*. [oak, str-wd. shrub. grass.] Annual, 4–16 in. (1–4 dm) high; basal leaves long-stemmed, elliptic to kidney-shaped; upper leaves disklike, fused to stem, from the middle of which rise tiny white or pinkish flowers. A delicious raw green. Coastal sage scrub, chaparral, foothill woods, etc., usually in moist, often shady or disturbed sites.

PRIMULACEAE, PRIMROSE FAMILY

254. Scarlet Pimpernel, *Anagallis arvensis*. [coast. oak, grass. shrub.] Annual with low, spreading, 4-sided stems, 2–16 in. (5–40 cm) long; leaves ovate to elliptic, sessile, opposite or in whorls of 3 along stem; flowers bright pinkish orange (sometimes blue), opening only when the sun shines. Poisonous. Open, disturbed places, ocean beaches. Native to Europe.

255. *Mosquito Bills or Henderson's Shooting Star, *Dodecatheon hendersonii*. [oak, shrub. grass.] Perennial; bare reddish stem rises 5–13 in. (13–34 cm) from fleshy white roots with ricelike bulblets; leaves basal, elliptic to ovate or obovate, long-stemmed; petals magenta to deep lavender or white with an upper zone of yellow, reversed to show purplish black stamen filaments. Usually in shady places. Inner South Coast Ranges from San Benito and Monterey cos. north, Cascade and Sierra Nevada foothills, Central Valley, San Bernardino Mtns.

RANUNCULACEAE, BUTTERCUP FAMILY

256. *White Virgin's Bower, *Clematis ligusticifolia*. [str-wd.] Climbing woody vine with tendrils that clasp limbs of trees and other vegetation; when in bloom covered with hundreds of cream flowers; leaves pinnately compound with 5–15 lanceolate to ovate leaflets; leaflets irregularly lobed or toothed, ¾–3 in. (2–8 cm) long; flowers in panicle; sepals white, densely hairy. The peppery-flavored stems and leaves were chewed by Indians as a remedy for colds and sore throats. Along streams.

257. Parry's Larkspur or Delphinium, *Delphinium parryi*. [oak, shrub. grass.] Perennial 12–35 in. (3–9 dm) tall; slender, erect, hairy stems bear deeply palmately divided leaves and end in a dense raceme of purplish blue, bilateral flowers; flowers have whitish hairs inside; sepals 5, the upper sepal extending into a backward-projecting spur. Grassy slopes in chaparral, coastal sage scrub, valley grassland, southern oak woodland, and yellow pine forests. Central western and sw. California to n. Baja.

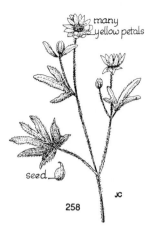

many
yellow petals

seed

258 JC

259 C

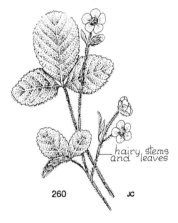

hairy stems
and leaves

260 JC

FLOWERS
WHITE

$\times \frac{1}{4}$

$\times \frac{1}{3}$

ER

6 - 12"   261

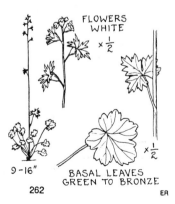

FLOWERS
WHITE

$\times \frac{1}{2}$

$\times \frac{1}{2}$

9 - 16"

BASAL LEAVES
GREEN TO BRONZE

262   ER

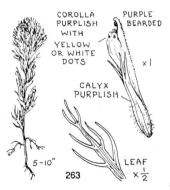

COROLLA
PURPLISH
WITH
YELLOW
OR WHITE
DOTS

PURPLE
BEARDED

$\times 1$

CALYX
PURPLISH

5 - 10"

263

LEAF
$\times \frac{1}{2}$

ER

258. **California Buttercup**, *Ranunculus californicus.* **[oak, grass. shrub.]** Perennial, 8–27½ in. (2—7 dm) tall, with slender roots; stems more or less prostrate to erect, branched or not; leaves smooth to hairy: basal leaves ovate, cordate, or round; upper leaves very deeply lobed; lobes linear to oblong, toothed; flower sepals greenish yellow and turned downward; petals yellow, generally 7–22; achenes more than 5 in rounded head, each with a recurved beak. Moist slopes and meadows in oak woodland, coastal scrub, grassland, and mixed evergreen forest.

ROSACEAE, ROSE FAMILY

259. ***Beach Strawberry**, *Fragaria chiloensis.* **[coast. shrub.]** Perennial from thick rootstalk, connected to others by runners; leaves leathery, shiny dark green above, gray-hairy below, divided into 3 obovate, toothed leaflets at the end of basal leaf-stalks; flowers 5-petaled, white; red berries sweet and juicy. Coastal beaches and grassland from Santa Barbara Co. north.

260. ***Wood Strawberry**, *Fragaria vesca.* **[oak, shrub.]** Perennial from short (not thick) rootstalk; leaves thin, divided into 3 roughly obovate, toothed leaflets at the end of basal leaf-stalks; leaflets sparsely hairy above, more hairy below; flowers 5-petaled, white; red berries delicious. Partially shaded places in woods. Whole region except Central Valley, the south coast below Santa Barbara Co., and the Western Transverse Ranges.

261. **Wedge-Leaved Horkelia**, *Horkelia cuneata.* **[oak, shrub. coast.]** Perennial 8–27 in. (2–7 dm) long with several resinous-smelling stems rising from a woody base; basal leaves consist of 5–12 pairs of toothed leaflets, each leaflet about ¾ in. (2 cm) long and sparsely to densely hairy; flowers white in open, headlike clusters. Coastal sage scrub, coastal strand, open chaparral, foothill woods. San Francisco Co. south to San Diego Co.

SAXIFRAGACEAE, SAXIFRAGE FAMILY

262. **Woodland Star**, *Lithophragma affine.* **[oak, shrub. sav.]** Perennial with stems 8–23 in. (2–6 dm) tall rising from slender rootstock bearing bulblets; stems feel sticky and hairy; basal leaves large, 3–5 lobed, teeth more or less sharp-tipped; stem leaves small; flowers in a simple raceme; petals white, 3-lobed at tip; 10 stamens. Open, grassy slopes in many plant communities. Not in Central Valley. *L. parviflorum* has the same range and habitat, but its petals are deeply lobed.

SCROPHULARIACEAE, FIGWORT FAMILY

263. **Purple Owl's Clover**, *Castilleja exserta.* **[grass. oak, shrub.]** Annual, 4–17½ in. (1–4.5 dm) tall, covered with stiff hairs; leaves divided into many threadlike segments; stems more or less reddish; flowers in a dense spike, pale to deep purple, with greenish to rose-purple bracts. Grassy slopes, open fields, valley grassland.

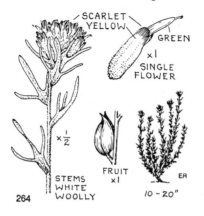

SCARLET
YELLOW
GREEN
×1
SINGLE
FLOWER
×½
STEMS
WHITE
WOOLLY
FRUIT
×1
10-20"
ER
264

265

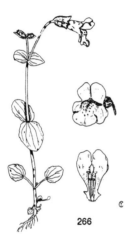

266

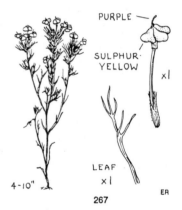

PURPLE
SULPHUR-
YELLOW
×1
LEAF
×1
4-10"
ER
267

268

ER

purple flowers
fruit
269

JC

264. Woolly Indian Paintbrush, *Castilleja foliolosa*. **[oak, shrub.]** Perennial, 12–24 in. (3–6 dm) high, much-branched, white-woolly throughout, may be woody below; leaves more or less linear, 0–3-lobed; scarlet bracts with yellow bands cover the dark green but pale reddish-margined flowers. On dry, open and rocky slopes in various plant communities. Coast Ranges (including San Francisco Bay area), Sierra Nevada foothills, Santa Catalina Island, and the central coast.

265. Chinese Houses, *Collinsia heterophylla*. **[oak, shrub. grass.]** Slender, erect annual, 4–20 in. (1–5 dm) high, simple or branched; leaves opposite and simple, lanceolate, toothed; rose-purple flowers cluster in widely spaced rings around the stem, forming fairylike "chinese houses"; the upper flower lip is white to lilac and bent upward. Common foothill, spring flower; likes shady places in many plant communities.

266. *Common Monkeyflower, *Mimulus guttatus*. **[str-wd. oak, shrub. grass.]** Usually perennial from a rootstock, sometimes annual, up to 39 in. (10 dm) or more tall; leaves opposite, ovate to round, often toothed; flowers yellow in raceme, often with reddish dots in the throat, 2-lobed upper lip bent upward, 3-lobed lower lip bent downward. Edible as a raw green. In wet places throughout the region.

267. Butter-And-Eggs or **Johnny-Tuck**, *Triphysaria erianthus*. **[oak, shrub. grass.]** Annual, generally 4–10 in. (10–35 cm) tall, purplish and finely hairy; leaves linear, the upper divided; flowers in dense spikes with leaflike bracts; corolla sack- or club-shaped, sulphur-yellow or white, with a purple, beaklike upper lip. Covers fields with yellow from March to May. Valley grasslands, foothill woods, coastal fields, open places.

SOLANACEAE, NIGHTSHADE FAMILY

268. Thorn Apple, *Datura wrightii*. **[oak, grass. shrub.]** Widely branched annual or perennial, 19–59 in. (5–15 dm) tall; stems with tiny soft whitish hairs; leaves ovate, coarsely lobed or entire; flowers violet-tinged, erect to nodding; fruit spiny, about 1 in. (2.5 cm) round. Sandy or gravelly open areas. Inner Coast Ranges, Sierra Nevada foothills, Tehachapi Mts., Central Valley, and all of cw. and sw. California.

269. White Horsenettle or **Silverleaf Nightshade**, *Solanum elaeagnifolium*. **[grass. oak, shrub.]** Perennial rising from deep rootstocks, under 39 in. (10 dm) tall, grows in colonies, covered with fine, star-shaped hairs, prickly; leaves bluish gray, somewhat yellowish, generally wavy edged, lanceolate; flowers star-shaped, blue to violet or lavender, with a slender yellow cone in the center when young, making this a striking flower. Dry, open, disturbed areas, roadsides, fields.

URTICACEAE, NETTLE FAMILY (often has stinging hairs, tiny green flowers)

270. *Hoary Nettle, *Urtica dioica* ssp. *holosericea*. [str-wd. oak] Perennial, gray-green, 39–117 in. (10–30 dm) tall with stout, erect stem arising from rhizome; leaves 2–4¾ in. (5–12 cm) long, opposite, toothed, lanceolate to narrowly ovate; achene ovate, tan. Stream banks, moist waste places, margins of deciduous woods. Whole region except n. Coast Ranges. An annual dwarf nettle, *U. urens* (under 23½ in./6 dm tall), is found in the same range. When boiled, the young shoots and leaves of both species make a good spinach substitute.

VIOLACEAE, VIOLET FAMILY

271. Douglas' Violet, *Viola douglasii*. [oak, shrub. grass.] Perennial under 8 in. (2 dm) tall, with stems clustered on a short, erect rootstock; leaves long-stalked, pinnately divided into segments which are also divided into linear-elliptic segments; petals 5, golden yellow with dark veins, the upper 2 petals maroon on the outside, the lower middle petal with a sack. Grassy slopes and flats, often on serpentine. Whole region except the s. coast below Santa Barbara Co. and the Western Transverse Ranges.

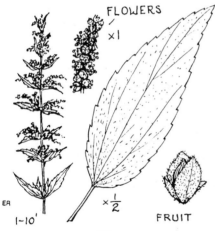

FLOWERS
×1

×½

ER

1~10'

FRUIT

270

flowers yellow

271

JC

TRACKS

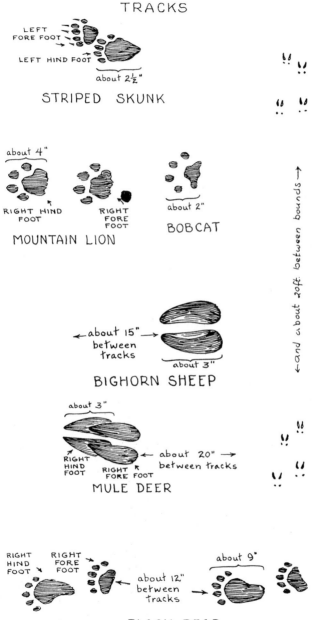

LEFT FORE FOOT

LEFT HIND FOOT

about 2½"

STRIPED SKUNK

about 4"

RIGHT HIND FOOT

RIGHT FORE FOOT

MOUNTAIN LION

about 2"

BOBCAT

←and about 20ft. between bounds→

←about 15"→ between tracks

about 3"

BIGHORN SHEEP

about 3"

RIGHT HIND FOOT

RIGHT FORE FOOT

←about 20"→ between tracks

MULE DEER

RIGHT HIND FOOT

RIGHT FORE FOOT

←about 12" between tracks→

about 9"

BLACK BEAR

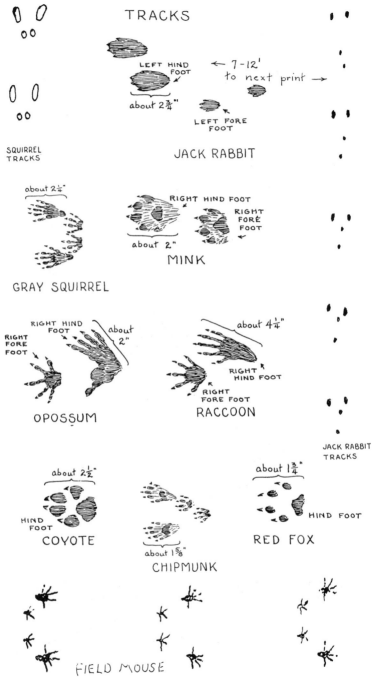

TRACKS

LEFT HIND FOOT

← 7-12'
to next print →

about 2¾"

LEFT FORE FOOT

SQUIRREL TRACKS

JACK RABBIT

about 2¼"

RIGHT HIND FOOT

RIGHT FORE FOOT

about 2"

MINK

GRAY SQUIRREL

RIGHT HIND FOOT

about 2"

RIGHT FORE FOOT

OPOSSUM

about 4¼"

RIGHT HIND FOOT

RIGHT FORE FOOT

RACCOON

JACK RABBIT TRACKS

about 2½"

HIND FOOT

COYOTE

about 1¾"

HIND FOOT

RED FOX

about 1⅝"

CHIPMUNK

FIELD MOUSE

4.

COMMON MAMMALS

Mammals are animals usually covered with hair or fur who give milk to their young. As most of the abundant species of mammals are entirely or mostly nocturnal, they are more likely to be seen at dusk or dawn, when it is hard to see them clearly. Therefore, when viewing a species illustration the reader should also note its accompanying measurements to correctly judge an animal's size. Besides this, as a basis for comparison, we use the four common mammals pictured below as examples. In describing animals illustrated, a "raccoon(+)" means larger than a raccoon, "rat(-)" is somewhat smaller than a rat, "mouse size" denotes same size as a mouse, and so on.

Wild mammals can best be approached by moving very slowly and quietly and wearing clothes colored like the surroundings. The illustratons of them are helpful for body shape and color pattern. Also study the descriptions and details about habits, noting particularly the habitats in which each mammal likes to live.

The purpose of this book is to acquaint the reader with the most common or widespread species within the Californian Wildlife Region. Many species found in neighboring regions (Pacific Coastal, Cascade, Sierra Nevadan, desert) are also found along the outskirts of our region, while others may live only in a small isolated area.

Gray fox.   Golden-mantled ground squirrel.

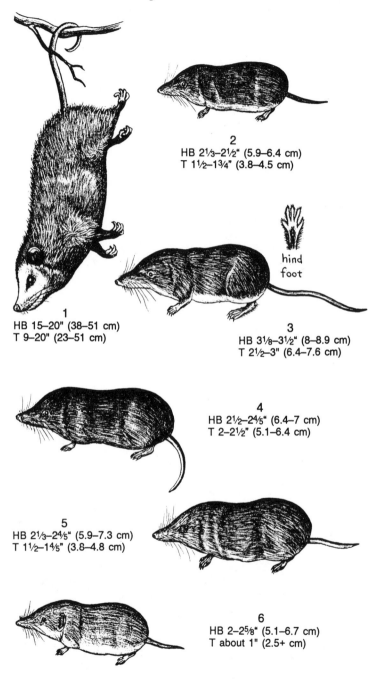

2
HB 2⅓–2½" (5.9–6.4 cm)
T 1½–1¾" (3.8–4.5 cm)

hind foot

1
HB 15–20" (38–51 cm)
T 9–20" (23–51 cm)

3
HB 3⅛–3½" (8–8.9 cm)
T 2½–3" (6.4–7.6 cm)

4
HB 2½–2⅘" (6.4–7 cm)
T 2–2½" (5.1–6.4 cm)

5
HB 2⅓–2⅘" (5.9–7.3 cm)
T 1½–1⅘" (3.8–4.8 cm)

6
HB 2–2⅝" (5.1–6.7 cm)
T about 1" (2.5+ cm)

POUCHED MAMMALS: ORDER MARSUPIALIA

A. OPPOSUMS: Family Didelphidae. Opossums, the only native marsupials in the U.S., have prehensile, round, scaly tails.

1. VIRGINIA OPPOSUM, *Didelphis virginiana*. **[sav. oak str.wd. grass]** Cat size. Short legs and a long, pointed nose; very thin, black ears may be whitish-tipped; thick, heavy body blackish to grayish to whitish; dull orange eye-shine. Active mainly at night. Omnivorous diet, including carrion. Pretends to be dead when attacked: "plays possum." Hab: edges of farms, woodlands, streamside woods; brush piles. R: western edge of California region.

INSECT EATERS: ORDER INSECTIVORA

A.SHREWS: Family Soricidae. Smallest of the mammals distinguished from mice by their long, pointed snout; their ears are completely or nearly hidden; small beady eyes; 5 toes on each foot—most mice have 4 toes on their front feet. Differences between shrew species are difficult to distinguish by amateurs. Shrews eat insects primarily, but sometimes they eat other small animals. They are ferocious hunters with voracious appetites. Being exceedingly nervous and active, they must feed frequently day and night or they will die. Their eyesight is very poor, but they possess an excellent sense of smell.

2. ADORNED or ORNATE SHREW, *Sorex ornatus*. **[grass mead. str.wd.]** Mouse(-). Sooty or grayish brown above, pale below; often with frosted hairs. Hab: near streams and in wet meadows of valley grasslands and foothill woodlands. R: wC above San Francisco Bay and Central Valley to Baja.

3. NORTHERN WATER SHREW, *Sorex palustris*. **[water str.wd.]** Mouse size. Large size for shrew; stiff hairs fringed on sides of hind feet increase surface area of foot, trapping air bubbles, which allows this shrew to actually run on water's surface; body blackish gray above, grayish below. Good swimmer; catches minnows, tadpoles, and water insects. Hab: found along mountain streams, marshes, ponds. R: cC to nC, inland to Sierra Nevada.

4. TROWBRIDGE SHREW, *Sorex trowbridgii*. **[str.wd. mead. oak]** Mouse size. Very distinct 2-colored tail, almost as long as head and body; dark to light brown all over. Hab: coastal mountains and hills from Santa Barbara Co. north usually within 40 miles of coast.

5. VAGRANT SHREW, *Sorex vagrans*. **[str.wd. marsh]** Mouse(-). Grayish brown with some silvery hairs, ash-gray below. Hab: marshes, meadows; also along streams in forests. R: nC, from San Francisco Bay north along coast.

6. GRAY or DESERT SHREW, *Notiosorex crawfordi* **[desert sage]** Mouse(-). Body lead gray washed brownish on top; tail 2-colored, dark at base and light at tip; ears stick out conspicuously from the fur. Hab: coastal sage or dry alluvial fans, desert scrub. R: sC, Baja.

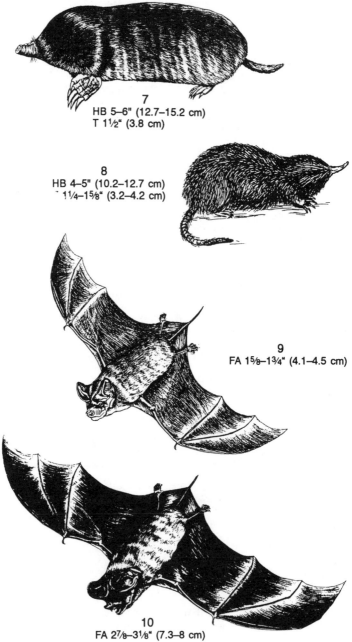

7
HB 5–6" (12.7–15.2 cm)
T 1½" (3.8 cm)

8
HB 4–5" (10.2–12.7 cm)
⁻ 1¼–1⅝" (3.2–4.2 cm)

9
FA 1⅝–1¾" (4.1–4.5 cm)

10
FA 2⅞–3⅛" (7.3–8 cm)

B. MOLES: Family Talpidae. Moles have soft fur and long noses. They spend most of their time burrowed underground. Low ridges of pushed up soil are left above their tunnels.

7. BROAD-FOOTED or CALIFORNIA MOLE, *Scapanus latimanus.* **[oak str.wd. grass sav. brush.]** Mouse(+). Brownish or grayish, seldom black; short slightly haired tail; naked snout with short hairs at base, nostril openings point upwards; front feet broader than long; eats insects and earthworms. Hab: likes soft soil in valleys and mountain meadows. R: most of California.

8. SHREW MOLE, *Neurotrichus gibbsii.* **[str.wd. grass water]** Mouse size. Smallest of moles; black or purplish black fur; tail bristly haired. Unlike other moles, it is often active above ground; taps ground with its nose, to detect the vibrations of insects it hunts. Makes little runways and tunnels in loose dirt and leaf mold. Hab: deep, soft soil in brushy areas or moist, weedy places. R: coastal areas from Monterey Co. north.

BATS: ORDER CHIROPTERA. Bats are flying mammals. All their limbs, including the tail, are connected together by membranes. The toes have hooked claws for hanging from tree limbs or cave ceilings. Bats always hang upside down when resting. Some hang in shaded places in trees by day, but most hang in hollows, attics, caves, or tunnels suitable to large bat colonies. Bats have poor vision, so depend on the shrill sounds they emit, often outside our hearing range, to know their surroundings by echo-location. This effective sonar system shows them exactly where their insect prey is flying. Some bats hibernate, others go south in winter. Forearm measurements (FA) are given for comparative size.

A. FREE-TAILED BATS, Family Molossidae. These bats have a tail that extends well past the edge of the tail membrane.

9. BRAZILIAN FREE-TAILED BAT, *Tadarida brasiliensis.* **[most habitats]** Mouse size. Smallest of the free-tails; short, chocolate brown fur; velvety tail more than half free from membrane; ears separate, with little bumps on front edge. Fast and high fliers, coming out at dusk to feed on insects, especially moths. Hab: forms large colonies in caves, cliff crevices, buildings; stays in low country or migrates south in the winter. R: all our area.

10. WESTERN MASTIFF BAT, *Eumops perotis.* **[brush. grass desert bldg.]** Rat(-). Largest of our bats; chocolate brown in color; tail more than half free from membrane. These bats give a call louder than any other bat. Mostly colonial; starts feeding at late dusk, mainly on wasps. Hab: roosts in buildings, crevices in cliffs, trees. R: coastal C from San Francisco Bay Area to nBaja.

11
FA 1⅛–1⅜" (2.9–3.5 cm)

12
FA 1⅜–1⅝" (3.5–4.1 cm)

14
FA 1⅔–1¾" (4.2–4.5 cm)

15
FA 1⅜–1⅝" (3.5–4.1 cm)

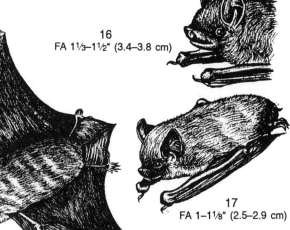

16
FA 1⅓–1½" (3.4–3.8 cm)

17
FA 1–1⅛" (2.5–2.9 cm)

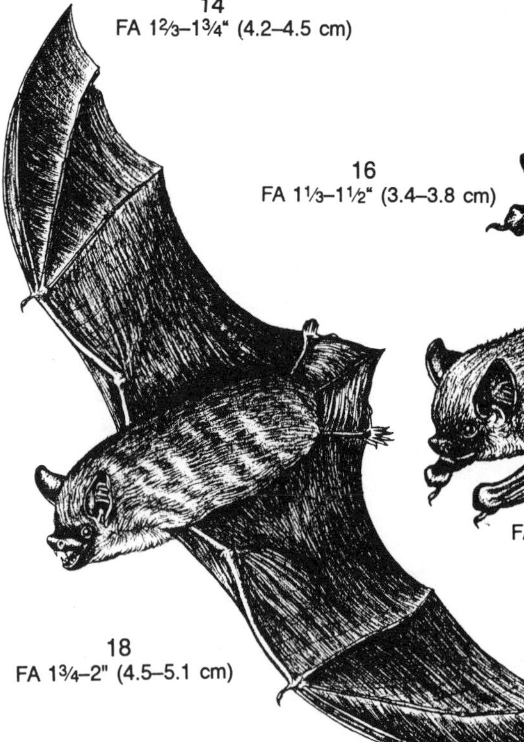

18
FA 1¾–2" (4.5–5.1 cm)

B. PLAIN-NOSED BATS, Family Vespertilionidae. Bats in this family have simple muzzles and tail enclosed in a membrane.

11. CALIFORNIA MYOTIS, *Myotis californicus.* **[most habitats]** Mouse(-). Light buff (in desert) to rich brown (along northwest coast) with hairs much darker at base; one of the smallest bats with small feet. Roosts several times during the night in different places—caves, rocks, mine tunnels, buildings, bridges. Hab: feeds near trees. R: all our area.

12. LONG-EARED MYOTIS, *Myotis evotis.* **[conif. mead.]** Mouse size. Distinctive large black ears, extending just beyond nose when laid down; golden brown fur. Usually solitary or in small groups; hunts late at night. Hab: likes open woods near ponderosa pine and spruce-fir forests. R: all our area.

13. SMALL-FOOTED MYOTIS, *Myotis ciliolabrum.* (not illus.) **[mead. str.wd. conif.]** Mouse size. FA 1¼–1⅜ in. (3.2–3.5 cm). Yellowish fur is long and silky; black mask over face; small feet; black ears. Appears early in evening, feeding low over brush or under trees. Wings partially spread when roosting. Hab: crevices, caves, tunnels, buildings, forested areas. R: C, except coastal regions north of Santa Barbara; nwBaja.

14. FRINGED MYOTIS, *Myotis thysanodes.* **[most except desert]** Mouse size. Buff-brown fur; conspicuous stiff-haired fringe along outer edge of tail membrane; comparatively large ears. Colonial. Hab: open woods; roosts in caves and buildings. R: most of C.

15. LONG-LEGGED MYOTIS, *Myotis volans.* **[conif. bldg.]** Mouse size. Dark to yellowish brown in color; distinctive round, short ears; small feet; underside of wing furred to elbow and knee. Flight less erratic than other myotis. Hab: roosts colonially, usually in buildings or rock crevices; coniferous and open forests. R: all our area.

16. YUMA MYOTIS, *Myotis yumanensis.* **[str.wd. bldg.]** Mouse size. Dull to yellowish brown hairs, darker at bases; membrane above hind legs hairy; whitish throat. Hunts rather late at night, flying low to the ground, mostly in open woods. Hab: colonial groups hang in clumps in caves, tunnels, buildings, dry areas. R: all our area.

17. WESTERN PIPISTRELLE, *Pipistrellus hesperus.* **[desert rocks]** Mouse(-). Smallest of our bats; ashy gray to yellowish gray color. Usually first evening bat, flies about sundown, with erratic flight. Drinks while skimming over water. Hab: caves, eaves, cliff crevices; common in deserts, usually near water. R: most of our area, except for coast north of San Francisco Bay.

18. BIG BROWN BAT, *Eptesicus fuscus.* **[all but desert]** Mouse(+). Common and widespread; pale brown (in desert) to glossy, bright brown; membranes, feet, and nose black; short ears; large size and fast flier with 13 in. wingspread. Hunts insects, mainly beetles. Hab: roosts singly or small groups in caves, buildings, tree hollows. R: all our area.

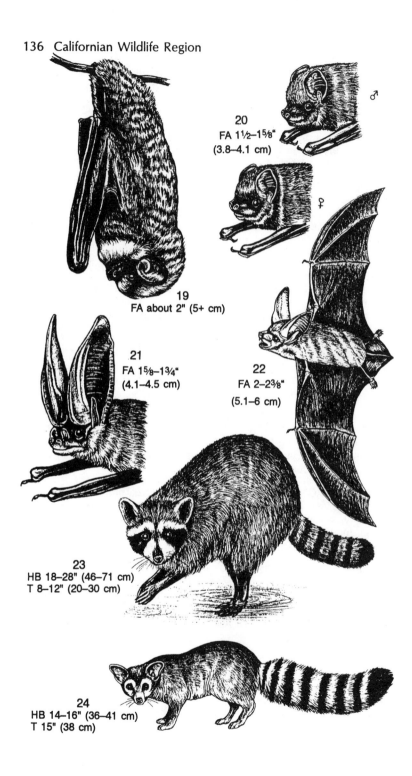

20
FA 1½–1⅝"
(3.8–4.1 cm)

♂

♀

19
FA about 2" (5+ cm)

21
FA 1⅝–1¾"
(4.1–4.5 cm)

22
FA 2–2⅜"
(5.1–6 cm)

23
HB 18–28" (46–71 cm)
T 8–12" (20–30 cm)

24
HB 14–16" (36–41 cm)
T 15" (38 cm)

19. HOARY BAT, *Lasiurus cinereus.* **[oak conif.]** Mouse(+). Fur reddish brown with white on tips, yellowish throat; tail membrane thickly furred on top; round ears; large size. Solitary; flies high, late at night. Hab: roosts in trees, rarely in caves; likes wooded areas. R: all our area.

20. WESTERN RED BAT, *Lasiurus blossevilli.* **[oak conif. str.wd.]** Mouse size. Rusty red to brick red fur, white-tipped; tail membrane covered with fur on top; female lighter-colored than male. Fairly straight, rapid flight; hunts only when dark. Often feeds in pairs, working back and forth over about a 100 yard area. Hab: likes woods; roosts in trees. R: throughout C and nBaja.

21. WESTERN or TOWNSEND'S BIG-EARED BAT, *Plecotus townsendii.* **[brush. conif. pin-jun.]** Mouse size. Grayish brown, with stomach fur buff-tipped; very large ears, over 1 in. (2.5) cm, connected across forehead. When roosting, ears fold back or are coiled over neck; 2 prominent lumps between eyes. Hab: roosts colonially in tight clusters in caves, tunnels, buildings, but solitary part of year. R: all our area.

22. PALLID BAT, *Antrozous pallidus.* **[desert bldg. conif.]** Mouse(+). Dull beige body and large, well-separated ears are distinctive. Flies slowly late at night. Feeds mainly in open areas, swooping low to ground; only bat that will land to grab beetles and other large insects. Colonial. Hab: different night hunting roosts than daytime sleeping roosts, usually in caves, rock crevices, buildings, deserts, canyons. R: most of our area.

FLESH EATERS: ORDER CARNIVORA

   A. RACCOONS and RINGTAILS, Family Procyonidae. Members of this family have ringed tails to some degree and 5 toes on each foot.

23. RACCOON, *Procyon lotor.* **[str.wd. oak sav. brush.]** Grayish tipped with black fur, dark ringed tail, and black mask over eyes are distinctive. Usually nocturnal; walks on soles of feet; keen eyesight; good swimmer and climber; very dexterous with hands. Omnivorous feeder on crayfish, mice, fruits, grain; often dips food in water. Snarls and growls when angry; mother twitters to young. Hab: stream borders and lakes near woods; dens in hollow trees, burrows. R: C, except for part of seC; nBaja.

24. RINGTAIL, *Bassariscus astutus.* Sometimes called a cacomistle, "civit cat," or "ringtail cat," but it is not a cat! **[brush. rocks oak str.wd.]** Cat size. Yellowish gray in color; long, bushy tail with 8 blackish brown rings; conspicuous white patches around eyes; foxlike face; thick fur between pads of feet; eye-shine yellowish green to red. Great explorer of rock, brush, and wood piles; nocturnal, very shy. Feeds on small rodents, insects, lizards, fruits. Has coughing bark when agitated, sometimes whimpers. Hab: brush, rocky ridges, cliffs, near water; dens in rock piles, old buildings, hollow trees. R: mountains and brushy areas of lower and middle altitudes.

25
male HB 6–9" (15–23 cm)
T 2¼–4" (5.7–10 cm)
female HB 5–7½" (13–19 cm)
T 2–3" (5–7.6 cm)

26
male HB 9–10½" (23–27 cm)
T 4–6" (10–15 cm)
female HB 8–9" (20–23 cm)
T 3–5" (8–13 cm)

27
male HB 13–17" (33–43 cm)
T 7–9" (18–23 cm)
female HB 12–14" (30–36 cm)
T 5–8" (13–20 cm)

28
HB 26–30" (66–76 cm)
T 12–17" (30–43 cm)

29
HB 18–22" (46–56 cm)
T 4–6" (10–15 cm)

30
HB 13–18" (33–46 cm)
T 7–10" (18–25 cm)

B. WEASELS, SKUNKS, AND THEIR KIND, Family Mustelidae.

This family has short legs, 5 toes on each foot, and scent glands. Active all year, they are nocturnal, solitary animals.

25. SHORT-TAILED WEASEL or ERMINE, *Mustela erminea*. **[str.wd. brush. grass]** Rat(-). Dark brown fur above, white below; white in winter in interior mountains, with black tail-tip. Commonly nocturnal, but hunts also in daylight for shrews, mice, and small birds, piercing skull, killing all the prey it can, storing the uneaten for later. Gives shrill shriek when alarmed. Hab: meadows, fields, woods, brush, usually near water; dens under roots and rock piles. R: nC from Tulare Co. north, mainly at higher altitudes on fringes of Central Valley.

26. LONG-TAILED WEASEL, *Mustela frenata*. **[most habitats]** Rat size. Slim head and long neck, tail and body are distinctive; uniform brown above, yellowish white below; has white patch(es) on forehead; black-tipped tail. Active in daylight, hunts at night, feeding mostly on small mammals, a few birds and reptiles, killing all it can catch, storing what it doesn't eat. Eats up to 40% of its body weight daily. Has high-pitched scream. Hab: often dens in brush, rock piles, old burrows; all land habitats close to water. R: most of our area, except hot deserts.

27. MINK, *Mustela vison*. **[str.wd. water]** Cat size. Glossy dark brown fur, except for white patch under chin; young minks have brownish red coat. Solitary, but may be part of family group. Hunts mainly at night; swims swiftly to catch fish, crayfish, and frogs, also small mammals (especially muskrats) and water birds. When scared or marking territory, anal glands secrete a very potent scent. Hab: streams and lakes; usually dens in holes in banks. R: C north of San Francisco, cC river valleys and Sierra Nevada foothills south to Fresno Co.

28. RIVER OTTER, *Lutra canadensis*. **[water str.wd.]** Raccoon(+). Velvety, dark brown fur on back, silvery gray below; broad nose, small ears, webbed feet; tail thick at base tapering to tip. A graceful swimmer, also at ease on land, it catches fish, often with teamwork. Sociable, very playful and affectionate, at times traveling in groups. Hab: streams and lakes, sometimes in nearby woods; dens in holes in banks with the entrance underwater. R: nC from San Francisco and cC to Tulare Co., west of the Sierra Nevada.

29. BADGER, *Taxidea taxus*. **[most habitats]** Raccoon(-). Heavy, flattened body, short legs, grizzly gray fur, a white stripe running over the top of head to the nose, white cheeks with a black patch in front of each ear. Feet are black with very long, powerful claws used to dig out dens of small rodents, its primary food, or new dens for itself. Usually out at night, sometimes by day. Has wobbly gait, flattens body when alarmed, backing up to face tormentor, hissing and growling savagely. Hab: open grasslands and deserts to mountain meadows and flats. R: all our area, except corner of nwC.

30. STRIPED SKUNK, *Mephitis mephitis*. **[str.wd. oak sav. rocks grass brush.]** Cat size. Black body; narrow white stripe on center of

31
HB 9–13½" (23–34 cm)
T 4½–9" (11.4–23 cm)

32
HB 5–6' (1.5–1.8 m)
shoulder height 2–3' (.6–.9 m)

33
HB 32–37" (81–94 cm)
T 11–16" (28–41 cm)

forehead; broad white patch on nape, dividing into a "V" at shoulders with 2 white stripes continuing down back; busy, white fringed tail. Warns by stamping feet. Tail up means "look out!" before it sprays an acrid scent. Does not hibernate; slow moving; omnivorous; hunts early morning and evening. Mothers teach young to hunt, often seen single file behind her. Hab: normally near water; dens in ground burrows, under wood or rock piles, under old buildings. R: all of our area, except very hot deserts and high mountains.

31. WESTERN SPOTTED SKUNK, *Spilogale gracilis.* **[brush. rocks oak]** Rat(+). Black with 4 broken white stripes along neck, back and sides; white spot on forehead; tail white-tipped. Generally nocturnal. Can climb trees to escape danger. Throws scent only in self- defense while standing on front feet. Eats mice, birds, insects, carrion, eggs, some vegetation. Hab: farmland, brush, open woods near streams; nests in burrows beneath rocks and wood piles or under old buildings—several may den together. R: most of our area except hot deserts and coast north of Santa Barbara.

C. BEARS, Family Ursidae. Bears are the largest carnivores. They have short tails and walk flat on the soles of their feet.

32. BLACK BEAR, *Ursus americanus.* **[str.wd. conif]** "Black" is only one of a variety of colors for this bear. Depending on locale, its color ranges from various shades of brown to black, often has a white patch on breast. Omnivorous diet includes fawns to rabbits, insects, carrion, garbage, roots, fruit and berries; hunts mainly at night, but sometimes by day; usually alone except for cubs with female. A clumsy walk is usual, but it can gain speeds of up to 33 mph (50 km/h). Uses smell first, hearing second, sight third for detecting prey or enemies. Gives deep growl when mad, a "woof-woof" snort for warning, and a whimper to call cubs. Hab: in or near woods in hills or mountains; dens in tree hollows, caves, or under thick, snow-covered brush in winter when dormant. R: in the forested mountain ranges of the state north of San Francisco and in the Sierra Nevada.

D. COYOTES and FOXES, Family Canidae. Canidae are doglike and have bushy tails. They walk on their toes and have long legs well adapted for running.

33. COYOTE, *Canis latrans.* **[all habitats]** Looks like a tawny medium-sized dog with rusty ears, legs, and feet; has pale belly and throat; dark-tipped, bushy tail; canine teeth long; nose more pointed than a dog's. Tail held low, even between legs, when running. Can cruise at 25 to 30 mph (40 km/h). Often gives high-pitched yaps in evening; in a wild area, a group may sing on a hilltop, where they feel secure. Hunts mainly at night for rodents and rabbits, but will eat nearly anything animal or vegetable; caches uneaten food. Coyotes generally pair; female makes a den to have her pups. Hab: almost every habitat—from dry deserts to forest edges and mountain tops. R: most of our area.

34
HB 15–20" (38–51 cm)
T 9–12" (23–30 cm)

35
HB 22–25" (56–64 cm)
T 14–16" (36–41 cm)

36
HB 21–29" (53–74 cm)
T 11–16" (28–41 cm)

37
HB 42–55" (107–140 cm)
T 30–37" (76–94 cm)

34. KIT FOX or SWIFT FOX, *Vulpes velox* **[desert grass]** Cat size. Fur soft, dense grizzled-buff with black-tipped overhairs above; whitish below; black-tipped tail, often with a black spot at upper base; large, triangular ears; can run up to 25 mph (40 km/h) for short stretches. Nocturnal and solitary, they mate for life and dig their own dens or enlarge upon an existing badger hole. They feed mainly on mice and rats. Hab: San Joaquin Valley and hills to west. R: cC to sC.

35. RED FOX, *Vulpes vulpes.* **[conif. brush. rock]** Raccoon size. Looks like a small, yellowish red bushy-tailed dog; has several color variations—cross phase with dark cross over shoulders and down center of back; black or silver phase in which body is mostly black with white-tipped body hairs, and intermediate stages; tail has some black hairs and is white-tipped; feet and lower legs are always black. Hunts mainly at night, sometimes during the day, for small mammals and insects, also likes fruit and berries; young are fed by both parents. Mates cleverly make a spare den to hide young in case first den is disturbed. Hab: likes a mixture of open country and forests. R: inland nC and cC (Sierra Nevada foothills and higher, some in Marysville Buttes).

36. GRAY FOX, *Urocyon cinereoargenteus.* **[oak brush. rocks str.wd. sav.]** Raccoon size. Grayish colored; underfur yellowish brown; rusty yellow on sides of neck, legs and feet; black stripe down center of black-tipped tail. Light throat and gray face act as a marvelous camouflage in brush. Hunts mainly at night for small mammals, also eats insects, nuts, corn and fruit. Very secretive. Climbs trees to escape enemies, eat fruit, or find birds' eggs or young. Voice: yowls, growls, yaps and barks. Hab: likes brushy areas, open woods, rocky country; dens in rocky caves, burrows, under logs. R: all our area.

E. CATS, Family Felidae. Members of this family are adept climbers having retractile claws; 5 toes on the front feet and 4 on the back feet. They have short faces, small rounded ears; eyes face forward with excellent night vision; long sleek bodies with strong legs; sensitive whiskers. Rough tongues to groom and rasp meat off bones; all purr and stalk silently on soft footpads.

37. MOUNTAIN LION or COUGAR, *Felis concolor.* **[brush. rocks str.wd. oak sav.]** Large, tawny cat, with long black-brown tipped tail; sides of nose and backs of ears darkish brown; eye shine golden-green; cubs are spotted. Also called a puma or panther, they are solitary, secretive, territorial, and great jumpers—up to 20 feet at a bound. Hunts mainly by night after deer, rabbits, domestic animals, rodents; caches kills in brush for later feeding, but won't eat tainted meat. Growls, yowls, and screams much louder than a house cat. Hab: in wilderness areas, mountain forests, rocky areas, chaparral; dens in caves or other sheltered spots. R: most of our area, except Central Valley.

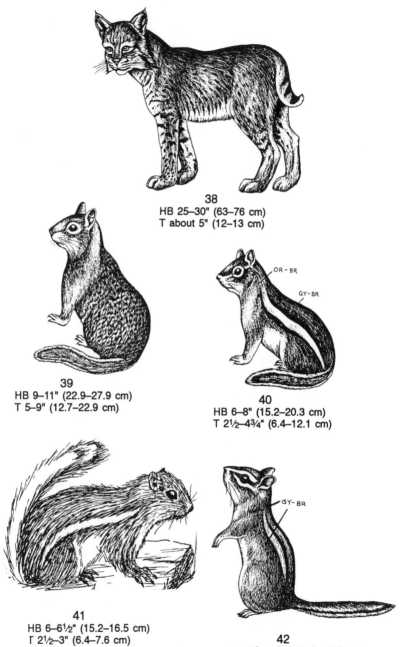

38
HB 25–30" (63–76 cm)
T about 5" (12–13 cm)

39
HB 9–11" (22.9–27.9 cm)
T 5–9" (12.7–22.9 cm)

OR–BR
GY–BR

40
HB 6–8" (15.2–20.3 cm)
T 2½–4¾" (6.4–12.1 cm)

41
HB 6–6½" (15.2–16.5 cm)
T 2½–3" (6.4–7.6 cm)

GY–BR

42
HB 4⅔–6½" (11.9–16.5 cm)
T 3½–5½" (8.9–14 cm)

38. BOBCAT or WILDCAT, *Felis rufus.* **[brush. oak str.wd. sav. rocks]** Raccoon size. Tawny fur above, dimly spotted with black; black on tip of distinctive short tail; whitish below with black spots; short pointed ear tufts. Generally solitary, hunts mostly at night, but sometimes in day, for small mammals and birds; will eat untainted carrion. Female are more exclusive about their home range (3–4 sq. km) than males. Hab: likes rocky areas and chaparral brush, but found in nearly every habitat; dens in rock crevices, hollow logs. R: all our area.

SPECIAL NOTE: Both of our wilderness cats play an important role in nature, keeping small mammal populations and deer herds down to normal sizes, which helps protect forests and crops. Heavy hunting and trapping of these beautiful wild animals should be discouraged.

GNAWING MAMMALS: ORDER RODENTIA. Rodents comprise about half of all mammal species. All the members of this order have 4 large incisor teeth for gnawing, 2 above and 2 below. Their eyes protrude on the side of the head to see both forward and behind.

A. SQUIRRELS and CHIPMUNKS, Family Sciuridae. Members of this family have 4 toes on the front feet and 5 toes on the back feet; their tails are usually bushy.

39. CALIFORNIA GROUND SQUIRREL, *Spermophilus beecheyi.* **[rocks grass sav. oak]** Cat size. Mottled gray and black in color, gray mantle over shoulders and sides of neck; a darker patch of fur extends triangularly from the head down the center of the back; dark tail bordered with white. Emits loud warning chirps. Hab: fields, pastures, slopes with scattered trees, rocky areas; avoids thick brush and dense woods. R: C, except deserts and highest mountains; nwBaja.

40. GOLDEN-MANTLED GROUND SQUIRREL, *Spermophilus lateralis.* **[brush. conif.]** Rat(-). Golden yellow head; 1 white stripe bordered with 2 black stripes on each side of the back, no stripes on sides of face like chipmunks; relatively short, hairy tail. Hab: mountain woods and chaparral. R: extreme nC and Sierra Nevada foothills and mountains south to Fresno Co.

41. SAN JOAQUIN ANTELOPE GROUND SQUIRREL (NELSON'S ANTELOPE SQUIRREL), *Ammospermophilus nelsoni.* **[sage grass desert]** Rat(-). Yellowish brown body with a creamy white line on each side of back; underside of tail also creamy white. The tail is curled over its back while scurrying around. Eats green vegetation, insects, also some vertebrates such as lizards. Forms colonies; makes many burrows with openings under bushes from which they exit with caution. If exposed to sun in temperatures above 90 degrees, it becomes frenzied, froths at the mouth, then dies. Hab: dry, sparsely vegetated areas. R: only found in San Joaquin Valley, and Kern Co.

42. MERRIAM'S CHIPMUNK, *Tamias merriami.* (Formerly *Eutamias merriami*) **[brush. conif. str.wd. rocks]** Mouse(+). Large, gray-brown chipmunk with indistinct stripes on back, below ear and head; light

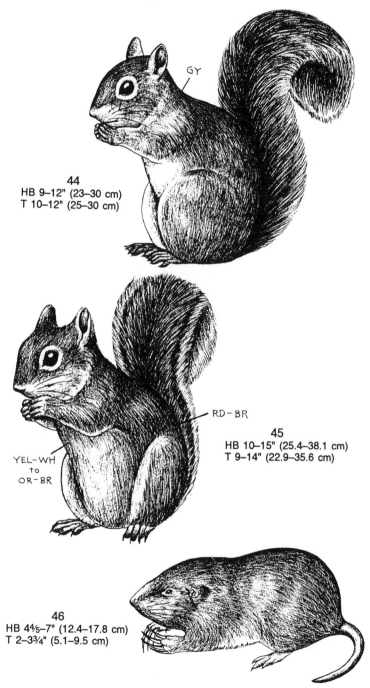

GY

44
HB 9–12" (23–30 cm)
T 10–12" (25–30 cm)

RD–BR

45
HB 10–15" (25.4–38.1 cm)
T 9–14" (22.9–35.6 cm)

YEL–WH
to
OR–BR

46
HB 4⅘–7" (12.4–17.8 cm)
T 2–3¾" (5.1–9.5 cm)

stripes are gray, dark stripes are brown. Hab: chaparral, oak, foothill and yellow pine woods, streamside thickets, rocky areas. R: cC coastal mountains, interior swC, foothills of Sierra Nevada north to San Joaquin Co., interior nBaja in low mountains.

43. SONOMA CHIPMUNK, *Tamias sonomae.* (Formerly *Eutamias sonomae*) (not illus.) **[brush. str.wd. oak conif.]** Mouse(+). HB 4⅘–6 in. (12–15 cm); T 4–5 in. (10–12.5 cm). Large dark, reddish brown and gray chipmunk, with ears of uniform color; indistinct body stripes, the lighter ones dull yellowish gray; head stripes reddish brown to brownish black; black spots behind eyes and below ears. Forages in bushes and on ground. Hab: clearings with brush, streamside thickets, chaparral; likes warm sunny slopes from sea level to 6000' (1,829 m). R: nwC from the coast to high inland mountains (Mt. Tamalpais just north of San Francisco to nwSiskiyou Co.).

44. WESTERN GRAY SQUIRREL, *Sciurus griseus.* **[oak str.wd.]** Cat size. All gray above with whitish belly; distinctive large, bushy fluffed tail as long as body; dusky feet. Especially active in the morning all year round, mostly in trees but fairly often on the ground. Hab: oak and oak-pine woods with open spaces. R: most of our area, except Central Valley and highest mountains.

45. FOX SQUIRREL, *Sciurus niger.* **[oak str.wd.]** Cat size. Rusty yellowish mixed with grayish above, pale yellow to orange belly; large bushy tail with orange tipped hairs. Some members of this species have a pure gray phase resembling the native gray squirrel. Forages on ground in open, some distance from trees. Eats all kinds of nuts—acorns are main food. Hab: open pine areas and oak woods. R: cC, wC (introduced in parks and woods of San Francisco Peninsula and several Central Valley cities).

B. POCKET GOPHERS: Family Geomyidae. Pocket gophers spend most of the time in underground burrows; they have thick bodies, short necks, and tails with fur-lined, reversible cheek pouches for holding food. The 2 huge, yellowish incisor teeth are always visible. Their large, curved front claws are effective digging tools; small ears and eyes help keep out dirt. Gophers push up mounds at an angle, not straight up like moles; their holes are plugged with dirt. They feed on various vegetable matter from shallow surface burrows.

46. VALLEY or BOTTA'S POCKET GOPHER, *Thomomys bottae.* **[most habitats]** Rat(-). Usually shades of brown, but color is variable; nearly black along parts of the Pacific Coast to nearly white in hot deserts; rounded ears have a similar sized dark patch behind them; valley specimens are larger than those found in the desert. Solitary, often fights if it meets another member of species. Hab: prefers grassy areas with rich loam, valleys, lower mountain meadows; less often in rocky places with sand or poor soil. R: most of our area except extreme neC.

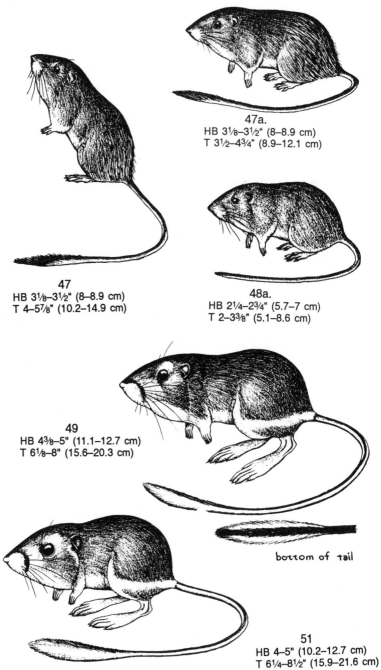

47a.
HB 3⅛–3½" (8–8.9 cm)
T 3½–4¾" (8.9–12.1 cm)

47
HB 3⅛–3½" (8–8.9 cm)
T 4–5⅞" (10.2–14.9 cm)

48a.
HB 2¼–2¾" (5.7–7 cm)
T 2–3⅜" (5.1–8.6 cm)

49
HB 4⅜–5" (11.1–12.7 cm)
T 6⅛–8" (15.6–20.3 cm)

bottom of tail

51
HB 4–5" (10.2–12.7 cm)
T 6¼–8½" (15.9–21.6 cm)

C. POCKET MICE and KANGAROO RATS, Family Heteromyidae. These small rats and mice have external, fur-lined cheek pouches; weak front feet; hind feet are large and powerful for jumping. The tail is usually very long to help direct the jump. Upper incisor teeth are grooved in front; nocturnal all-night feeders and burrowers, well adapted to dry areas, as they absorb moisture from the seeds they eat. All have underground burrows for their young, storing food, and sleeping.

47. CALIFORNIA POCKET MOUSE, *Chaetodipus californicus.* **[brush. oak]** Mouse size. Very long, crested tail; rump with spinelike hairs; color olive-brown speckled with yellow-brown. Hab: hills and slopes covered with chaparral or live oak woods. R: coastal C from San Francisco south into interior nBaja. **a. SAN DIEGO POCKET MOUSE or SHORT-EARED POCKET MOUSE,** *Chaetodipus fallax.* Similar except darker brown and has shorter tail. R: swC in San Diego vicinity.

48. SAN JOAQUIN POCKET MOUSE, *Perognathus inornatus.* **(not illus.) [brush.]** Mouse(-). HB 2½–3⅛ in. (6.5–8 cm); T 2⅘–3 in. (7–7.5 cm). Buff colored, soft hair is distinctive. Hab: dry grassy and weedy areas with very fine soil. R: in Sacramento and San Joaquin valleys, wcC. **a. LITTLE POCKET MOUSE,** *Perognathus longimembris.* Very similar. R: sC.

49. AGILE or PACIFIC KANGAROO RAT, *Dipodomys agilis.* **[brush.]** Mouse(+). Medium size; cinnamon brown color with white belly and white patch above eyes, dark back stripe extending to tip of tufted tail; 5 toes on each hind foot. Very active jumper and great seed hunter. Hab: sandy or gravelly soil of washes or slopes and chaparral. R: coastal swC, nwBaja. South and east from Santa Barbara. San Bernardino and San Gabriel mountains. **a. NARROW-FACED or SANTA CRUZ KANGAROO RAT,** *Dipodomys venustus* is found only in a mountainous strip near the ocean from Santa Cruz Co. to San Luis Obispo Co.

50. BIG-EARED KANGAROO RAT, *Dipodomys elephantinus.* **(not illus.) [brush.]** HB 5 in. (12.5 cm); T 7–8 in. (18–20.5 cm). Striking looking, cinnamon colored rodent with unusually big ears, 5 toes on hind foot, tail strongly crested with long hairs. Hab: chaparral. R: Gabilan Mts., Pinnacles Natl. Mon. of Monterey and San Benito cos.

51. HEERMANN'S KANGAROO RAT, *Dipodomys heermanni.* **[grass oak brush.]** There are 2 types of *heermanni*, lighter colored to the south and to the north, darker with a distinctive fluffy, dark, white-tipped crest on the tail. Nocturnal; likes moonless nights, so is rarely seen. Hab: thinly wooded slopes; flat, arid grasslands; open rocky areas with sparse chaparral. R: coast from San Francisco through Sonoma Co., inland to Sierra Nevada foothills (except in highly cultivated areas of Central Valley), and north to the limit of our area; found on the coast around San Luis Obispo and Santa Barbara cos.

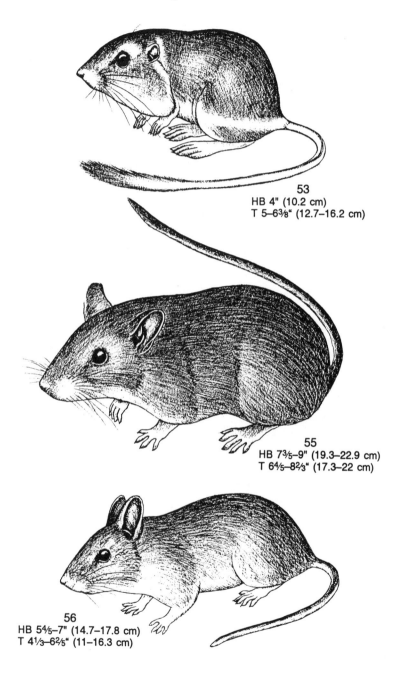

53
HB 4" (10.2 cm)
T 5–6⅜" (12.7–16.2 cm)

55
HB 7⅗–9" (19.3–22.9 cm)
T 6⅘–8⅔" (17.3–22 cm)

56
HB 5⅘–7" (14.7–17.8 cm)
T 4⅓–6⅖" (11–16.3 cm)

52. GIANT KANGAROO RAT, *Dipodomys ingens.* (not illus.) **[grass desert]** HB 5⅝–6 in. (14.5–15 cm); T 7–8 in. (18–20.5 cm). Largest kangaroo rat with dusky tipped, white and dark striped tail markings; 5 toes on each hind foot. Nocturnal. Eats seeds and green plants. Hab: sandy loam with sparse plant cover; 2-4 entrances to burrow system, which houses a nest chamber as well as seed caches. R: sC, wSan Joaquin Valley.

53. MERRIAM'S KANGAROO RAT, *Dipodomys merriami.* **[desert]** One of the smallest kangaroos of our area; color varies from dark brown to pale yellowish buff above, white below; tail has brownish black tuft and long crest. Eats seeds and some greenery. Hab: gravelly to rocky desert soil with sparse vegetation; female is territorial; lives in shallow burrows; stores seeds. R: sC, seC, Baja. **a. STEPHENS' KANGAROO RAT,** *Dipodomys stephensi.* Found solely in San Jacinto Valley of Riverside and San Bernardino cos.

54. FRESNO or SAN JOAQUIN KANGAROO RAT, *Dipodomys nitratoides.* (not illus.) **[grass desert]** HB 3⅗–4 in. (9–10 cm); T 4⅘–6 in. (12–15 cm). Dark yellowish buff distinguished by small size and 4 toes on each hind foot. Hab: dry alkaline plains with scattered low grass and brush. R: San Joaquin and adjacent valleys (Merced Co. south to Kern Co.).

D. RATS and MICE, Family Muridae. These rodents are small to medium-sized. All have 5 toes on hind feet; 2 gnawing and 6 cheek teeth on both upper and lower jaws.

1. NEW WORLD RATS and MICE, Subfamily Sigmodontinae.

a. WOODRATS are distinguished by their hairy tail, and white throat and breast. They store food in stick lodges.

55. DUSKY-FOOTED WOODRAT, *Neotoma fuscipes.* **[brush. oak str.wd.]** About rat sized. Usually larger than other similar species; grayish brown above, light gray underneath; tail paler beneath than above; hind feet spotted with dusky hairs. Eats nuts, acorns, seeds, fruits, green leaves, fungi. Builds large stick lodges in conical pile, as high as 8 ft. (2.5 m) with similar diameter, often placed against tree or shrub; very territorial. Hab: dense chaparral, streamside thickets, deciduous or mixed woods. R: C, except for deserts, Central Valley, and high mountains; nwBaja.

56. DESERT WOODRAT, *Neotoma lepida.* **[rocks desert brush.]** Rat(-). Sometimes called a "pack rat," tawny colored back; belly tawny to grayish; hair bases slate colored. Piles rubbish up for a house next to cacti or rocky cliffs and crevices. Eats cacti and other available green vegetation. Hab: rocky slopes scattered with cactus and other low vegetation, arid sandy places, desert basins in the Central Valley, sagebrush scrub of the sw coast, inland chaparral. R: csC, sC and Baja.

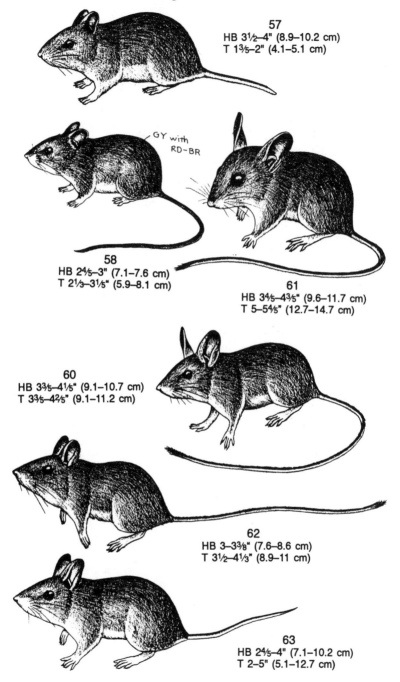

57
HB 3½–4" (8.9–10.2 cm)
T 1⅗–2" (4.1–5.1 cm)

GY with
RD~BR

58
HB 2⅘–3" (7.1–7.6 cm)
T 2⅓–3⅕" (5.9–8.1 cm)

61
HB 3⅘–4⅗" (9.6–11.7 cm)
T 5–5⅘" (12.7–14.7 cm)

60
HB 3⅗–4⅕" (9.1–10.7 cm)
T 3⅗–4⅖" (9.1–11.2 cm)

62
HB 3–3⅜" (7.6–8.6 cm)
T 3½–4⅓" (8.9–11 cm)

63
HB 2⅘–4" (7.1–10.2 cm)
T 2–5" (5.1–12.7 cm)

b. GRASSHOPPER MICE are distinguished by a short, white-tipped tail, stout body, and short fur. They inhabit prairies and deserts; are nocturnal, and active all year.

57. SOUTHERN GRASSHOPPER MOUSE or SCORPION MOUSE, *Onychomys torridus*. **[brush. sage grass]** Mouse size. Pinkish cinnamon or grayish above; white belly. Voice a shrill whistle. Feeds mainly on invertebrates, sometimes other mice. Hab: prairies, grasslands, sagebrush, sandy soil; lives in used burrows. R: cC to sC, except coast; nBaja.

c. HARVEST MICE are small brown mice resembling house mice, but their tails are covered with short hairs. They have a distinct groove down front of upper incisors; nocturnal; active all year.

58. WESTERN HARVEST MOUSE, *Reithrodontomys megalotis*. **[most habitats]** Mouse size. Tawny to brown above; whitish to dark gray below. Feeds on seeds, insects; stores food. Hab: grasslands to open desert, usually in areas of dense vegetation near water; hides its stick nest in thick weeds or grass. R: all our area.

59. SALT MARSH HARVEST MOUSE, *Reithrodontomys raviventris*. (not illus.) **[salt marsh]** HB 2⅗–3⅕ in. (6.5–8 cm); T 2⅕–3⅖ in. (5.5–8.5 cm). Brown washed with strong tawny or buff and black above; pinkish cinnamon below. Makes nest in vegetation and does not have a burrow. Hab: salt marshes. R: San Francisco Bay Area and Sacramento River Delta.

d. WHITE-FOOTED MICE are medium-sized mice with white feet, brown or tawny backs, white or creamy white bellies, and rather long tails. They are nocturnal, preferring woods, prairies, rocks, buildings. Most nest on the ground, but some nest in trees.

60. BRUSH MOUSE, *Peromyscus boylii*. **[brush. rocks]** Mouse size. Sides tawny tinged; well-haired, tufted tail is as long as body. Feeds on acorns, manzanita berries, cutworms, and insects; stores food. Nests under rocks or debris. Hab: chaparral, arid and semi-arid areas, rocky places; climbs in brush. R: most of our region.

61. CALIFORNIA MOUSE, *Peromyscus californicus*. **[brush. oak bldg.]** Mouse(+). Largest mouse of this genus; tail blackish above; ears large. Monogamous; territorial. Stores acorns. Hab: live oak slopes, heavy chaparral, also uses buildings as nesting sites. R: csC, cC Sierra Nevada foothills, swC, nwBaja.

62. CANYON MOUSE, *Peromyscus crinitus*. **[rocks sage]** Mouse size. Tail long and well-haired with small tuft at end; long, silky fur. Hab: canyon walls, rocky slopes in arid environments; nests or burrows under rocks. R: sC (Kern Co. south) into neBaja, away from coast.

63. DEER MOUSE, *Peromyscus maniculatus*. **[most habitats except water]** Mouse size. Variable in color from dark red-brown to pale

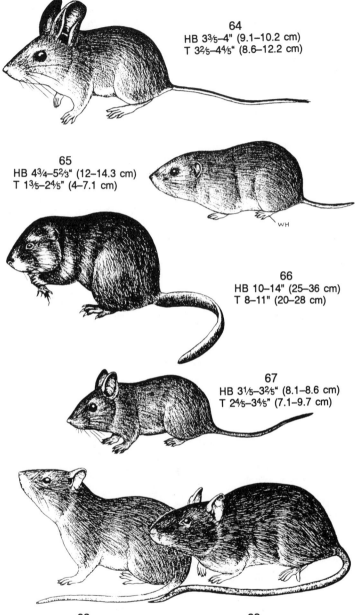

64
HB 3⅗–4" (9.1–10.2 cm)
T 3⅖–4⅘" (8.6–12.2 cm)

65
HB 4¾–5⅔" (12–14.3 cm)
T 1⅗–2⅘" (4–7.1 cm)

WH

66
HB 10–14" (25–36 cm)
T 8–11" (20–28 cm)

67
HB 3⅕–3⅖" (8.1–8.6 cm)
T 2⅘–3⅘" (7.1–9.7 cm)

68
HB 7–10" (17.8–25.4 cm)
T 5–8" (12.7–20.3 cm)

69
HB 7–8" (17.8–20.3 cm)
T 8⅖–10" (21.3–25.4 cm)

grayish buff; tail markedly bicolored. Feeds on seeds, nuts, insects; stores food. Hab: nearly every dry-land habitat; may be found under logs, in burrows, in stumps, or in buildings. R: C and Baja.

64. PIÑON MOUSE, *Peromyscus truei.* **[brush. rocks pin-jun.]** Mouse(+). Large ears; tail sharply bicolored. Hab: rocky ground with scattered piñon and juniper; climbs trees. Main diet is piñon nuts and juniper berries. Stores food. Makes a grass or shredded bark nest in tree hollows or under rocks. R: most of our area, except Central Valley, extreme swC, and nwBaja.

2. VOLES, Subfamily Arvicolinae, are generally grayish brown with long, soft fur; relatively short tail; small, black, beadlike eyes. They usually make narrow runways through the grass and shallow tunnels underground or under the snow in the winter. Their brown droppings reveal their presence.

65. CALIFORNIA VOLE, *Microtus californicus.* **[marsh brush. grass]** Mouse(+). Grayish brown, almost black when near the coast, reddish in desert; tail bicolored; feet pale. Eats mainly grass and green vegetation. Hab: saline and freshwater marshes, damp grassy meadows, hills with grass and scattered brush. R: most of C, except deserts and nw corner.

66. COMMON MUSKRAT, *Ondatra zibethicus.* **[marsh water]** Rat(+). Very rich brown fur; silvery belly; the naked tail is flattened. This aquatic rodent with webbed hind feet feeds mainly on water plants and animals; builds a brush house like a beaver's, but smaller, or digs a tunnel in a bank with the entrance below the water line. Hab: cattail marshes, edges of ponds, lakes, and slow streams, open water. R: nwC, neC. Introduced into marshes and slow streams of the Central Valley.

3. OLD WORLD MICE and RATS, Subfamily Murinae. These rodents are dull grayish brown to black in color, with long, naked tails.

67. HOUSE MOUSE, *Mus musculus.* **[bldg. grass]** This small, grayish brown mouse with a buff or gray belly has a scaly tail and short fur. Hab: common in buildings, farms or fields; harmful to stored grain and food products; its gnawing characteristic makes it destructive to buildings. R: almost everywhere near or in towns, villages, and farms.

68. NORWAY RAT (COMMON RAT, SEWER RAT), *Rattus norvegicus.* **[bldg. grass]** Distinctive dull gray-brown color and scaly tail. Gives impression of being smelly and dirty. Has been the cause of Bubonic and other plagues; contaminates food with its droppings. Feeds on almost anything from stored grain to farm poultry it has killed. These rats are communal and may work together. Hab: cities and towns around bases of buildings, some farms and fields. R: worldwide.

69. BLACK RAT (SHIP RAT, ROOF RAT), *Rattus rattus.* **[bldg.]** Two color phases: black and brown; belly usually grayish, never white; scaly tail longer than head and body. Hab: lives mostly in buildings, rarely in fields; almost always near the coast. R: common in C coastal cities.

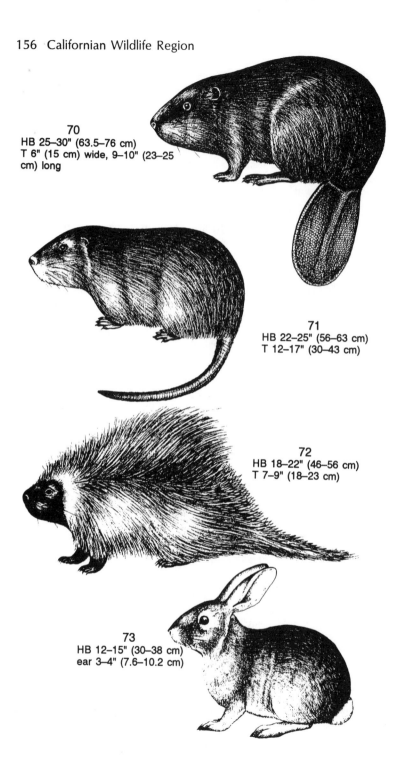

70
HB 25–30" (63.5–76 cm)
T 6" (15 cm) wide, 9–10" (23–25 cm) long

71
HB 22–25" (56–63 cm)
T 12–17" (30–43 cm)

72
HB 18–22" (46–56 cm)
T 7–9" (18–23 cm)

73
HB 12–15" (30–38 cm)
ear 3–4" (7.6–10.2 cm)

E. BEAVER, Family Castoridae. Castor is the only living genus in this famly; it is the largest rodent in our area.

70. BEAVER, *Castor candensis.* **[water str.wd.]** Raccoon(+). Has large, plump, brown body and flat, paddlelike, scaly tail used to warn against danger by violently slapping the water; also for steering while swimming. A mud and stick dam across a stream forms the beaver pond. The house is conical and formed with sticks and mud-clay so closely intertwined that even a bear can rarely break into one. It is occupied by the family group of parents and young up to two years of age. Beavers feed mainly on the bark of willows, alders, and cottonwoods; some food is stored in the house for winter; very intelligent animal. Hab: streams and lakes with proper shore trees. R: cC to nC (more numerous toward Sierra Nevada).

F. NUTRIA, Family Myocastoridae. Nutria are large beaverlike rodents, distinguished by their round, scaly tail.

71. NUTRIA, *Myocastor coypus.* **[water marsh]** Cat(+). A large rodent, dull gray-brown in color; long, round, almost hairless tail; webbed hind feet. Visible mainly at night. Blunt nose and glistening black eyes. Prefers aquatic plants for food. Hab: swamps, marshes, ponds, lakes; burrows in banks with entrance above water; also makes winter platforms and summer nests with sticks in dense vegetation and shallow water. R: found in some waterways of the Central Valley.

G. AMERICAN PORCUPINE, Family Erethizontidae.

72. PORCUPINE, *Erethizon dorsatum.* **[pin-jun. str.wd.]** Raccoon(-). Heavy body, short legs, and skin covered with sharp quills used for defense are distinctive; usually dark colored; dark red eye-shine. Active at night; often seen in tree tops. Frequently alone in summer, sometimes in groups in winter. Eats bark of trees, buds, and twigs. Grunts, groans, and gives high-pitched sounds. Loves to chew on salty things; often a camp pest by gnawing on boots, saddles, even at handles. Hab: coniferous and piñon forests, sometimes brushy areas; dens in caves or in hollow trees. R: eastern two-thirds of C except sC.

RABBITS and HARES: ORDER LAGOMORPHA

A. RABBITS and HARES, Family Leporidae. Members of this family have long ears, long hind legs, and a short, white, cottony tail; bulging eyes on side of head; vegetarian.

73. DESERT or AUDUBON COTTONTAIL, *Sylvilagus audubonii.* **[grass oak rocks desert]** Cat(-). Gray fur mottled with golden brown; tail and belly hairs pure white to roots; ears black tipped, larger and broader than similar species; lots of white under tail. Active from late afternoon through the night, also during the day. Hab: open plains, foothills, desert brush, sparse piñon or juniper; uses fallen trees, burrows of other animals, and heavy brush for shelter. R: most of our area, except parts of nC.

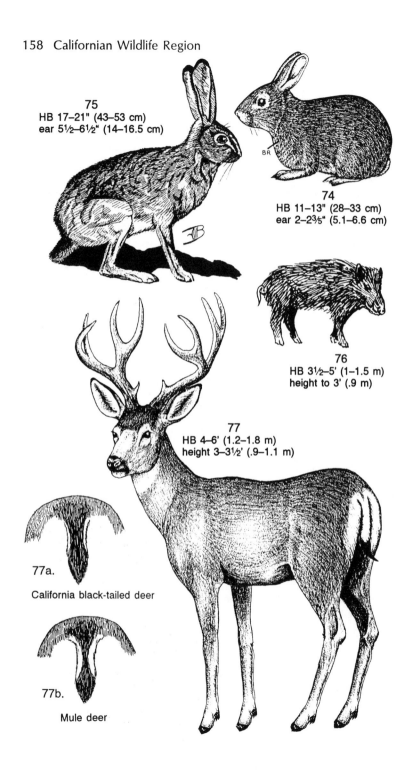

75
HB 17–21" (43–53 cm)
ear 5½–6½" (14–16.5 cm)

74
HB 11–13" (28–33 cm)
ear 2–2⅗" (5.1–6.6 cm)

76
HB 3½–5' (1–1.5 m)
height to 3' (.9 m)

77
HB 4–6' (1.2–1.8 m)
height 3–3½' (.9–1.1 m)

77a.

California black-tailed deer

77b.

Mule deer

74. BRUSH RABBIT, *Sylvilagus bachmani.* **[brush.]** Cat(-). Body, ears, and tail of this rabbit are smaller than other rabbits in our area; brown all over to its small white tail. Active most of the day and night, least at midday, foraging very close to its hide-out. Hab: chaparral, thick brush. Secretive and shy, almost always hiding in dense foliage through which it makes tunnels; rarely uses burrows. R: w two-thirds of C (not in Central Valley), including west flank of Sierra Nevada; nwBaja.

75. BLACK-TAILED JACKRABBIT, *Lepus californicus.* **[grass brush. oak desert]** Raccoon(-). Large, black-tipped ears; fur gray with sprinkling of black; top of tail black; powerful hind legs allow travel at speeds of 30–35 mph (48–56 kmph). Its run consists of long jumps with frequent high leaps to see what is around. Never runs into ground holes as do true rabbits. Hab: croplands, sagebrush, piñon woods, wide grassy spaces, arid lands with scattered plant life. During the heat of the day, it rests in a depression it has dug under a bush for shelter. R: most of our area.

EVEN-TOED HOOFED MAMMALS: ORDER ARTIODACTYLA

A. SWINE, Family Suidae.

76. WILD BOAR or FERAL PIG, *Sus scrofa,* **[oak brush.]** HB 3½–5 ft. (1–1.5 m); height to 3 ft. (.9 m). Coarse, thin hair; variable in color, most often black; upper tusks turn upward; naked snout. Fast runner, trots; can swim; poor eyesight but excellent sense of smell and hearing. Omnivorous, acorns being its favorite, even eats carrion. Reverted to wild state from domestic stock. Hab: brush, chaparral. R: scattered in C coastal and cC mountains, also Butte Co. **Boars and sows with piglets are dangerous. Stay clear of them!**

B. DEER, Family Cervidae.

77. MULE DEER, *Odocoileus hemionus.* **[brush. str.wd. oak]** Winter color is bluish gray with lighter undercoat giving a bluish cast; in summer, the color may range from golden brown to reddish brown; some have a whitish rump patch; fawns spotted; tail either white with a black tip or entirely black on top; large ears continuously whisk around to catch warning sounds; long slim legs. Male has equally branched antlers that are shed in late winter. Active at night in moonlight, early mornings, and evenings. Easily makes great bounding leaps over most obstacles to escape enemies in rough areas; wise bucks learn to slip low through brush if hunted. Does and fawns bleat; males utter a guttural grunt or a shrill roar when deeply frightened or angry. Hab: mixed oak and coniferous forests in summer; pastures or meadows edged by woods, grassy areas mixed with bushes and trees, and chaparral in winter. R: most of C and Baja.

a. Black-tailed Deer. (tail shown in top picture) Found near the coast from San Luis Obispo Co. north; also south through the Sierra Nevada foothills to Madera Co.

b. California Mule Deer. (tail shown in bottom picture) Found near the coast in Santa Barbara and Ventura cos.; also in San Bernardino Mountains and north in the Sierra Nevada to Oregon.

c. Southern Mule Deer. Found from Riverside Co. south.

78. DWARF or TULE ELK, *Cervus nannodes.* (not illus.) **[brush. grass]** HB 5½–7 ft. (1.5–2 m); height 4–5 ft. (1–1.5 m). Long neck hairs form grizzled, grayish brown throat mane in males; back buffy gray with a yellowish rump patch. Male much larger than female; very large, spreading antlers on male in autumn. Feeds on grasses, bark, twigs, and herbs. R: some small herds have been introduced and are located as shown by dots on the map below.

C. GOATS and SHEEP, Family Bovidae.

79. FERAL GOAT, WILD GOAT, *Capra hircus.* **[sav. oak brush. rocks]** (not illus). HB 4–5 ft. (1–1.5 m); height to 3⅓ ft. (1 m). Various colors; horns flattened from side to side and spirally twisted or curved backwards. Reverted to wild state from domestic stock. R: in coastal mountains from Ventura to Monterey cos.

80. BIGHORN SHEEP, *Ovis canadensis.* **[brush. rocks desert alp.]** Color varies from brown to grayish brown with white on rump, belly, back of legs, muzzle, and around the eye; short tail. Males have massive, spiraled horns; female's are short and slender and do not complete a curl. Grazes on a variety of vegetation and must have water in desert areas. An excellent rock climber, jumper, and swimmer who prefers cliffs and rocky areas not frequented by humans. Hab: rocky slopes, ridges, and cliffs in a variety of climates from desert to alpine meadows. R: Sierra Nevada, eC mountains, sC desert.

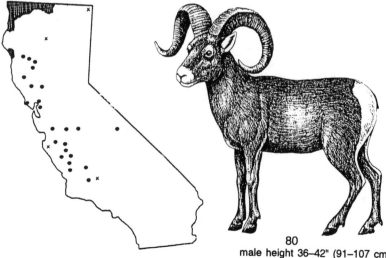

Locations of tule elk.

80
male height 36–42" (91–107 cm)
female height 30–36" (76–91 cm)

5.
COMMON BIRDS

Because birds have wings, they can move easily from one region to another. Some are resident all year, some are winter visitors, others spring and fall migrants. Unless noted, a bird is assumed to be an all year resident. The bird descriptions cover only important characteristics. Additional information is given when particularly interesting or useful such as change in plummage colorations in some birds. The illustrations are usually of the male since the male is easier to identify and the female is often present with the male. Note the kinds of wildlife areas or habitats a bird is found in as well as types of bills, feet, and tracks (page 163), sizes and shapes of bodies, and manners of feeding, flying, and behaving (page 237). The page illustrations of birds are not always in proportion to actual sizes. For this reason five familiar birds are used as examples. But the apparent bulk of a bird, its wingspread, tail, neck, legs, and beak lengths all affect estimates of size to the comparitive birds below. The actual measurements usually give a size range to allow for individual differences as well as variances in regional subspecies.

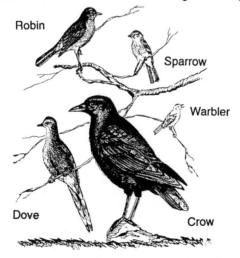

Robin

Sparrow

Warbler

Dove

Crow

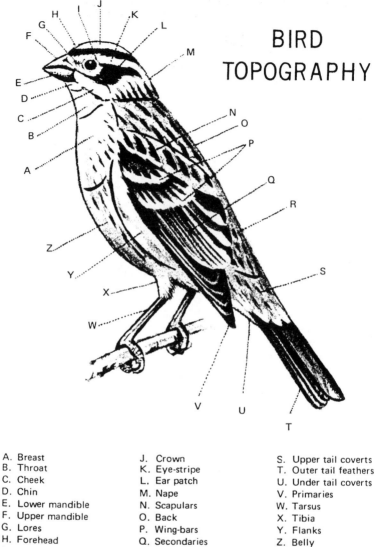

BIRD TOPOGRAPHY

A. Breast	J. Crown	S. Upper tail coverts
B. Throat	K. Eye-stripe	T. Outer tail feathers
C. Cheek	L. Ear patch	U. Under tail coverts
D. Chin	M. Nape	V. Primaries
E. Lower mandible	N. Scapulars	W. Tarsus
F. Upper mandible	O. Back	X. Tibia
G. Lores	P. Wing-bars	Y. Flanks
H. Forehead	Q. Secondaries	Z. Belly
I. Eye-ring	R. Rump	

Often birds do not remain in view long enough to identify them while thumbing through the bird chapter. A basic knowledge of bird topography will help to quickly pinpoint identifying marks while the bird is still in sight. If your fieldbook is not handy, notes should be taken using the proper descriptive terms. A few identification aids jotted on a scrap of paper are far superior to trusting one's memory.

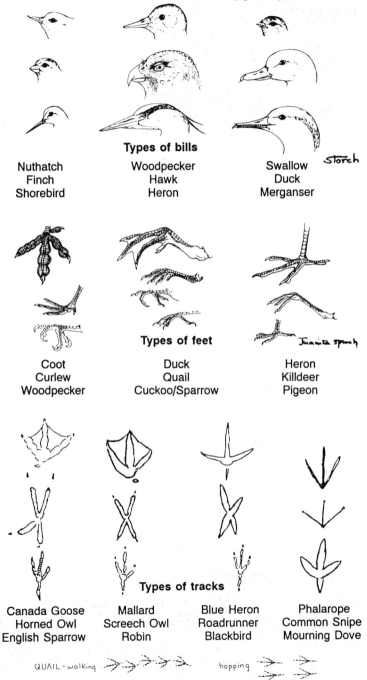

Types of bills

Nuthatch	Woodpecker	Swallow
Finch	Hawk	Duck
Shorebird	Heron	Merganser

Storch

Types of feet

Coot	Duck	Heron
Curlew	Quail	Killdeer
Woodpecker	Cuckoo/Sparrow	Pigeon

Juanita Spark

Types of tracks

Canada Goose	Mallard	Blue Heron	Phalarope
Horned Owl	Screech Owl	Roadrunner	Common Snipe
English Sparrow	Robin	Blackbird	Mourning Dove

QUAIL - walking   hopping

Abbreviations used in the bird chapter: Hab = habitat; BR = breeding or summer range; WR = winter range; Res = where resident; M = where migrant; TL = length from head to tip of tail; C = California; n = northern; s= southern; w = western; e = eastern; c = central.

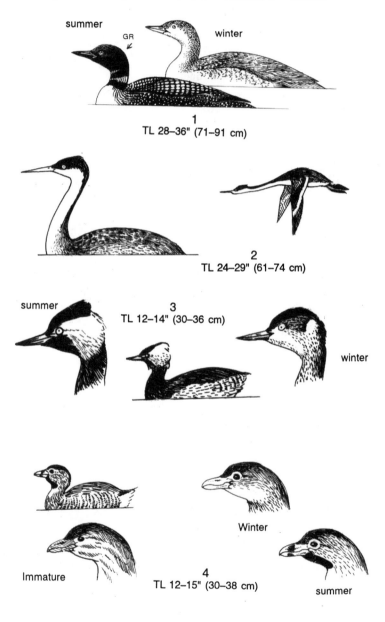

summer

GR

winter

1
TL 28–36" (71–91 cm)

2
TL 24–29" (61–74 cm)

summer

3
TL 12–14" (30–36 cm)

winter

Immature

Winter

4
TL 12–15" (30–38 cm)

summer

LOONS: ORDER GAVIFORMES

A. LOONS, Family Gaviidae. These birds are expert swimmers with large, webbed feet which they use to dive and catch fish under water; their legs appear far at the rear of their bodies. They fly with rapid, steady wingbeats, taking to the air from the water while paddling their feet. In flight the head is held lower than the body.

1. COMMON LOON, *Gavia immer*. **[water]** Crow(+). Varies in size. Large, heavy body; dark, thick pointed bill held horizontally. During breeding has white spots on black back, also two black and white partial neck rings; winter, dark brownish on top of head and body; year round white breast and belly. Voice: a yodel-like laugh. Hab: some inhabit interior lakes and rivers; winter, along lakes and rivers near the coast or on coastal ocean water. WR: along Pacific Coast of C and Baja. **a. PACIFIC LOON,** *Gavia pacifica*; **b. RED-THROATED LOON,** *Gavia stellata*; **c. YELLOW-BILLED LOON,** *Gavia adamsii*. These also winter along C coast.

GREBES: ORDER PODICIPEDIFORMES

A. GREBES, Family Podicipedidae. Grebes are swimming and diving birds with flat-lobed toes, short legs at the back end of their bodies, and very short tails. They take off from water by running over the surface first. Their flight is weak.

2. WESTERN GREBE, *Aechmophorus occidentalis*. **[water]** Crow(+). This is a very long-necked, large-sized, black and white grebe. It has a remarkable courtship dance while paddling and flying on top of the water, wailing and whistling. Makes floating nests. Hab: marshes, lakes, ocean, bays. WR: Pacific Coast to sC and Baja, inland to lakes.

3. EARED GREBE, *Podiceps nigricollis*. **[water]** Robin(+). Small size; thin, upturned bill and rump held high above the water distinguish this grebe. Winter colors are blackish above and whitish below, with white cheeks; during breeding season it has yellowish brown ear tufts; brownish below. Very gregarious. Hab: ponds, lakes; winter, ocean, bays. WR: wC, Central Valley, Baja. BR: sC, Central Valley. **a. HORNED GREBE,** *Podiceps auritus* WR: C coast, occasionally inland where there are lakes or large rivers. **b. RED-NECKED GREBE,** *Podiceps grisengena*. WR: Pacific Coast to sC.

4. PIED-BILLED GREBE, *Podilymbus podiceps*. **[water]** Robin(+). Small, thick-bodied with chickenlike bill which is white in winter and black-banded during breeding; general color brownish with brown stripes on white sides; white tail. Usually solitary. Hab: ponds, lakes, marshes, slow streams; winters in brackish estuaries and bays. Res: C south to nBaja.

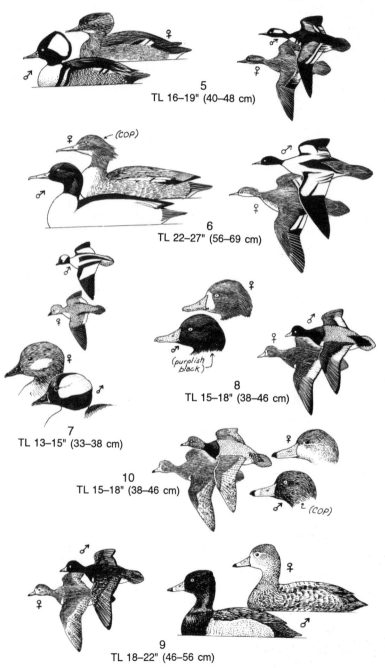

5
TL 16–19" (40–48 cm)

6
TL 22–27" (56–69 cm)

(COP)

(purplish black)

8
TL 15–18" (38–46 cm)

7
TL 13–15" (33–38 cm)

10
TL 15–18" (38–46 cm)

(COP)

9
TL 18–22" (46–56 cm)

WATERFOWL AND ALLIES: ORDER ANSERIFORMES

A. DUCKS, GEESE, and SWANS, Family Anatidae

1. a. MERGANSERS, Tribe Mergini. These are diving and fish-eating ducks with long, serrated bills for catching fish; their flight is rapid and straight with the body and neck held in a horizontal position.

5. HOODED MERGANSER, *Lophodytes cucullatus*. **[water]** Crow size. Male can lower and lift its high black and white crest; female with bushy reddish brown crest. Nests in trees. Hab: wooded ponds or rivers, streams, estuaries, sheltered bays. WR: C coast, nwBaja; inland to rivers and ponds.

6. COMMON MERGANSER, *Mergus merganser*. **[water]** Crow(+). Greenish black head without crest, long, narrow, hooked bill, and much white on body and wings of male are distinctive; female has reddish head. Voice: low, short "crucks." Hab: lakes, ponds, rivers; likes small islands and low shrubs. BR: nC, parts of cC. WR: most of our area.

b. SEA DUCKS. These diving ducks are rather heavy and short-necked. They are found along the coast.

7. BUFFLEHEAD, *Bucephala albeola*. **[water]** Dove(+). Male distinctive with large white area on puffy, greenish head; female dark gray above with white oval patch in middle of head. Female nests in tree cavities. Hab: lakes, ponds, rivers, sheltered salt bays, estuaries. An unusual diving duck because it can fly up from water without paddling. WR: C, all our area, nBaja. **a. COMMON GOLDENEYE,** *Bucephala clangula*. Similar in appearance and also winters in all our area.

2. BAY OR DIVING DUCKS, Tribe Aythyini. These ducks winter in protected river and bay mouths. All species dive from the surface and swim under water. Their diet has more fish and other animal food than other ducks. When rising from the water they first patter along the surface to take off.

8. LESSER SCAUP, *Aythya affinis*. **[water]** Crow(-). Male's head, neck, and chest have glossy purplish iridescence; female has sharp white area on face. Can stay under water a long time probing the bottom for food. Hab: bays, lakes, estuaries. WR: C and Baja. **a. GREATER SCAUP,** *Aythya marila*, is a winter visitor, but mainly C coast.

9. REDHEAD, *Aythya americana*. **[water]** Crow size. Male has large round reddish head; whitish bill with black tip; black chest, gray on back and sides; female brownish. Nests in marshes. Hab: salt bays, estuaries. WR: in most of our area. BR: Inland in isolated areas.

10. RING-NECKED DUCK, *Aythya collaris*. **[water]** Crow(-). Male has distinctive purple head and neck, black back, whitish ring at base of bill; female with characteristic narrow white eye-ring. Hab: in deep bodies of fresh water. Flies fast and low over water. WR: near coast on lakes and ponds of wooded areas.

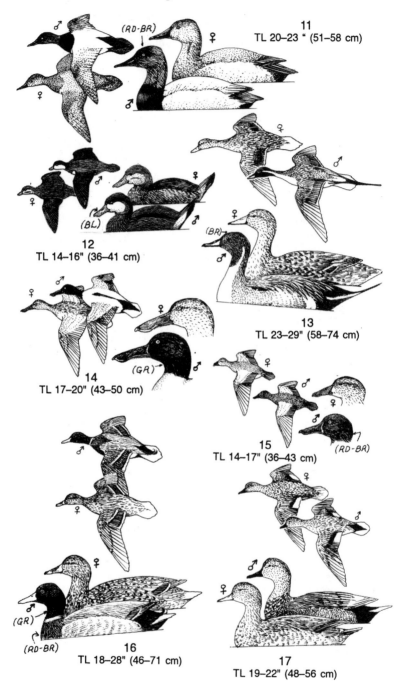

11
TL 20–23 " (51–58 cm)

(RD-BR)

12
TL 14–16" (36–41 cm)

(BL)

(BR)

13
TL 23–29" (58–74 cm)

14
TL 17–20" (43–50 cm)

(GR)

15
TL 14–17" (36–43 cm)

(RD-BR)

16
TL 18–28" (46–71 cm)

(GR)

(RD-BR)

17
TL 19–22" (48–56 cm)

11. CANVASBACK, *Aythya valisineria.* **[water]** Crow(+). Distinctive long, dark bill; male with reddish head and neck, black chest, white back and sides, black in rear; female grayish brown. Hab: estuaries, bays, lakes. WR: most of our area.

4. STIFF-TAILED DUCKS, Tribe Oxyurini. These ducks are small, thick-necked; their uptilted tails are often held straight up.

12. RUDDY DUCK, *Oxyura jamaicensis.* **[water]** Dove(+). During breeding, the male's reddish brown body, purple-black top of head, blue bill and broad white checks are distinctive; male in winter and female's body gray, striped with brown. Rapid wingbeats of the short rounded wings create a fast but uneven flight. Female lays very large eggs in a basket-like, floating nest hidden in reeds. Hab: ponds, lakes, bays with marsh vegetation for vegetarian diet. Res: most of our area.

5. SURFACE-FEEDING DUCKS, Tribe Anatini. These ducks dabble and tip their tail end up in shallow water looking for water plants and insects. Most do not dive, but they are fast fliers.

13. NORTHERN PINTAIL, *Anas acuta.* **[water]** Crow(+). Male distinctive with long, sharp black and white pointed tail, white neck and breast, dark brown head, and rippled gray pattern on back and sides; female plain, splotched dark brown on light brown. Voice: short whistle call. Nests on ground some distance from water. Hab: prairies or grassland, marshes, lakes, ponds. WR: most of C. BR: some breed in the Central Valley.

14. NORTHERN SHOVELER, *Anas clypeata.* **[water]** Dove(+). Large spatula-like bill distinctive, used to strain small food from water; male with iridescent green head, white on back, breast and rump, and reddish sides; female is mottled dark brown. Hab: likes muddy or shallow fresh water, ponds, marshes, sloughs, salt bays. Res: cC. WR: most of our area.

15. CINNAMON TEAL, *Anas cyanoptera.* **[water]** Dove size. Male glossy dark cinnamon except for back; blue patch on forepart of wings; female mottled brown. Hab: reed beds, sluggish streams, rivers, ponds, marshes, shallow lake edges. Res: most of our area. **a. GREEN-WINGED TEAL,** *Anas crecca.* WR: most of our area. **b. BLUE-WINGED TEAL,** *Anas discors.* WR: cC along coast, and in Central Valley.

16. MALLARD, *Anas platyrhynchos.* **[water]** Crow(+). Male easily identified by all green head and neck; white collar and brownish red chest, metallic purple wing patch, yellow-green bill, silver-gray peppered back, with lighter sides and belly; female brownish with dark markings. Hab: lakes, ponds, flooded fields, marshes; Res: most of our area.

17. GADWALL, *Anas strepera.* **[water]** Crow(+). Male has mottled brown head, rippled gray body, blackish bill and tail coverts; female is mottled brown, showing white when swimming. Unusual to this tribe because it dives. Hab: ponds, marshes, lakes, grassy areas. Will wander away from water into fields to feed. Res: most of our area, particularly inner valleys.

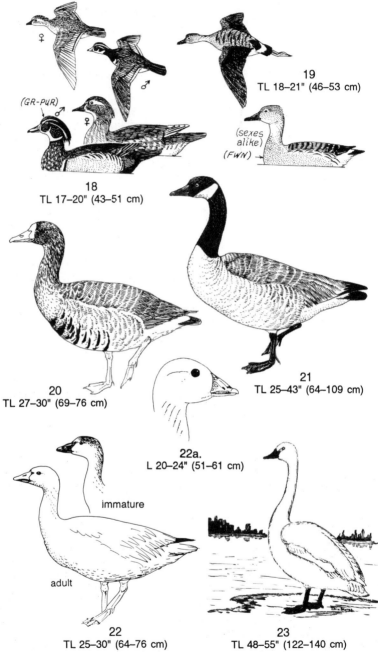

♀

(GR-PuR)

♂   ♀

18
TL 17–20" (43–51 cm)

19
TL 18–21" (46–53 cm)

(sexes alike)
(FWN)

20
TL 27–30" (69–76 cm)

21
TL 25–43" (64–109 cm)

22a.
L 20–24" (51–61 cm)

immature

adult

22
TL 25–30" (64–76 cm)

23
TL 48–55" (122–140 cm)

6. WOOD DUCKS, Tribe Cairinini. These are the only ducks with a long crest extending down the back of the head.

18. WOOD DUCK, *Aix sponsa.* **[water, str.wd.]** Crow size. Male beautifully colored in winter and spring with metallic green head crested with violet, lined with white; breast reddish brown; female generally gray brown with white eye-ring and swept-back bluish gray crown; male looks similar to female in summer and fall. Nests in trees. Hab: slow moving streams of quiet waters near woods. Res: Central Valley and Coast Ranges. WR: extends to Los Angeles Co.

7. WHISTLING DUCKS, Tribe Dendrocygnini. These goose-like ducks with long legs give a shrill, whistling call. They are not divers.

19. FULVOUS WHISTLING DUCK (TREE DUCK), *Dendrocygna bicolor.* **[water]** Crow size. Yellowish brown head and body; whitish throat, streaked brown; barred brown wings; long gray legs. Builds grass nests in marshes, seldom in trees. Mainly forages on land. Hab: likes marshes, meadows, cultivated fields. BR: Merced to Imperial Valley of sC.

8. GEESE, Tribe Anserini. Geese are large, heavy-bodied, gregarious birds, with necks longer than ducks; the sexes look alike.

20. GREATER WHITE-FRONTED GOOSE, *Anser albifrons.* **[water, grass]** Crow(+). Gray-brown with black bands on belly, white in front of eyes; pink bill; orangish feet. Voice: squeal-like "wah-wahwahwah" cry. Hab: marshes, lakes, pastures, flooded fields, bays. WR: Central Valley and San Francisco Bay area.

21. CANADA GOOSE, *Branta canadensis.* **[water, grass]** Crow(+). Long black neck and head with white cheeks, body brown above and gray below, white rump are distinctive. Flocks form V's. Forages on marsh vegetation, meadow grass, and grain fields. Voice: deep honking cry. Hab: lakes, fields, ponds, bays, marshes, rivers, meadows, little islands. WR: widespread coastal C, Central Valley to nBaja.

22. SNOW GOOSE, *Chen caerulescens.* **[water, grass]** Crow(+). In white phase, pure white with black wingtips; feet pink; bill pinkish with black edges; head and upper neck occasionally stained rust color. Quite noisy in flight; flies in V-shaped flocks. Hab: freshwater marshes and lakes; feeds in cultivated fields and grassland. WR: C coast, inland Central Valley, sC, nBaja. **a. ROSS'S GOOSE,** *Chen rossii.* Resembles Snow Goose. WR: Central Valley.

9. SWANS, Tribe Cygnini. Swans are large, white, long-necked birds, very graceful swimmers! Both sexes look alike.

23. TUNDRA SWAN (WHISTLING SWAN), *Cygnus columbianus.* **[water]** Crow(+). White color and very large size distinguish this swan; feet and bill black. Neck is held out straight when flying in V-shaped flocks. Voice: a soft "woo woo" and whistlelike notes. Hab: rivers, lakes, large ponds, bays, and estuaries. WR: Central Valley and coastal nC.

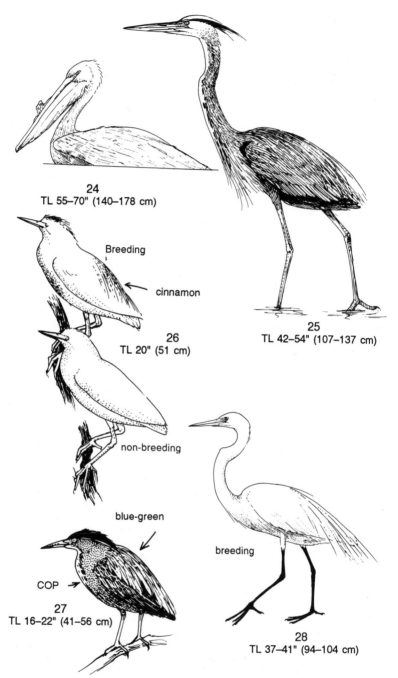

24
TL 55–70" (140–178 cm)

Breeding

cinnamon

26
TL 20" (51 cm)

non-breeding

25
TL 42–54" (107–137 cm)

blue-green

breeding

COP

27
TL 16–22" (41–56 cm)

28
TL 37–41" (94–104 cm)

PELICANS: ORDER PELICANIFORMES. Toes joined by webbing.

A. PELICANS, Family Pelecanidae. Pelicans are big fish-eating birds with very large, long bills and a large pouch below the bill to hold fish. When flying the head is pulled back on the shoulders.

24. AMERICAN WHITE PELICAN, *Pelecanus erythrorhynchos*. **[water]** Crow(+). Adult all white except for yellow-brown bill. Juveniles whitish with black on back of head and grayish bill. Flocks fly in line; flaps, then glides in flight; 8 to 9 foot wingspread. They wade in shallows in teams forming arcs to trap and catch fish. Hab: bays, lagoons. WR: wcC to sC along coast and Central Valley; nBaja.

HERONS AND THEIR ALLIES: ORDER CICONIIFORMES

A. HERONS AND BITTERNS, Family Ardeidae. All are long-legged wading birds, stalking fish, frogs, and crayfish. They strike with long bills for the catch. Most make nests in colonies in trees. They fly with long neck drawn back against the body, and legs straight out behind.

25. GREAT BLUE HERON, *Ardea herodias*. **[grass, water, str.wd.]** Crow(+). Head white with long black feather crest; bill yellow; grayish blue body with black markings. This largest of the dark herons flies above streams with slow, powerful wingbeats. At its chosen fishing spot, it stands still and waits in shallow to medium-deep water to strike prey. Voice: deep, rough croaking calls, "rhaank, rhaank." Nests in trees or hidden in reeds. Hab: shores, tidal flats, streams. Res: most of our area; nBaja.

26. CATTLE EGRET, *Bubulcus ibis*. **[grass, water]** Crow(+). All white most of year, but reddish brown on head, shoulders, and breast in summer; in breeding season legs are pinkish or orangish. Hab: usually seen feeding in flocks in pastures or marshes; often seen on top of cattle. Res: sC. WR: coastal C, Central Valley. BR: isolated places in Central Valley and nC.

27. GREEN-BACKED HERON (GREEN HERON), *Butorides virescens*. **[water, str.wd.]** Crow(+). Bluish green feathers on back, black on sides and tail, reddish brown neck, black crest on head and upper neck; small heron with shorter, bright orange or yellow legs. Rapid flight with deep wingbeats. Voice: a repeated "kwuk-kwuk-kwuk" or "schwenk." Hab: abundant in fresh, brackish, and salt water, along wooded streams, in small ponds, marshes. Res: most of our area.

28. GREAT EGRET (COMMON EGRET), *Casmerodius albus*. **[str.wd. water]** Crow(+). All white with glossy black legs and feet and yellow bill; no crest on head. When flying, neck looks like an open "S." Hab: fresh and salt water marshes, mudflats, rice fields, ponds, streams. Res: cC. WR: wC to nBaja. **a. SNOWY EGRET,** *Egretta thula*. Similar, but has thin black bill and is smaller. Res: Central Valley, C coast.

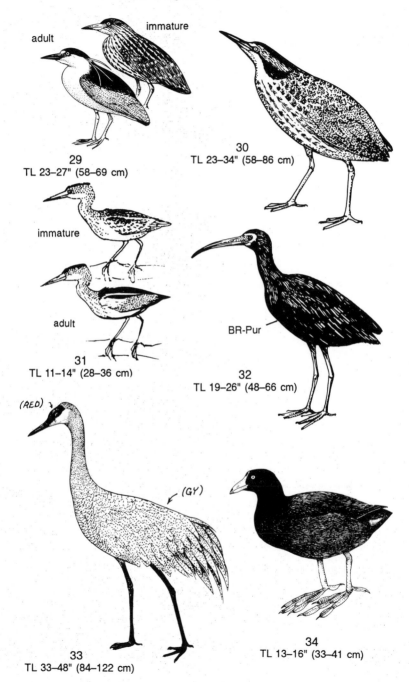

adult

immature

29
TL 23–27" (58–69 cm)

30
TL 23–34" (58–86 cm)

immature

adult

31
TL 11–14" (28–36 cm)

BR-Pur

32
TL 19–26" (48–66 cm)

(RED)

(GY)

33
TL 33–48" (84–122 cm)

34
TL 13–16" (33–41 cm)

29. BLACK-CROWNED NIGHT HERON, *Nycticorax nycticorax.* **[water]** Crow(+). The only heron with a black back and top of head; in breeding several white plumes extend back from head; eyes red. Roosts in trees during the day and forages at night. Stalks food in water with slow movements or long waits. Voice: short hoarse "cwa-cwa." Hab: marshes and wooded streams. Res: most of our area.

30. AMERICAN BITTERN, *Botaurus lentiginosus.* **[water]** Crow(+). Bitterns are hard to see in the freshwater marshes as their colors camouflage with the cattails and rushes, especially when they freeze with the bill pointing straight up like a cattail stalk. Black blotch on side of head, otherwise brown and white streaked and spotted. In mating season they give a deep, hollow, croaking, pumping noise. Hab: common most of the year in marshes with tall vegetation. Res: coastal nC and Central Valley. WR: extends to Baja.

31. LEAST BITTERN, *Ixobrychus exilis.* **[water]** Dove size. Distinctive buffy wing patch on upper part of rust-colored wings; back black with a white stripe. A weak flier, but can run, climb, and hide with great dexterity. Voice: soft cooing call. Hab: likes reedy ponds and marshes. BR: localized areas in cC. Res: sC to Baja.

B. IBISES AND SPOONBILLS, Family Threshkiornithidae. These are long-legged marsh birds with bills that are thin and curved or flat and spoonlike. They flock together and nest in trees.

32. WHITE-FACED IBIS, *Plegadis chihi.* **[water]** Crow(+). In breeding season adult has a broad white line on chin and around each eye; head and body reddish brown with glossy greenish bronze tail and wings; juvenile mostly brown; long thin, down-curving bill; flocks fly in V's or straight lines, with alternate gliding and flapping. Hab: rice fields, marshes, swamps. BR: cC, sC. WR: scattered populations in sC and cC.

CRANES AND THEIR ALLIES: ORDER GRUIFORMES

A. CRANES, Family Gruidae. Cranes have long legs and long necks that extend straight out in flight. Tail feathers down-curved.

33. SANDHILL CRANE, *Grus canadensis.* **[water, grass]** Crow(+). Adult birds very large, gray with white cheeks and throat, red cap; juveniles more brown. Glides and then flaps in flight with rapid upstroke of wings. Voice: rolling and shrill "goroooo-ah-ah-ah." Hab: marshes, prairies, fields. WR: cC.

B. RAILS, GALLINULES, AND COOTS, Family Rallidae. These hen-shaped marsh birds have strange grunting, whispering voices.

34. AMERICAN COOT, *Fulica americana.* **[water, grass]** Dove size. Slate gray body and wings; juveniles lighter gray; white patch under tail and white bill. Buoyantly bobs head back and forth when swimming, making funny upward jumps before diving under the surface. Trails legs during heavy flight. Gregarious. Hab: marshes, lakes, winter fields, bays. Res: throughout our area.

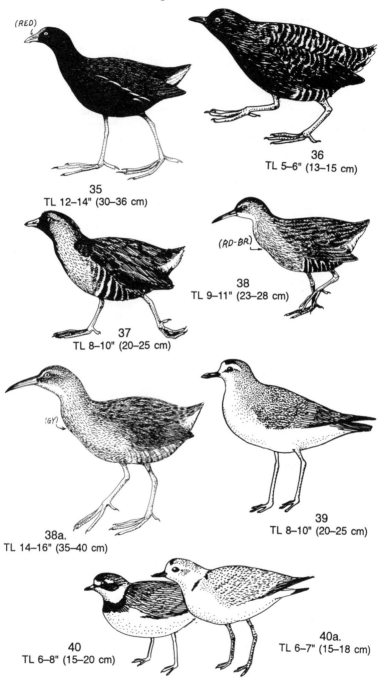

(RED)

35
TL 12–14" (30–36 cm)

36
TL 5–6" (13–15 cm)

(RD-BR)

38
TL 9–11" (23–28 cm)

37
TL 8–10" (20–25 cm)

(GY)

38a.
TL 14–16" (35–40 cm)

39
TL 8–10" (20–25 cm)

40
TL 6–8" (15–20 cm)

40a.
TL 6–7" (15–18 cm)

35. COMMON MOORHEN (GALLINULE), *Gallinula chloropus.* **[water, grass]** Dove size. Bright red on front of face with chickenlike, yellow-tipped red bill, black head, blue-gray belly, and white markings on flank distinguish this bird. Henlike "cluck-cluck" call. Hab: Feeds on insects, fruits, and seeds, hiding in thick vegetation; freshwater marshes, reedy ponds. Res: cC, nBaja. WR: extends to coastal and sC.

36. BLACK RAIL, *Laterallus jamaicensis.* **[water, grass]** Warbler size. Mostly blackish except for white markings and a reddish brown nape; olive legs. Voice: "nikee-dooo" note. Hab: salt marshes on the Pacific Coast and freshwater savanna lands. Res: San Francisco Bay area, isolated areas of sC.

37. SORA, *Porzana carolina.* **[water, grass]** Sparrow size. Short, strong, chickenlike yellow bill; chunky body gray and white-marked below; brown with black markings on wings; black face and throat during breeding. Weak short flight when flushed; feet dangle as it lands. Voice: whistled "ker-wee" call; a whinnying descending musical note. Hab: flooded fields, fresh marshes with deep grass or reeds. Res: San Francisco Bay to Central Valley. WR: extends south to wBaja.

38. VIRGINIA RAIL, *Rallus limicola.* **[water, grass]** Robin size. Reddish brown in front, on wings, and bill; juveniles very dark brown with long, black and white bands on sides and belly. Usually runs secretly through grass and cattails; rarely attempts a weak, fluttering flight. Hab: hides in fresh and brackish marshes with deep grass or reeds. Res: all our area.
a. CLAPPER RAIL, *Rallus longirostris,* is similar, but larger. Res: San Francisco and Monterey Bay area, Santa Barbara Co. south to wBaja.

SHOREBIRDS, GULLS, AND ALLIES: ORDER CHARADRIIFORMES

A. PLOVERS, Family Charadriidae. These are small to medium-sized shorebirds with characteristically short bills, often swelling at the tips. Their neck and tail are short. They are very active birds, moving in short starts and stops, swift in flight, and fast at seizing insects and other prey. Their nests are on the ground.

39. MOUNTAIN PLOVER, *Charadrius montanus.* **[grass, shrub]** Robin(-). Seen in flight, the white wing-band and black tail-band with white border are distinctive; otherwise drab brown above, pale below. Hab: semi-arid grassland, plateaus, fields. WR: Central Valley, sC, nBaja.

40. SEMIPALMATED PLOVER, *Charadrius semipalmatus.* **[water]** Sparrow size. Narrow, dark band across white breast; white band in front of and above eyes; white collar; back, wings, and tail grayish brown; legs orange-yellow. When feeding, it flies more than runs from place to place. Mixes with other shorebirds. Hab: mudflats, beaches. M: common migrant in spring and fall. WR: coastal C. **a. SNOWY PLOVER,** *Charadrius alexandrinus.* Looks similar, but paler. Res: C coast to nwBaja. BR: isolated areas of sC.

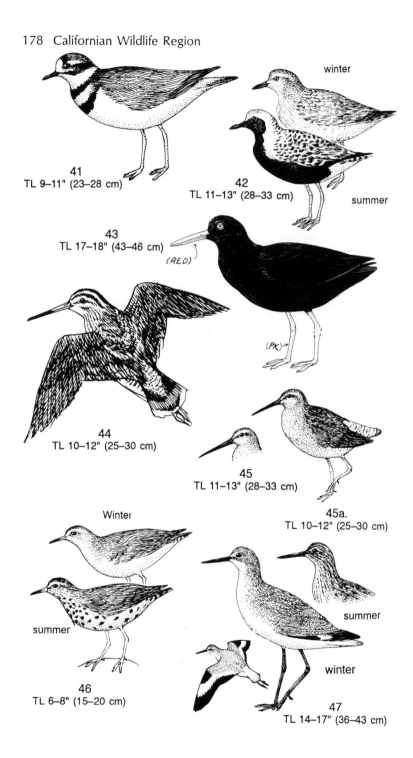

41
TL 9–11" (23–28 cm)

winter

summer

42
TL 11–13" (28–33 cm)

43
TL 17–18" (43–46 cm)

(RED)

(PK)

44
TL 10–12" (25–30 cm)

45
TL 11–13" (28–33 cm)

45a.
TL 10–12" (25–30 cm)

Winter

summer

46
TL 6–8" (15–20 cm)

summer

winter

47
TL 14–17" (36–43 cm)

41. KILLDEER, *Charadrius vociferus.* **[grass, water]** Robin size. Two black bands on white neck distinctive; wings and back brown with white and black on edges of wings. Female leads intruder from nest by acting injured. Voice: plaintive "kee-dee-kee-dee." Hab: fields and pastures near water, lawns, river banks, mudflats, shores of lakes and ponds, rare on sea coasts. Res: throughout our area.

42. BLACK-BELLIED PLOVER, *Pluvialis squatarola.* **[water]** Robin(+). During breeding distinctive white rump and nape with black chest and throat; during winter the underparts are light colored, the back is speckled gray-brown. Hab: beaches, mudflats, marshes. WR: coastal C, Central Valley, nwBaja.

B. OYSTERCATCHERS, Family Haematopodidae

43. BLACK OYSTERCATCHER, *Haematopus bachmani.* **[water]** Crow size. Mainly black with long red bill and reddish eyelids, pinkish legs and feet. Male displays itself by walking up to the female with head held low. Flocks fly in V's. Hab: rocky shores, occasionally beaches. Res: along Pacific Coast.

C. PROBING SHOREBIRDS: SANDPIPERS, PHALAROPES, Family Scolopacidae

1. SNIPES, DOWITCHERS, Subfamily Scolopacinae. These are small medium-sized wading birds with slender wings, long bare legs, and long bills. They are usually gregarious.

44. COMMON SNIPE, *Gallinago gallinago.* **[water]** Robin(+). Looks like a dowitcher, but is more brownish streaked on the back and head, and shows orange tail and brown rump in flight; long straight bill. Flight a continued quick zigzag. Hab: wades in wet meadows, marshy banks of lakes and rivers. WR: most of our area.

45. LONG-BILLED DOWITCHER, *Limnodromus scolopaceus.* **[water]** Robin(+). Distinguished by long straight bill, mottled brown back; sides of breast and belly rusty brown and lightly barred. Winter birds gray overall except for white tail and rump. Feeds fast with rapid down-driving motion. Voice thin "keeek" call. Hab: beaches, mudflats, marshes, fields. WR: C coast to nBaja, Central Valley. **a. SHORT-BILLED DOWITCHER,** *Limnodromus griseus,* is similar in appearance, but with shorter bill; winters along Pacific Coast.

46. SPOTTED SANDPIPER, *Actitis macularia.* **[water]** Sparrow(+). In winter, white below and brown above, black line through eye; spotted on breast and belly during breeding. Voice: sharp "peet" or "pee-weet-weeet" call similar to other sandpipers. Hab: seashores, lakeshores, and rivers. BR: nC. WR: coastal C, Central Valley, nBaja.

47. WILLET, *Catoptrophorus semipalmatus.* **[water]** Crow size. Known immediately in flight by wide white band entirely across the middle of the otherwise black wings. When wings are folded it looks like any

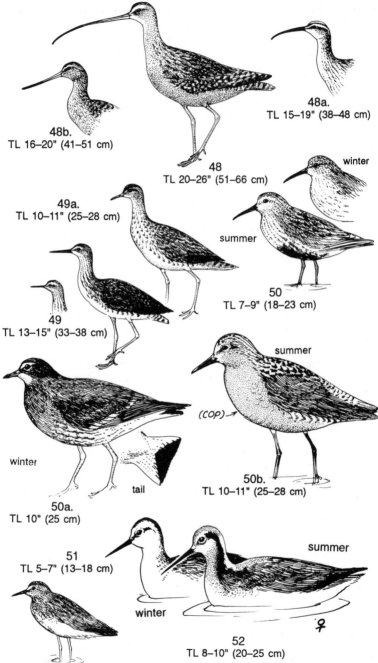

48b.
TL 16–20" (41–51 cm)

48a.
TL 15–19" (38–48 cm)

48
TL 20–26" (51–66 cm)

49a.
TL 10–11" (25–28 cm)

winter

summer

49
TL 13–15" (33–38 cm)

50
TL 7–9" (18–23 cm)

summer

(COP)

winter

tail

50a.
TL 10" (25 cm)

50b.
TL 10–11" (25–28 cm)

51
TL 5–7" (13–18 cm)

summer

winter

52
TL 8–10" (20–25 cm)

♀

common gray wader. Body lightly mottled brown on gray, nearly white below; bluish legs. Usually migrates in small flocks or with 2 mates. Voice: a "pill-will-willet." Hab: salt or freshwater marshes, mudflats. WR: C coast south to coastal Baja. M: primarily along coast inland to salt marshes of cC.

48. LONG-BILLED CURLEW, *Numenius americanus*. **[water, grass]** Crow size. Very long, down-curved bill; body brownish, mottled dark brown, lighter below; underwing linings reddish brown. Camouflaged to look like ground and plants. Nests in meadows or pastures. Hab: tidal flats, salt marshes, beaches. WR: coastal C, Central Valley, nwBaja. **a. WHIMBREL,** *Numenius phaeopus*. Like Long-billed Curlew but bill shorter. WR: Pacific Coast of C, nwBaja. **b. MARBLED GODWIT,** *Limosa fedoa*. Bill also looks very similar to Long-billed Curlew; body shorter. WR: along coast San Francisco Bay area to nwBaja.

49. GREATER YELLOWLEGS, *Tringa melanoleuca*. **[water]** Crow(-). Very thin, long bill; distinctive long, yellow legs; tail banded with black; back a checkered gray. Hab: along Pacific Coast in marshes, near ponds, streams, mudflats. WR: wC, Central Valley. **a. LESSER YELLOWLEGS,** *Tringa flavipes*, is similar but smaller in size and migrates along coast from San Francisco Bay area south.

2. CALIDRIDINE SANDPIPERS, Subfamily Calidridinae. Most sandpipers move in and out with the waves along the ocean and bay shores, picking at tiny marine life in the sand or water.

50. DUNLIN, *Calidris alpina*. **[water]** Robin(-). Plump, short-necked with long, slightly downturned bill; winter plumage is grayish above, with black trim on wings, wide white bands shown in flight and black stripe on tail; spring plumage is reddish brown on back and black on belly. Hunched-over body when feeding. Hab: beaches, tidal flats, muddy pools. WR: C coast, Central Valley, nwBaja. Two similar sandpipers with shorter bills are: **a. SURFBIRD,** *Aphriza virgata*. WR: C coast, nwBaja. **b. RED KNOT,** *Calidris canutus*. WR: coastal C from San Francisco Bay area south to nwBaja.

51. LEAST SANDPIPER, *Calidris minutilla*. **[water]** Sparrow size. Thin, short bill, yellow legs, and small size are distinctive; brown mottled above, with thin black stripe down center of tail. Hab: wet meadows, mudflats, marshes, rarely sandy beaches. WR: C coast, Central Valley, nwBaja. Other similar sandpipers: **a. SANDERLING,** *Calidris alba*. WR: C coast, nwBaja. **b. WESTERN SANDPIPER,** *Calidris mauri*. WR: coast of C, nwBaja.

3. PHALAROPES, Subfamily Phalaropodinae. When feeding, these birds spin like gyroscopes to stir up live food in the water.

52. WILSON'S PHALAROPE, *Phalaropus tricolor*. **[water]** Robin(-). Looks like a sandpiper, but has lobed toes for use in swimming; during breeding, has a reddish brown area down neck to wings bordered by black; throat and behind the neck white; during winter, dark gray above

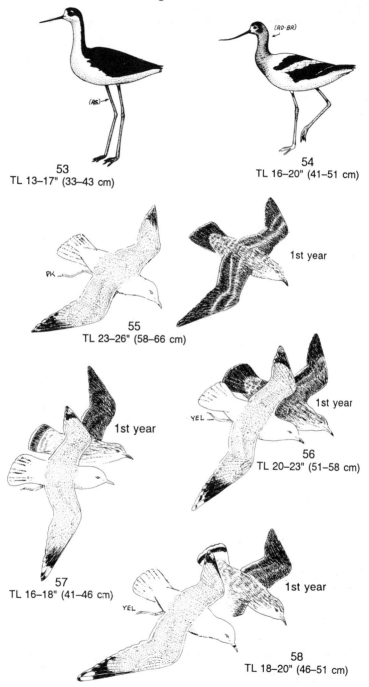

53
TL 13–17" (33–43 cm)

54
TL 16–20" (41–51 cm)

1st year

55
TL 23–26" (58–66 cm)

1st year

1st year

56
TL 20–23" (51–58 cm)

57
TL 16–18" (41–46 cm)

1st year

58
TL 18–20" (46–51 cm)

with white below; Hab: shallow lakes, fresh and saltwater marshes, mudflats, sea coasts. M: summer visitor to Central Valley migrates south. **a. RED PHALAROPE**, *Phalaropus fulicaria*. **b. RED-NECKED PHALAROPE**, *Phalaropus lobatus*. Both winter on sC coast.

D. AVOCETS AND STILTS, Family Recurvirostridae. This family is characterized by very slender, upturned bills for probing in the sand and very long legs.

53. BLACK-NECKED STILT, *Himantopus mexicanus*. **[water]** Crow(-). Bill and red legs are very slender; black above and white below. Voice: startlingly shrill yipping notes. Hab: lakes, mudflats, grassy fresh and saltwater marshes. Res: coastal C from San Francisco Bay south to nwBaja, lower Central Valley, sC. BR: extends to upper Central Valley.

54. AMERICAN AVOCET, *Recurvirostra americana*. **[water]** Crow size. Distinctive light orange head and neck; during breeding, deeper orange; otherwise black and white with blue-gray legs. Hab: beaches, rivers, shallow lakes, ponds, mudflats. Res: San Francisco Bay area inland to Central Valley, coastal to sC.

E. GULLS and TERNS, Family Laridae. Gulls land on water, while terns plunge in head-first to catch fish. Gulls have generally square tails, while terns usually have forked and pointed tails. Both have long wings, the tern's being narrower. Gulls have stout hooked bills, while terns have stout but long, pointed bills. Gulls have deliberate, powerful flight, while the flight of terns is more buoyant and swift. Both have webbed feet.

55. HERRING GULL, *Larus argentatus*. **[water]** Crow(+). The only large gull with black-tipped wings and pink legs; back and wings mainly gray. Voice: shrill and startling squeal or scream. Hab: beaches, dumps, farmlands, rivers, piers. WR: coastal C and Central Valley. **a. THAYER'S GULL**, *Larus thayeri*. WR: coastal C and Central Valley.

56. CALIFORNIA GULL, *Larus californicus*. **[water, bldg.]** Crow(+). Similar to Herring Gull, but legs turn greenish in second year; also somewhat smaller. Voice: loud "keee-arr" squeal. Hab: seashores, bays, estuaries, lakes, rivers, farms, cities, piers. WR: coastal C and Central Valley.

57. MEW GULL, *Larus canus*. **[water]** Crow size. Adult has distinctive thin, yellow bill; greenish yellow legs; juvenile looks like Ring-billed Gull. Voice: very high-pitched mewing calls. Hab: tidal rivers, coastal waters, mudflats, and inland to lakes. WR: Pacific Coast of C and Baja.

58. RING-BILLED GULL, *Larus delawarensis*. **[water]** Crow size. Distinctive black ring around yellow bill; otherwise similar to California Gull. Hab: bays, seacoasts, lakes, rivers, irrigated fields. WR: most of our area.

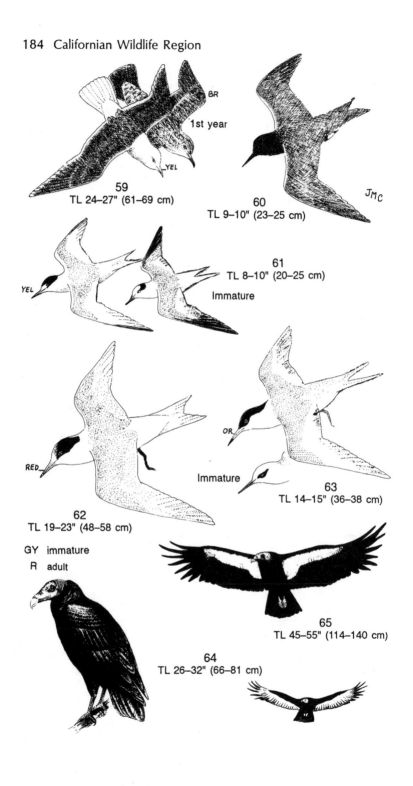

59
TL 24–27" (61–69 cm)

60
TL 9–10" (23–25 cm)

61
TL 8–10" (20–25 cm)

Immature

62
TL 19–23" (48–58 cm)

63
TL 14–15" (36–38 cm)

Immature

GY immature
R adult

64
TL 26–32" (66–81 cm)

65
TL 45–55" (114–140 cm)

59. WESTERN GULL, Larus occidentalis. **[water, bldg.]** Crow(+). Dark gray-black on wings and back with white fringes on wings; tail and head white; feet pinkish white. Hab: coastal cliffs, beaches, piers, tidal rivers; common on Pacific beaches, rare inland. Res: along Pacific Coast.

60. BLACK TERN, Chlidonias niger. **[water]** Robin size. Dark colors distinctive; the only black headed and bodied tern. Has zigzag, darting flight after insects over water; rarely dives. Hab: lakes, marshes, coasts. M: summer visitor along Pacific Coast and inland. BR: cC.

61. LEAST TERN, Sterna antillarum. **[water]** Robin size. Small size, white forehead, and very rapid wingbeat distinctive; gray back and wings with black edges. Feeds by sweeping down to surface to grab small fish. Voice: rapidly repeated "ket-ket-ket" notes. Hab: beaches, sea coasts, bays, estuaries, inland on large rivers. BR: along the Pacific Coast from San Francisco Bay area south to Baja.

62. CASPIAN TERN, Sterna caspia. **[water]** Crow size. Distinctive large size and blood red bill; head is spotted gray and dark in winter, which is when they are seen in our area. Has over a 4–foot wingspan. A fierce robber of other sea birds' fish. Hab: sea coasts, bays, lakes. WR: coastal sC to Baja. BR: isolated areas in cC. **a. COMMON TERN,** Sterna hirundo, is a rare winter migrant in the same area. **b. ROYAL TERN,** Sterna maxima. Similar to the Caspian Tern except for orange bill. BR: San Diego area. WR: Monterey coast and south.

63. FORSTER'S TERN, Sterna forsteri. **[water]** Crow(-). Top of head and neck solid black, but rest of body white or light gray; wing tips frosty white; tail is deeply forked. Hab: salt and freshwater marshes near the coast, estuaries, lakes, beaches. WR: Pacific Coast from San Francisco area south to Baja. BR: San Francisco Bay to Central Valley.

EAGLES, HAWKS, VULTURES AND FALCONS: ORDER FALCONIFORMES

A. VULTURES, Family Cathartidae. Vultures feed almost entirely on dead animals and birds.

64. TURKEY VULTURE, Cathartes aura. **[oak, grass, shrub, des. str.wd.]** Crow(+). Often called a buzzard; has bare reddish head; juveniles have blackish heads. Can coast for hours on wind currents, flies with wings uptilted at a 10 degree angle, slightly V'd, tilting quickly from side to side; wingspread of 6 feet. Sharp eyes see dead carcasses or other vultures descending to feast. Hab: open areas, deserts, grassland; perches in dead trees. Res: coastal C, Baja. BR: throughout our area.

65. CALIFORNIA CONDOR, Gymnogyps californianus. Crow(+). Res: only a few condors were left in San Luis Obispo and Ventura cos. of sC...now in zoos, trying to save them from extinction. Their wingspread is about 9 feet.

66
TL 21–25" (53–64 cm)

immature

adult

67
TL 15–17" (38–43 cm)

68
TL 30–40" (76–102 cm)

GY- BR

OR–RED

69
TL 19–25" (48–64 cm)

RD- BR

70
TL 16–22" (41–56 cm)

B. KITES, EAGLES, HAWKS, Family Accipitroidae

1. OSPREY, Subfamily Pandioninae. A fish-eating hawk; hovers high over water, then plunges down feet first, often completely under water, to seize fish. Wingspread of 4½ feet to nearly 6 feet.

66. OSPREY, *Pandion haliaetus.* **[water]** Crow(+). When flying, a large black patch shows at the crook of whitish wing; undertail has 4 bands against white; plummage dark above, white below and on head; black streak through eye. Nest is a large pile of sticks on top of high conifers or stumps. Hab: seashore, marshy lagoons, rivers, lakes. WR: Pacific Coast into Baja. BR: isolated area in cC.

2. a. KITES, Subfamily Accipitrinae, have long, pointed wings and long tails; they regularly hover in flight; their flight pattern is very graceful.

67. BLACK-SHOULDERED KITE (WHITE-TAILED KITE), *Elanus leucurus.* **[str.wd. water, sav. grass]** Crow(-). White and dark grayish markings, except juveniles have brown streaks on breast; black wing patch at lower shoulder of wing; long white tail. Flies with wing tips pointed downward, soaring and hovering. Feeds on rodents, snakes, and insects. Hab: grassland and marshes. Res: most of our area.

b. EAGLES. These accipiters' wingspan may reach 7 feet.

68. GOLDEN EAGLE, *Aquila chrysaetos.* **[sav. oak]** Crow(+). General rich brown color with golden tinge on back, wings, and neck in the adult; juveniles have white on underwing linings and base of tail. Preys mainly on rabbits and rodents, hurtling down at high speed and leveling to a glide as it strikes. Hab: open country, open woods of mountains, canyons, plains. Res: most of our area, though rare except in the Central Valley, mostly in wild country.

c. BUTEO OR BROAD-WINGED SOARING HAWKS have rounded, broad wings and a fanlike tail. Also known as buzzard hawks, they soar and wheel high in the sky.

69. RED-TAILED HAWK, *Buteo jamaicensis.* **[oak, grass, rocks, str.wd. shrub]** Crow(+). Usually rounded, red tail above with paler color below; brown belly and forepart of underwings; juveniles have tail finely streaked with brown. May perch on high tree limbs; soars but rarely hovers. Voice: high, shrill scream. Hab: open woods, savanna, rare in dense forests; nests in trees; hunts mammals and birds in open areas by diving from a soaring position. Res: common throughout our area. Two other Buteos common throughout our area as winter residents are: **a. ROUGH-LEGGED HAWK,** *Buteo lagopus.* White tail with broad black band. WR: throughout our area. **b. FERRUGINOUS HAWK,** *Buteo regalis.* Has whitish on pale rufous tail. WR: all our area.

70. RED-SHOULDERED HAWK, *Buteo lineatus.* **[str.wd.]** Crow(+). Reddish shoulder patches and black and white bars on tail and along

71
TL 18–23" (46–58 cm)

♂ GY
♀ BR

72
TL 16–24" (41–61 cm)

73
TL 10–14" (25–36 cm)

74
TL 14–20" (36–51 cm)

75
TL 11–13" (28–33 cm)

outer parts of wings are distinctive; belly and front part of underwings are light orangish brown; juveniles are brownish streaked below; wings are longer and less broad than those of the Red-tailed Hawk. Hab: nests in wet woodlands and along rivers; hunts for rodents, small birds, and insects. Res: wC, and Central Valley.

71. SWAINSON'S HAWK, *Buteo swainsoni.* **[sav. grass]** Crow(+). Brown underneath, except in light phase; banded tail; reddish brown around neck and breast; face and throat white; juveniles are streaked with brown in front and on back. Slightly uplifts wings as it glides. Often migrates in flocks. Hunts for gophers, rats, and insects by diving down from a perch to the ground or from low flight. Hab: cultivated lands, open oak-pine woods. BR: Central Valley.

d. HARRIERS have long, rounded wings and a long tail; they regularly forage low to the ground, tilting to both sides while harrying prey.

72. NORTHERN HARRIER (MARSH HAWK), *Circus cyaneus.* **[water, grass]** Crow(+). White rump against dark back and tail distinctive; male is gray, whitish below except for black tail bars; female is brown with brown streaks below; longer wings than accipiters (below); long tail. Hovers over marshes and grassy areas, then dives to catch rodents. When gliding, the wings are held rather high. Hab: marshes, prairies, cultivated fields. Res: cC, nBaja. WR: our entire area.

e. ACCIPITERS OR BIRD HAWKS. The female is larger than the male. Both have short, rounded wings and long tails.

73. SHARP-SHINNED HAWK, *Accipiter striatus.* **[oak]** Dove size. Long, brownish, square-tipped tail with black bands; bluish gray above; short rounded wings. Sails for short distance, then beats its wings quickly in a sudden rush as it seizes a small bird. Being able to make quick sharp turns in flight, this small hawk can hunt in wooded areas. Hab: mountain woods. WR: all our area

74. COOPER'S HAWK, *Accipiter cooperii.* **[str.wd. oak]** Crow size. Wide rounded tail and large head; slate gray above, rich reddish brown breast bars; juveniles have brownish streaks on breasts. Fast, powerful catcher of large birds and rats. Voice: loud "kek-kek-kek." Hab: coniferous forests, open woods, canyons, river groves. Res: most of our area except Central Valley. WR: Central Valley.

C. FALCONS AND ALLIES, Family Falconidae. Falcons have long streamlined tails and pointed wings.

75. MERLIN (PIGEON HAWK), *Falco columbarius.* **[str.wd. grass]** Dove(+). Black cap not adjoined to a black facial pattern; male has dark bluish gray wings and back; female has brown on head and back; dark bars on tail. Hunts shorebirds, mice, pigeons, and insects, swooping low with steady wing beats. Hab: open woods, plains, marshes, grassland, deserts, sea coasts, cliffs. WR: most of our area.

76
TL 17–20" (43–51 cm)

77
TL 15–21" (38–53 cm)

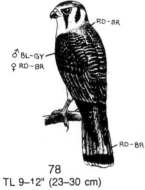

RD-BR

♂ BL-GY
♀ RD-BR

RD-BR

78
TL 9–12" (23–30 cm)

TNY

79
TL 14–20" (36–51 cm)

80
TL 7–8½" (18–22 cm)

81
TL 13–17" (33–43 cm)

76. PRAIRIE FALCON, *Falco mexicanus.* **[rocks, grass, des.]** Crow size. Black patches at base on underside of wings are distinctive; paler brown color than other falcons; more white on head. Has swift, strong, low flight; attacks birds in open areas, rarely in woods. Nests on cliffs. Hab: open woods of mountains, plains, deserts. Res: interior dry areas. WR: all our area.

77. PEREGRINE FALCON, *Falco peregrinus.* **[rocks, water]** Crow size. Dark facial pattern and back are distinctive. Swift chaser of birds. Population was declining, but they are on the increase again. Hab: open areas, cliffs, sea coasts, cities, deep woods. WR: coastal and wC, south into Baja.

78. AMERICAN KESTREL (SPARROW HAWK), *Falco sparverius.* **[oak, grass, des. str.wd.]** Robin(+). Rusty brown back, tail, and whiskers distinctive; black and white patterned face. Hunts from trees or poles or hovers and dives for insects. Voice: sharp "killy-kully" cry. Hab: open areas, edges of woods, farms, cities, highways. Res: throughout our area.

OWLS: ORDER STRIGIFORMES. Large eyes face forward, surrounded by a circle of feathers.

   A. BARN OWLS, Family Tytonidae. Barn owls have light colors and their faces are heart-shaped and monkeylike.

79. COMMON BARN OWL, *Tyto alba.* **[rocks, bldg. grass, oak, water]** Crow size. Wingspread 40 to 47 inches. Large owl, white in front with light speckling, brownish mottling on back and wings. Has peculiar movement of head, back and forth. Nocturnal; flies frequently, landing on backs of rats and mice in the dark. Voice: gives ghostlike wheezy cry; sharp hiss when disturbed. Often nests in old buildings. Hab: open woods, marshes, farmyards. Res: most of our area.

   B. OTHER OWLS, Family Strigidae. Large-headed, short-necked birds of prey with hooked bills and strong talons. Quiet moth-like flight. Mostly nocturnal.

80. NORTHERN SAW-WHET OWL, *Aegolius acadicus.* **[oak]** Crow size. More white on brown streaked breast than most small owls; no ear tufts; quite tame. Secretive hunter after dark. Hab: oak woods, pine forests, alder thickets, scrub, old buildings. Res: coastal C. WR: most of C.

81. SHORT-EARED OWL, *Asio flammeus.* **[water, grass]** Crow(-). Ears difficult to see; brown and fawn streaked and mottled; large black patch at bend of wing distinctive. Often out in daytime; irregular side-to-side flight as it pursues small mammals before diving. Hab: prairies, meadows, farms, marshes, open woods, dunes. WR: throughout our area. Res: coastal nC.

82
TL 13–16" (33–41 cm)

83
TL 18–25" (46–64 cm)

85
TL 7–10" (18–25 cm)

84
TL 6–7½" (15–19 cm)

RD-BR

87
TL 16–19" (41–48 cm)

86
TL 9–11" (23–28 cm)

82. LONG-EARED OWL, *Asio otus.* **[str.wd. oak]** Crow(-). Wings unusually long with wingspread 36 to 43 inches; ear tufts long and close together; breast and belly streaked downward with black. Groups together in winter. Nests in dense trees or in caves of cliffs. Hab: mixed coniferous and deciduous forests, generally near water. WR: locally throughout our area. BR: coastal from San Francisco Bay south.

83. GREAT HORNED OWL, *Bubo virginianus.* **[most habitats]** Crow(+). Wingspread 35 to 55 inches. Ear tufts larger and farther apart than other owls; large size; eyes yellow; demeanor fierce and dominating; belly horizontally barred in black. Hunts everything up to the size of a skunk and fox. Voice: 4 to 7 deep low hoots, 3 or 4 times in a row. Makes large nests on cliffs, in trees or caves. Hab: almost everywhere except cities and deserts. Res: throughout our area.

84. NORTHERN PYGMY OWL, *Glaucidium gnoma.* **[oak]** Sparrow size. No ear tufts, two black spots on hind side of neck that look like eyes, long tail with 5 bright white bars, and blackish brown streaking on flanks are distinctive. Hunts both by day and night and is a terror among songbirds and woodpeckers as it darts through bushes. When perched, it may appear to be a pine cone. Hab: dense wooded canyons and hardwood or mixed forests. Res: coastal wC from San Francisco Bay area south to Santa Barbara, csC.

85. WESTERN SCREECH OWL, *Otus kennicottii.* **[oak, str.wd. bldg. des.]** Robin size. Usually grayish in our area, mottled with white on front; ear tufts rather short and wide apart. May nest in woodpecker holes. Hab: oak and streamside woods, groves on farms, or in towns. Res: most of our area.

86. BURROWING OWL, *Speotyto cunicularia.* **[grass, sav. des.]** Robin(+). Long bare legs, light sandy mottled color, white stripe on chin; frequent bobbing motion. Hunts mainly in daylight by short swoops, then dives on prey. Uses ground squirrel or prairie dog holes for nests; often stands erect near the hole. Hab: open grassland, savanna, prairie, lower elevations. Res: most of our area.

87. SPOTTED OWL, *Strix occidentalis.* **[oak]** Crow size. No ear tufts. Dark brown back and wings thickly covered with white spots; dark bars across lighter breast and belly. Hab: rather rare in western dense old growth coniferous forests and woodlands, thickly wooded canyons. Res: coastal wC to sC.

FOWL-LIKE BIRDS: ORDER GALLIFORMES

A. GROUSE, PHEASANTS, TURKEYS, QUAIL AND PARTRIDGES, Family Phasianidae. Members of this family have a chickenlike bill; the wings are typically short and rounded. In flying, they burst up suddenly from the ground into full flight, usually traveling only a short distance close to the ground. Primarily ground birds, **Phasianidae** forage with much scratching of their feet.

RED

BR

RD-BR

88
TL 36–48" (91–122 cm)

GY

89
TL 12–15" (30–38 cm)

♂

♀

90
TL 9–11" (23–28 cm)

91
TL 10–12" (25–30 cm)

GY

RD-BR

RED

92
TL 30–36" (76–91 cm)

93
TL 12–14" (30–36 cm)

JMC

88. WILD TURKEY, *Meleagris gallopavo.* **[oak, str.wd. sav.]** Crow(+). Slimmer, but it looks like the domestic turkey, with blue head and red wattles on neck of male; reddish brown on top of tail. A good runner, seldom flies. Hab: likes clearings in woods or open forests; found in scattered open oak and deciduous-coniferous woods. Res: wC, cC, ncC.

89. CHUKAR, *Alectoris chukar.* **[des. shrub]** Dove size. Quail-looking with red bill and legs; white throat bordered with black; distinctive brown streaks on sides; bluish gray on top; tail with outer parts reddish brown. Forms coveys of two or three dozen birds. Voice: "chu-kar" call. Hab: dry mountains, deserts, brushy, rocky, or grassy areas, plateaus, canyons. Res: wcC from San Francisco Bay area south to Santa Barbara.

90. CALIFORNIA QUAIL, *Callipepla californica.* **[shrub, grass]** Dove size. Plump and gray with black and white design on head and throat of male; scaled dark and light belly; the top-knot feather curves forward; female has unique streaked throat. Usually in large coveys. A sentinel stands watch when the flock feeds. Roosts in low brushy trees at night. Flushes explosively when disturbed. Call sounds like "Chi-ca-go." Hab: semi-desert scrub, sagebrush, thickets, chaparral, woods' edges, farms, parks. Res: much of our area.

91. MOUNTAIN QUAIL, *Oreortyx pictus.* **[shrub, oak]** Dove size. Very long straight top-knot feather, bright white bars on reddish brown side are distinctive; reddish brown throat patch; female duller in color than male. Hard to flush, as they take cover in thick brush. Voice: gives a soft "whoook" note. Hab: mixed forests, mountain brush. Res: inland wC from Monterey south to Baja.

92. RING-NECKED PHEASANT, *Phasianus colchicus.* **[grass, str.wd.]** Crow(+). Scarlett wattle, purple, red, dark blue, green markings on head of male, and white ring around its neck are distinctive; both sexes have very long, pointed tails and mottled brown body. Fast running; explodes into flight. Hab: fields, marsh edges, brushy areas. Res: interior cC, locally to sC.

KINGFISHERS AND ALLIES: ORDER CORACIIFORMES

A. KINGFISHERS, Family Alcedinidae. Kingfishers have long, sharp, strong bills and large heads. They dive for fish.

93. BELTED KINGFISHER, *Ceryle alcyon.* **[water, rocks, str.wd.]** Dove(+). Has a big head with a rough feather top-knot, distinctive gray-blue and white coloration on throat and belly, and a powerful bill; female has reddish brown across center of belly. Often seen perched on a limb above water or flying up and down streams or lakes; may hover before diving to catch a fish. Voice: noisy, rattling, dry call. Hab: near water (fresh and salt), wooded creeks; nests in holes in banks. Res: coastal to sC. WR: most our area.

94
TL 10–13" (25–33 cm)

95
TL 20–24" (51–61 cm)

96
TL 12–14" (30–36 cm)

97
TL 8–9½" (20–24 cm)

98
TL 10½–11½" (27–29 cm)

99
TL 6½–7½" (17–19 cm)

CUCKOOS, ROADRUNNERS: ORDER CUCULIFORMES

A. CUCKOOS, Family Cuculidae. Long-tailed, slender birds with two toes forward and two that point backward. Sexes look alike.

94. YELLOW-BILLED CUCKOO, *Coccyzus americanus.* **[str.wd.]** Dove(+). Very large white spots against black of undertail coverts are distinctive on long tail; body dark brown above with reddish brown on the wings. Eats hairy caterpillars. Hab: thick undergrowth of streamside woods, where they are more often heard than seen, orchards. BR: isolated areas in cC to Baja (rare).

95. GREATER ROADRUNNER, *Geococcyx californianus.* **[shrub, des.]** Crow(+). Bushy-looking bird with a high brown crest and long tail; long, fast running legs; short wings; rarely flies; white crescent on open wing. Catches snakes, lizards, and large insects. Voice: dovelike song, pitched downward. Hab: arid country with scattered brush, chaparral, deserts. Res: all our area except northern coast.

WOODPECKERS: ORDER PICIFORMES

A. WOODPECKERS, Family Picidae. All woodpeckers have strong, sharp bills and the habit of digging into wood, mainly for wood-boring insects; stiff tails useful as props; toes arranged two forward, two back; wavering flight pattern.

96. NORTHERN FLICKER (RED-SHAFTED RACE), *Colaptes auratus.* **[str.wd. oak]** Dove(+). Brown crown without red on nape; gray face and throat; side whiskers red; reddish under wings and tail; wings flash reddish orange in flight. Probes trees for insects and grubs; also catches ants on the ground. Voice: the cry of all flickers is a loud and repeated "flick-flick-flicker-flicker" or "quicker." Hab: open areas near trees. Res: throughout our area.

97. ACORN WOODPECKER, *Melanerpes formicivorus.* **[oak, sav.]** Robin size. Distinctive red cap, white rump, black chin, white and yellow throat, and easily-seen white wing patches. Gathers great amounts of acorns and other nuts which it stores in tight fitting holes that are re-used every year. Often in flocks, noisily talking. Hab: oaks, oak-pine canyons, foothills. Res: wC to nwBaja.

98. LEWIS' WOODPECKER, *Melanerpes lewis.* **[oak]** Robin(+). Dark with reddish face and rose-colored belly. Unorthodox woodpecker: it flies like a crow, gathers in large flocks; catches insects in the air or on the ground, does very little tree hammering, and stores its nuts in other's holes or crevices. Hab: open oak or pine forests, orchards. Res: cC to San Luis Obispo Co.

99. NUTTALL'S WOODPECKER, *Picoides nuttallii.* **[oak, str.wd.]** Sparrow(+). Distinctive black face, black and white pattern on side of head, and black and white stripes on back; male has red cap. Hab: live oak woods, streamside woods, orchards. Res: most of our area.

RED

♀

100
TL 9–10" (23–25 cm)

♂

Red

Red

Red

Red-naped
form

Red-
breasted
form

101
TL 8–9" (20–23 cm)

YEL

GY

102
TL 14–16" (36–41 cm)

♀

104b
TL 5½–6½" (14–17 cm)

104
TL 13–14" (33–36 cm)

103
TL 13–14" (33–36 cm)

GY

104a.
TL 12" (30 cm)

105
TL 11–12" (28–30 cm)

100. HAIRY WOODPECKER, *Picoides villosus*. **[oak, str.wd.]** Robin size. Comparatively long bill, wide white stripe down back, and white-spotted wings are distinctive; male has red area on back of head. Hab: deciduous, mixed, coniferous forests, wooded towns, and parks. Res: most of C, except for Central Valley and seC. **a. DOWNY WOODPECKER**, *Picoides pubescens*. Small sized bird with similar markings. Res: all our area except seC.

101. RED-BREASTED SAPSUCKER, *Sphyrapicus ruber*. **[str.wd.]** Robin size. Red cap, throat, and nape; yellow belly; white, lengthwise stripe on wings; barred back. Feeds on sap by drilling parallel holes in live trees, eating tiny insects in the sap. Shy in actions. Hab: mixed deciduous or coniferous forests, orchards, parks. WR: most of our area.

PIGEONS AND DOVES: ORDER COLUMBIFORMES

A. PIGEONS AND DOVES, Family Columbidae. Pigeons and doves are distinguished by plump bodies, small heads, short legs, pointed wings, fanned or tapered tails, and swift flight. They characteristically bob their heads when walking and have low, cooing voices. Mainly they are seed, grain, acorn, and fruit eaters.

102. BAND-TAILED PIGEON, *Columba fasciata*. **[oak, str.wd.]** Crow(-). Distinctive broad gray band on widely-curved tail; white neckband against greenish black upper back; gray rump. Voice: repeated "whoo-coo-coo" call with a low and owl-like pitch. Lays only one egg in a loose twig nest on the ground or in a bush. Hab: oak woods, sometimes in coniferous forests, orchards, cultivated fields. Res: wC.

103. ROCK DOVE (DOMESTIC PIGEON), *Columba livia*. **[bldg. rocks]** Dove size. White rump and black tailband are distinctive, but it has many color variations, including all white. Glides with angled-up wings. Voice: soft, gurgling "coo-roo-roo." Hab: in or near cities and farms, also buildings, widespread along rocky sea coasts, cliffs. Res: throughout our area.

104. SPOTTED DOVE, *Streptopelia chinensis*. **[bldg. str.wd.]** Dove size. Very dark body with gray head; black and white spots form neckband; white side borders on tail. Hab: parks and riverside woods. Res: swC, Santa Barbara. **a. RINGED TURTLE-DOVE**, *Streptopelia risoria*. Res: this escaped cage bird is a resident in the Los Angeles area. **b. COMMON GROUND DOVE**, *Columbina passerina*. In flight, wings flash rufous red. Hab: open country and towns. Res: small area in swC, Baja.

105. MOURNING DOVE, *Zenaida macroura*. **[grass, oak, str.wd.]** Dove size. Distinctive slim brownish body and long tapering tail with white fringes on black outer parts. Its swift, direct flight gives forth a whistle from the wings. Feeds in flocks on fruits, seeds, nuts, and insects. Nests in pairs; mates are very faithful. Voice: sad, but beautiful "oooah-coo-coo-coo" heard in spring and summer. Hab: open woods, grassland, coastal scrub, mesquite, farms, suburbs, desert near water. Res: widespread throughout our area.

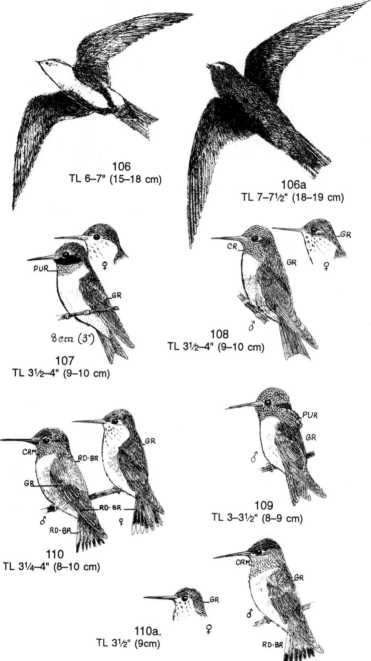

106
TL 6–7" (15–18 cm)

106a
TL 7–7½" (18–19 cm)

PUR
♀
GR
8 cm (3")
107
TL 3½–4" (9–10 cm)

CR
GR
GR
♀
♂
108
TL 3½–4" (9–10 cm)

CRM
RD-BR
GR
GR
RD-BR
♂
RD-BR
♀
110
TL 3¼–4" (8–10 cm)

PUR
GR
♂
109
TL 3–3½" (8–9 cm)

CRM
GR
♂
RD-BR

GR
110a.
TL 3½" (9cm)
♀

SWIFTS, HUMMINGBIRDS: ORDER APODIFORMES

A. SWIFTS, Family Apodidae. Swifts feed almost entirely on flying insects, usually caught high in the sky in their wide mouths. Their stiff, slender wings, unlike a swallow's, appear to beat alternately, "twinkling" like bats. Sexes look alike.

106. WHITE-THROATED SWIFT, *Aeronautes saxatalis.* **[rocks, shrub]** Sparrow(+). Striking black and white pattern unique. Voice: excited shrill "jeejeejee" call. Occasionally nests in tall buildings. Hab: open country and plains, mountains with cliffs. Res: most of our area except Central Valley. **a. BLACK SWIFT,** *Cypseloides niger.* Black all over. BR: cC coast, sC, interior mountains.

B. HUMMINGBIRDS, Family Trochilidae. Hummingbirds with their long, slender bills for probing flowers in search of nectar and tiny insect food are the smallest of North American birds. Their rapid wingbeat makes a humming sound. Very quarrelsome; some feathers iridescent; voice a squeak or lisping "tsip."

107. BLACK-CHINNED HUMMINGBIRD, *Archilochus alexandri.* **[str.wd. oak, shrub]** Warbler(-). Green body; the only "hummer" with a black throat; purple bar just below throat in male; female mainly greenish with white breast. May capture insects like a flycatcher. Hab: lightly wooded areas, chaparral, suburban gardens in foothills. BR: Central Valley, swC, nwBaja.

108. ANNA'S HUMMINGBIRD, *Calypte anna.* **[shrub, oak]** Warbler(-). Male has red iridescent throat and front of head; bronze with green body; green tail of female is broadly tipped with white; has a few red feathers on throat. Voice: male, when serenading, flies in a deep arc, making popping noises at the bottom of the arc. The Anna is the only hummer to live in only one state—California. By mid-winter they are the only ones that stay. The nest is covered with moss and lichen and lined with plant down. Hab: open woods, chaparral, gardens, meadows. Res: most of our area.

109. COSTA'S HUMMINGBIRD, *Calypte costae.* **[shrub, des.]** Warbler(-). Metallic violet cap and throat; gorget is very distinctive in male, often showing ragged feather outline at back of neck or on side; bronze-green bodied female is similar to Black-chinned Hummingbird. Hab: deserts, mesas, sagebrush, chaparral in hills. BR: southern third of the state.

110. RUFOUS HUMMINGBIRD, *Selasphorus rufus.* **[oak, shrub]** Warbler(-). Male has very distinctive reddish brown back and orange-red throat; female greenish with light reddish brown sides. Male makes courting dive within a few inches of female with a shrill sound. Hab: flowering gardens, wooded brushy areas, mountain meadows. M: throughout our area: coastal areas in spring, mountains in fall. **a. ALLEN'S HUMMINGBIRD,** *Selasphorus sasin.* Male has iridescent green cap and upper back; otherwise very similar to the Rufous. BR: coastal C north of Ventura.

112
TL 8–9" (20–23 cm)

JMC

113
TL 7–8" (18–20 cm)

CRM
GR
♂
♀

111
TL 2¾–3¼" (7–8 cm)

BR
OL.

114
TL 7–8" (18–20 cm)

111. CALLIOPE HUMMINGBIRD, *Stellula calliope.* **[oak, shrub]** Warbler(-). The smallest "hummer"; male has purple feathers on its throat, forming streaks against white; female has greenish and white streaks on its throat, pale buff on sides, and bronze-green on top. Male shows off to female by flying back and forth in a long shallow curve. They defend female and territory by plunging down to "buzz" the intruder. Hab: mixed forests, brushland, meadows, canyons, mountains. BR: mountains of C, except along coast. M: lowlands of C and Baja.

GOATSUCKERS (NIGHTJARS): ORDER CAPRIMULGIFORMES

A. NIGHTHAWKS AND POORWILLS, Family Caprimulgidae. These birds have small bills but very large mouths lined with hairs which are made for catching swift insects in flight; they hunt at dusk and in the dark. They have large flat heads and long wings; flight is moth-like; they nest on the ground.

112. LESSER NIGHTHAWK (TRILLING NIGHTHAWK), *Chordeiles acutipennis.* **[grass, des.]** Robin(-). White throat streak; body barred and mottled blackish brown; white patch on wing is closer to tip; flies low to the ground at lower altitudes. Hunts insects at dusk and dawn in open areas. Hab: dry, brushy country. BR: Central Valley and interior sC.

113. COMMON POORWILL, *Phalaenoptilus nuttallii.* **[shrub, des.]** Robin(-). A night bird with a mottled brown body; white on square tail forming 2 blocks in corners; rounded wings. Flutters up like a huge moth from the ground when flushed. Voice: soft "poo-woo" or "poor-will" call repeated endlessly. Unique among birds, the poorwill hybernates in rock crevices, Joshua limbs, or under shrubs during cold months when the insects it feeds on are absent. From the normal 106 degrees, torpid body temperatures have been reported from 64 to 56 degrees. For a four year period, Dr. Jaeger observed a poorwill hybernating each winter in the same rock niche. The Indian name translates as "the sleeping one." Hab: roadsides, chaparral, deserts. BR: most of C, except Central Valley. Res: cwC (Monterey Co.) to sC, Baja.

PERCHING BIRDS: ORDER PASSERIFORMES

A. TYRANT FLYCATCHERS, Family Tyrannidae. The large head and short legs are typical of this family. They often perch on exposed branches or wires, flying up in a quick circle to catch insects, and then back to perch. The smaller species do tail flipping.

114. OLIVE-SIDED FLYCATCHER, *Contopus borealis.* **[oak, str.wd. sav.]** Robin(-). Stout-bodied, large-headed; white strip down the middle of its dark chest; cottony white area pokes out behind its wing; otherwise olive-brown. Hab: coniferous and deciduous forests, burns, dead snags. BR: San Francisco Bay area south to Monterey, scC, cBaja.

115
TL 6–6½" (15–17 cm)

116
TL 5½–6" (14–15 cm)

116a.
TL 5¾" (15 cm)

117
TL 8–8½" (20–22 cm)

118
TL 6½–7" (17–18 cm)

119
TL 7–8" (18–20 cm)

120
TL 8–9" (20–23 cm)

121
TL 7–8" (18–20 cm)

120a.
TL 8–9" 20–23 cm)

115. WESTERN WOOD-PEWEE, *Contopus sordidulus.* **[oak, str.wd.]** Sparrow size. An olive-gray bird with 2 white wing-bars and a high-topped head. Voice: a nasal "pe-yee" note. Hab: oak woods, streamside groves, open conifers. BR: C and nBaja except Central Valley and seC.

116. WESTERN FLYCATCHER (PACIFIC SLOPE FLYCATCHER), *Empidonax difficilis.* **[str.wd.]** Warbler(+). Olive-brown on top, yellowish underneath, oval eye rings, 2 white wing bars. Hab: perches high in shady moist woods, canyons. BR: wC, portions of Central Valley, ncBaja. **a. WILLOW FLYCATCHER,** *Empidonax traillii.* Similar in size and appearance to above. BR: most of cC.

117. ASH-THROATED FLYCATCHER, *Myiarchus cinerascens.* **[shrub, oak, des. str.wd.]** Sparrow(+). Olive-gray back, ash colored throat, light belly, slightly yellowish on sides, reddish brown tail; head is a little bushy in appearance. Hab: semi-arid country, chaparral, open woods. BR: most of our area except Central Valley.

118. BLACK PHOEBE, *Sayornis nigricans.* **[str.wd. rocks, bldg.]** Sparrow(+). Black, but white belly and edges of tail. Voice: strident "fee-bee fee-bee" call rising then dropping to a sharp "seep." Nests under bridges, near water. Hab: middle to low elevations, shady streams, rocky canyons, farmyards. Res: C west of Sierra Nevada, south into Baja.

119. SAY'S PHOEBE, *Sayornis saya.* **[grass, rocks, shrub]** Sparrow(+). Gray-brown head and back, 2 dullish white wing bars, pale orangish brown belly and undertail coverts. Nests in cliffs, abandoned ranch buildings. Hab: open arid country, deserts, brushy plains, ranches. Res: San Francisco Bay area to sC except coast. WR: extends to the coast and Central Valley.

120. WESTERN KINGBIRD, *Tyrannus verticalis.* **[grass, sav.]** Robin(-). White outer rims on black tail feathers, yellow on breast and belly, pale gray throat; grayish on head and upper back. Hab: likes savannas, agricultural lands, roadsides. BR: most of our area except along coast. **a. CASSIN'S KINGBIRD,** *Tyrannus vociferans.* Similar in size and appearance. Hab: open country near brush or woods, likes to perch up high. BR: cC coast and inland. Res: extends further south into nwBaja.

B. LARKS, Family Alaudindae. The slender bills, small horns on their heads, long hind claws, light colors, grassland habitat, and tendency to walk instead of hop are distinctive of larks. Gregarious.

121. HORNED LARK, *Eremophila alpestris.* **[grass, des.]** Sparrow(+). Black breast band, yellow to white neck, curved black patch through and under eye, 2 black feather horns atop head, gray-brown above, paler below. Voice: high-pitched, irregular tinkling song, frequently repeated as the bird rises high in the air. After migration, it returns every year to the same place. Nests in grass-lined hollows on the ground. Hab: cultivated areas, prairies, open fields, and urban. Res: throughout our area.

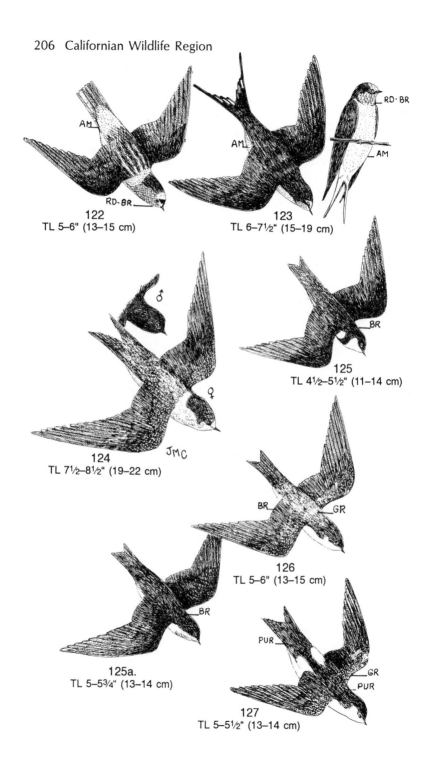

122
TL 5–6" (13–15 cm)

123
TL 6–7½" (15–19 cm)

124
TL 7½–8½" (19–22 cm)

125
TL 4½–5½" (11–14 cm)

126
TL 5–6" (13–15 cm)

125a.
TL 5–5¾" (13–14 cm)

127
TL 5–5½" (13–14 cm)

C. SWALLOWS, Family Hirundinidae. Tails are notched or deeply forked. They have a short bill and wide mouth to capture insects in flight. Swallows are often seen perched on wires and are strong, graceful fliers, usually at lower elevations than swifts.

122. CLIFF SWALLOW, *Hirundo pyrrhonota*. **[rocks, grass, bldg.]** Sparrow size. Indigo blue above, creamy below; tail barely notched; rusty rump and white patch in front of blue cap; chocolate brown throat. Glides in long curves, then strokes swiftly up to roost. Colonial—a vast array of juglike mud nests are hung under eaves and cliff overhangs. Hab: near water in open to semi-wooded country, farms, cliffs, canyons. BR: length of C and nBaja, except se corner of our area.

123. BARN SWALLOW, *Hirundo rustica*. **[grass, rocks, bldg.]** Sparrow size. Deep steel blue swallow with deeply forked, white spotted tail; orange-brown underparts. They fly close to the ground hunting insects in the air. Barns are a favorite place to build their softly lined mud and grass nests. Hab: likes to be near water, suburbs, farms. BR: most of our area north of Bakersfield, spotty breeding south of Santa Barbara.

124. PURPLE MARTIN, *Progne subis*. **[oak, sav. bldg.]** Robin(-). Male has purple-blue body and head, with black on wings and tail; female and juveniles are mainly brownish. Hab: towns, farms, or semi-open country near water; likes colonial nest boxes, tree holes. BR: San Francisco Bay area south to Monterey, Central Valley. M: summer visitor to nC and Central Valley.

125. BANK SWALLOW, *Riparia riparia*. **[str.wd. oak, rocks, grass]** Sparrow size. Our smallest swallow has a unique brown breast band sharply marked against white underparts; brown elsewhere. Flight irregular, fluttery. Hunts insects near water. Nests in holes in sand, gravel pits, steep river banks. Except for Kingfishers, this is the only bird that digs a tunnel 18 to 36 inches long with its feet and bill in a bank for its nest. Being colonial, a bank may be honeycombed with their tunnels. Hab: near water, fields. BR: cnC. M: throughout our area. **a. NORTHERN ROUGH-WINGED SWALLOW,** *Stelgidopteryx serripennis*. Similar size, behavior, appearance—except no breast band. BR: C south into nBaja.

126. TREE SWALLOW, *Tachycineta bicolor*. **[str.wd. water]** Sparrow size. Blue-green back, white below; white throat; juveniles are brown above and look like those of the Bank Swallow and Northern Rough-winged Swallow. Nests in holes in dead trees or snags. Hab: open country near water, meadows, wires. BR: nC, Central Valley. WR: sC coast, Baja. Res: cC coast and Central Valley.

127. VIOLET-GREEN SWALLOW, *Tachycineta thalassina*. **[rocks, oak, bldg.]** Sparrow size. Iridescent dark green and purple upperparts, white undersides, white on both sides above tail; juveniles have brown back and wings. Colonial, generally returns each year to the same nesting place. Nests in tree cavities, woodpecker holes, cliff crevices, or nest boxes. Hab: open coniferous, deciduous or mixed forests. BR: most of our area. WR: cwC, swC, nwBaja.

129
TL 21–27" (53–69 cm)
W 4–4½ ft.

128
TL 17–21" (43–53 cm)

131
TL 12–13½" (30–34 cm)

130
TL 11–13" (28–33 cm)

133
TL 5–5½" (13–14 cm)

132
TL 16–18" (41–46 cm)

D. CROWS, MAGPIES AND JAYS, Family Corvidae. This family is comprised of medium to large, usually very talkative, raucous voiced, omnivorous birds with short, rounded wings in the jays and magpies; longer, more pointed wings in the crows and ravens. Ravens are more solitary than crows, but do operate in flocks. Sexes look alike.

128. AMERICAN CROW, *Corvus brachyrhynchos.* **[str.wd. oak, grass]** Crow size. All black with purplish gloss. Frequently flies in flocks; when soaring, wings are pitched up at an angle. Eats insects and small rodents, fruit and grains; also a scavenger. Voice: distinctly loud "caw-caw" cry, sometimes "cahr." Hab: open fields, farms, orchards, open woods, river groves, city edges. Res: most of our area, except deserts or higher mountains.

129. COMMON RAVEN (NORTHERN RAVEN), *Corvus corax.* **[rocks, des. str.wd.]** Crow(+). All black with ruffled feathers on throat; heavy, powerful bill; larger than the crow. Glides and soars more than crows. Very intelligent and often playful with each other in the sky. Mates remain together. They gurgle to each other while preening necks. Eats most everything, including carrion. Voice: deep, hoarse croak. Likes canyon walls and cliffs for nesting. Hab: open to forested lowlands, mountains; prefers to be near water and larger trees. Res: most of our area except Central Valley.

130. SCRUB JAY, *Aphelocoma coerulescens.* **[oak, shrub, str.wd.]** Dove size. No crest; blue streaked, white throat surrounded by a broken blue band; deep blue wings, rump, head, and tail; brownish back, pale gray underneath; white streak over eye. Short flight ends with upsweep to branch. Hab: oaks, piñon-juniper, chaparral, pine-oaks, streamside woods, orchards. Res: most of our area.

131. STELLER'S JAY, *Cyanocitta stelleri.* **[oak, str.wd.]** Dove size. High, blackish blue crest, back, lower top of tail and basal wing feathers; blue on wings, lower back, tail and underneath; wings and tail lightly barred. Hab: coniferous forests, pine-oak and deciduous forests, streamside woods. Res: C except for lowlands and deserts.

132. YELLOW-BILLED MAGPIE, *Pica nuttalli.* **[oak, str.wd. grass]** Crow size. Yellow bill; black and white body; flowing, iridescent, greenish black, long tail. Gregarious and very talkative. Hab: farms, grassland, edges of brush, but mostly in oaks interspersed with grass. Res: C in Sacramento and San Joaquin valleys, and Coast Range valleys from San Francisco south to Santa Barbara Co.

E. TITMICE AND CHICKADEES, Family Paridae. This family has mostly small birds with small sharp bills. Sexes look alike and are usually found in small flocks. They feed mainly on insects in trees and often nest in tree cavities.

133. PLAIN TITMOUSE, *Parus inornatus.* **[oak, str.wd.]** Warbler size. Plain gray-white below, brown-gray above; eye-ring white; pointed crest. Actively forages alone or in pairs. Voice: "tzick-a-dee-dee" notes;

134a
TL 5–5¾" (13–15 cm)

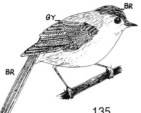

135
TL 3½–4" (9–10 cm)

136
TL 5–6" (13–15 cm)

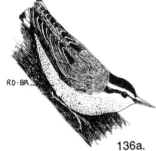

136a.
TL 4½" (11 cm)

137
TL 3¾–4½" (10–11 cm)

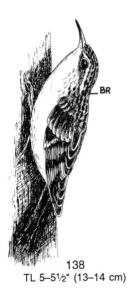

138
TL 5–5½" (13–14 cm)

melodious "sweedy-sweedy" song. Hab: oaks, piñon-juniper woods, streamside woods. Res: mountains and hills of C south into ncBaja (low to mid elevations).

134. CHESTNUT-BACKED CHICKADEE, *Parus rufescens.* (not illus.) **[str.wd.]** Warbler size. Distinctive reddish brown back and sides; white cheeks; black cap and throat. Very active, often hanging upside down when feeding. Forages high in foliage of trees. Associates frequently with other small birds. Nests are often in cavities of trees near ground. Hab: moist coniferous forests or streamside oak woods. Res: along coast from San Luis Obispo Co. north. **a. MOUNTAIN CHICKADEE,** *Parus gambeli.* **[oak, str.wd.]** Res: inland from coast—Santa Barbara to San Diego cos.

F. BUSHTITS, Family Aegithalidae. Short-billed insect-eaters with long tails. These plain, dull gray, tiny, social birds are barely larger than hummingbirds.

135. BUSHTIT, *Psaltriparus minimus.* **[oak, str.wd. shrub]** Warbler(-). Gray back with brown cap. Usually moves from tree to tree in twittering flocks. A pair weaves an 8 to 10 inch gourd-shaped nest of moss and lichen, beginning from the top downward. The down-lined nest is hung in foliage near the tip of a branch with the entrance near the top. Hab: oak scrub, chaparral, broad-leaved and mixed woods. Res: most of our area.

G. NUTHATCHES, Family Sittidae. Nuthatches are large-headed birds with short tails. They are tree climbers with strong bills and feet, often going down trees upside down foraging for insects in tree bark. Sexes are similar.

136. WHITE-BREASTED NUTHATCH, *Sitta carolinensis.* **[oak]** Sparrow size. Male has black cap and collar; blue-gray back and tail with black markings; white breast and belly. Hab: conifer to mixed deciduous woods. Res: C, except hot Central Valley and seC; ncBaja. **a. RED-BREASTED NUTHATCH,** *Sitta canadensis.* Similar, with rusty breast and belly, black streak through eye. Res: all our area.

137. PYGMY NUTHATCH, *Sitta pygmaea.* **[oak]** Warbler(-). Gray-brown cap comes down to eye. Slate gray above, creamy white below. Hab: pine woods. Res: coastal cC, interior swC, ncBaja.

H. CREEPERS, Family Certhiidae. Creeps up tree trunks hunting insects.

138. BROWN CREEPER, *Certhia americana.* **[oak]** Sparrow size. Brown above with white streaks; long, sharp, down-curved bill. Stiff-pointed, long tail feathers support the creeper against trees. Spirals up trees probing for insects, then flies to bottom of next tree. Hab: coniferous forests, deciduous woodlands; in winter, open woods, parks. Res: coastal C in mountains. WR: extends to lower altitudes.

139
TL 5½–5¾" (14–15 cm)

140
TL 4½–5½" (11–14 cm)

141
TL 5–6" (13–15 cm)

142
TL 5–5½" (13–14 cm)

143
TL 4½–5" (11–13 cm)

144
TL 4–4½" (10–11 cm)

145
TL 7–8½" (18–22 cm)

I. WRENS, Family Troglodytidae. Wrens are small quick-moving, brownish birds with finely-barred, rounded, narrow tails often cocked upward. They have sharp, slender bills and feed mostly on insects. Sexes look alike.

139. CANYON WREN, *Catherpes mexicanus.* **[rocks]** Warbler(+). White throat and breast; reddish brown belly with a few white dots; head and back dotted white on brown. Hab: canyons, sheer rock cliffs, old stone buildings. Res: C inner Coast Ranges, south into Baja.

140. MARSH WREN (LONG-BILLED WREN), *Cistothorus palustris.* **[water]** Warbler size. Upper back has white streaks on brown; heavy white stripe through eye. Hab: keeps well hidden in marshes with cattails, bullrushes, and reeds. Res: C coast to Santa Barbara Co., Central Valley. WR: extends to swC and Baja.

141. ROCK WREN, *Salpinctes obsoletus.* **[rocks]** Sparrow size. Gray-brown with light eye stripe; fine brown streaks on pale breast; buff corners on outer tail feathers. Often shows bobbing motion. Nest is concealed in a rock crevice with a pathway to the nest of small pebbles and rock chips. Hab: semi-arid rocky canyons and slopes, concrete walls. WR: cC lower elevations. Res: rest of C.

142. BEWICK'S WREN, *Thryomanes bewickii.* **[oak, str.wd. shrub]** Warbler(+). Long, white eye stripe; dark barring on tail; white underparts. Characteristically jerks long tail. Sometimes odd nesting places are chosen: the farm junkyard, outbuildings, pockets of coats left out, stumps, watering pots, tin cans. Hab: brush, woods of foothills and lowlands, gardens, farmyards. Res: widespread in most of our area.

143. HOUSE WREN, *Troglodytes aedon.* **[shrub. str.wd. oak, bldg.]** Warbler size. Rusty brown above; dark barred tail; underpart of wings and eye-ring creamy. Aggressively drives other birds from good nesting holes. Hab: thickets, farmlands, gardens; likes nest boxes. Res: most of our area. BR: extending north and east. WR: from cC south.

144. WINTER WREN, *Troglodytes troglodytes.* **[oak, str.wd.]** Warbler size. Distinguished by stubby tail and dark brown barring on belly. Frequent bobbing action. Other names for the Winter Wren are "Wood Wren" and "Mouse Wren," apt names for a bird that creeps like a mouse through tangled thickets of undergrowth in coniferous and mixed wood forests. Hab: prefers to be near water. Res: nC to cC in mountains. WR: extends south along coast to Los Angeles Co.

J. DIPPERS, Family Cinclidae. Strong legs and waterproofing oil glands aid these birds in diving, swimming, and walking under water of mountain streams to feed on aquatic life.

145. AMERICAN DIPPER, *Cinclus mexicanus.* **[water]** Robin(-). Also called a "Water Ouzel." Sooty gray-blue plumage; chunky wren-like body; very short tail. Flies close to the water with rapid wingbeats. Named dipper from a unique, quick, bobbing motion of dipping up and

146
TL 6–6½" (15–17 cm)

147
TL 4½–5" (11–13 cm)

148
TL 3½–4" (9–10 cm)

148a.
TL 4" (10 cm)

149
TL 6½–7½" (17–19 cm)

down on rocks with its legs partially bent. Dives underwater to walk or run on the stream bottom; also flies underwater propelled by its wings. Builds large moss nests near water. Hab: close to fast moving mountain streams, rapids. Res: inland from Ventura Co. south to San Diego Co., along coast and inland from San Luis Obispo Co. north.

K. THRUSHES, KINGLETS, AND GNATCATCHERS, Family Muscicapidae

1. WRENTITS, Subfamily Timaliinae. Wrentits are small, wrenlike birds with very long, cocked-up tails and short, curved bills.

146. WRENTIT, *Chamaea fasciata.* **[shrub, str.wd.]** Sparrow size. All brown color, streaked breast. Does not migrate, never leaves its small brushy area. Seldom seen, as they slip through brush, but its song can be heard year-round. Voice: song of many rapidly repeated, ringing notes, condensed into a long trill. Hab: chaparral, brush, garden shrubs. Res: all our area to Sierra Nevada foothills except Central Valley.

2. KINGLETS AND GNATCATCHERS, Subfamily Sylviinae. Thin-billed and small insectivorous birds; very active and quick. Gnatcatchers are long-tailed and kinglets have short, forked tails.

147. BLUE-GRAY GNATCATCHER, *Polioptila caerulea.* **[oak, shrub, str.wd.]** Warbler(-). Distinctive white eye-ring and blue-gray back; tail white underneath with a black line down the middle. Often twitches long tail sideways. Forages for insects in the foliage. Hab: open oak-pine woods, chaparral. BR: nC south to nwBaja (mainly mountains). WR: Central Valley and seC.

148. GOLDEN-CROWNED KINGLET, *Regulus satrapa.* **[oak, str.wd.]** Warbler(-). Bright orange (male) or yellow (female) crown bordered by black; white band above the eye; back is olive colored; wings have 2 white bars; flicks wings. Moves as a group feeding on insects found in foliage. Hab: coniferous forests in spring and summer; deciduous woods and brush in winter. Res: nC and south in Sierra Nevada. WR: extends south to nwBaja except for San Joaquin Valley. **a. RUBY-CROWNED KINGLET,** *Regulus calendula.* Similar, male has distinct white eye-ring and red cap. WR: throughout our area.

3. THRUSHES, Subfamily Turdinae. This subfamily has beautiful singers. They eat insects, worms, and fruit. Bluebirds nest in bird boxes or cavities in trees; most thrushes build stick, moss, and leaf nests in trees. All young have spotted breasts.

149. HERMIT THRUSH, *Catharus guttatus.* **[oak, str.wd. shrub]** Sparrow(+). Reddish brown tail contrasts with olive-brown back and spotted breast. Frequent, unique rising of tail. Voice: Different pitches of long, ethereal, and flutelike notes. A bird of the undergrowth, they live near or on the ground. Hab: open, humid coniferous or mixed woods; during winter, streamside woods, thickets. WR: most of our area, csC.

150
TL 6½–8" (17–20 cm)

151
TL 9–10" (23–25 cm)

152
TL 6–7" (15–18 cm)

152a.
TL 7" (18 cm)

153
TL 9–11" (23–28 cm)

154
TL 9–11" (23–28 cm)

155
TL 11–13" (28–33 cm)

155a.
TL 10–11" (25–28 cm)

150. SWAINSON'S THRUSH, *Catharus ustulatus.* **[str.wd.]** Sparrow(+). Olive-brown back, spotted breast; light brown eye-ring. Hab: willow or alder thickets, coniferous forests. BR: coastal C. M: widespread.

151. VARIED THRUSH, *Ixoreus naevius.* **[oak, str.wd.]** Robin size. Orange wing-bars and eye-stripe, plus black (in male) or gray (in female) breast band distinguish this bird from robins. Hab: dense, humid coastal forests; in winter it likes streamside woods and ravines, chaparral. WR: cC and Central Valley.

152. WESTERN BLUEBIRD, *Sialia mexicana.* **[str.wd. grass, oak]** Sparrow(+). Male has blue throat, head, tail, and wings; reddish brown back and breast; female and juveniles are browner and have grayer throats. Hab: open deciduous and mixed forests, streamside woods, savanna, farms; in winter semi-open woodland, brush. Res: mostly mountains and coast in C; nwBaja. WR: extends to lower elevations. **a. MOUNTAIN BLUEBIRD,** *Sialia currucoides.* Similar, except all blue without rusty breast and shoulders. WR: most of our area except coast.

153. AMERICAN ROBIN, *Turdus migratorius.* **[grass, str.wd.]** Male has distinctive red breast; blackish head with white eye-ring; dark gray back and wings; white throat with brown streaks. Their nests are mud lined, with eggs "robin's egg blue." Earthworms are their specialty, but they are also fond of berries. Voice: a carol of rising and falling short phrases. Hab: greenbelts, farmland, thickets, open deciduous, coniferous and streamside woods, savanna; in winter, lowland areas. Res: C. WR: sC, Baja.

L. MOCKINGBIRDS AND THRASHERS, Family Mimidae. Called mimic-thrushes, though not all mimic other birds. All are fine singers. They are long-tailed and their bills are often curved. Insects and fruits are their main diet.

154. NORTHERN MOCKINGBIRD, *Mimus polyglottos.* **[sav. des.]** Robin(+). Gray with large white patches on wings, sometimes flashed from a standing position or in flight; tail is blackish with white sides. Voice: excellent mimic—from birds, cats, to a squeaky wheelbarrow; high clear flutelike song of many varied notes and phrases; may sing in flight, often sings at night, especially at nesting time. Hab: farms, towns, open areas with scattered trees, thick brush, streamsides. Res: most of our area.

155. CALIFORNIA THRASHER, *Toxostoma redivivum.* **[oak, shrub, des. str.wd.]** Robin(+). Overall brown to gray-brown, belly paler; light streak over eye; long down-curved bill. Beak is used for digging. Voice: loud, cheerful song of many varied phrases; good imitator. Hab: lowlands and coastal brushy areas, foothills, streamside woods, thickets, parks. Res: most of our area. **a. LE CONTE'S THRASHER,** *Toxostoma lecontei.* Similar but pale gray body; very pale belly. Hab: deserts (creosote and associated scrubs). Res: scC and sides of San Joaquin Valley.

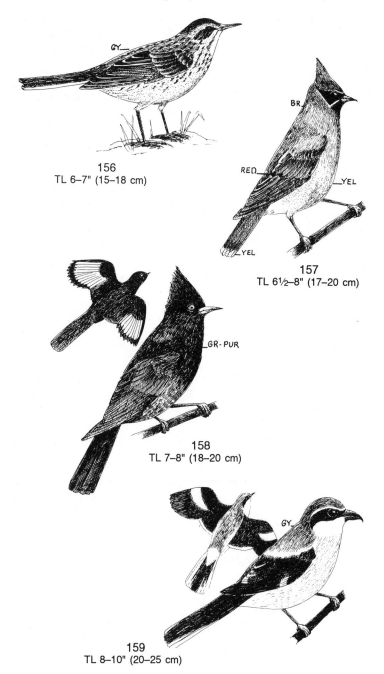

156
TL 6–7" (15–18 cm)

157
TL 6½–8" (17–20 cm)

158
TL 7–8" (18–20 cm)

159
TL 8–10" (20–25 cm)

M. PIPITS, Family Motacillidae. Walks methodically rather than with a hop; long hind claw; bobs tail up and down. They feed and nest on the ground.

156. AMERICAN PIPIT (WATER PIPIT), *Anthus rubescens.* **[grass]** Sparrow size. Long slim body; grayish brown marked above, brownish streaked below; dark tail trimmed white; slender bill; black legs; long, light stripe over eye. Hab: prefers low, open grassland, cultivated areas. WR: and M: in flocks over most of our area.

N. WAXWINGS, Family Bombycillidae. Waxwings are crested, gregarious, fruit-eaters. They often move in noisy flocks, and have red waxlike tips on secondary wing feathers.

157. CEDAR WAXWING, *Bombycilla cedrorum.* **[oak, str.wd. shrub]** Sparrow(+). Sharp grayish tan crest; black and white face mask; yellow-tipped short tail; yellowish belly; red waxlike spots on wings. Generally, large flocks winter in most of our area to eat fruit and berries. Hab: likes berry-producing trees and shrubs, open woods. WR: C, most of our area south to Baja. **a. BOHEMIAN WAXWING,** *Bombycilla garrulus.* Similar in habits, but larger and grayer; without yellow belly. WR: most of our area where berries are available except extreme sC.

O. SILKY FLYCATCHERS, Family Ptilogonatidae. Silky flycatchers have a high crest and a long dark tail.

158. PHAINOPEPLA, *Phainopepla nitens.* **[oak, des.]** Sparrow(+). Male glossy black with large white patches on outer part of wings that flash in flight; females and juveniles are grayish; head is crested. Short flights are made from high perches to catch insects. Often seen in small flocks. Eats mistletoe, berries—especially red pepper tree berries, supplementing diet with insects. Nests are frequently built in the middle of a clump of mistletoe. Hab: prefers hot country with mesquite, desert scrub, open oak woods. Res: most of our area except coast from Monterey north and Central Valley.

P. SHRIKES, Family Laniidae. Hook-tipped bills.

159. LOGGERHEAD SHRIKE, *Lanius ludovicianus.* **[sav. grass, des. shrub]** Robin size. Black mask over eyes with a thin white line above and a large patch below; white rump; body and top of head gray; wings and tail black. A fierce predator using thorns and barbed-wire points on which to impale small mice, birds, large insects. Sits perfectly still perched on wires and fence posts watching for prey. Hab: all year in open woods, savanna, deserts, and low scrub areas. Res: most of our area.

Q. STARLING, Family Sturnidae. Starlings look like short-tailed Brewer blackbirds, but in winter they are speckled all over the front with white dots.

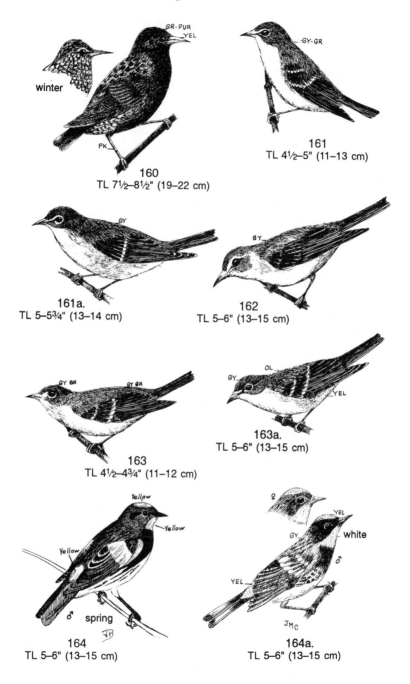

winter

GR-PUR
YEL
PK

160
TL 7½–8½" (19–22 cm)

GY-GR

161
TL 4½–5" (11–13 cm)

GY

161a.
TL 5–5¾" (13–14 cm)

GY

162
TL 5–6" (13–15 cm)

GY BR   GY BR

163
TL 4½–4¾" (11–12 cm)

GY   OL
YEL

163a.
TL 5–6" (13–15 cm)

Yellow
Yellow
Yellow
♂ spring

164
TL 5–6" (13–15 cm)

♀
YEL
GY   white
♂
YEL
JMC

164a.
TL 5–6" (13–15 cm)

160. EUROPEAN STARLING, *Sturnus vulgaris.* **[grass, oak, bldg.]** Robin(-). Glossy, purplish black, with a green tint; spotted back; yellow bill; short tail. Spotted almost all over in winter. Swift direct flight with triangular body look. Bullies other birds. Hab: farms, cities, parks, open groves, open country, desert scrub; frequents wires, poles, fence posts. Res: most of C and nBaja.

R. VIREOS, Family Vireonidae. Vireos are generally plain to olive-colored birds. They do not rapidly flit about like a warbler, but are rather slow moving as they pick crawling insects from foliage. Their bills are heavier than a warbler's.

161. BELL'S VIREO, *Vireo bellii.* **[str.wd. oak]** Warbler size. Mouse gray; 2 narrow wing-bars; whitish eye-ring. Forages low in tangled brush for caterpillars, spiders and other insects. Hab: willows, streamside woods, dense brush, desert areas near water. BR: from coastal slopes and interior cC into nwBaja. **a. GRAY VIREO,** *Vireo vicinior*, resembles Bell's Vireo but without wing bars. Hab: piñon-juniper slopes, scrub oak, chaparral. BR: Summer in interior sC.

162. WARBLING VIREO, *Vireo gilvus.* **[str.wd. oak]** Warbler size. Mouse gray with darker wings and tail; whitish underparts; broad white eye-stripe. Voice: distinctive long warbling song, with deep undertone. Hab: streamside woods, parks, aspen groves, shade trees, scrub. BR: C, except Central Valley and seC. M: widespread.

163. HUTTON'S VIREO, *Vireo huttoni.* **[oak, str.wd.]** Warbler size. Grayish olive; incomplete eye-ring with a black spot above the eye; 2 white wing-bars separated by black. Moves slowly through tree canopy, stopping after every move to search for insects. Hab: deciduous, mixed forests, prefers live oak brush. Res: along C coast and west edge of Sierra Nevada foothills. **a. SOLITARY VIREO,** *Vireo solitarius.* Very similar, slightly larger. Hab: coniferous and mixed forests. BR: throughout C except Central Valley, sw coast, and extreme seC. M: throughout our area.

S. WOOD WARBLERS, ORIOLES, BLACKBIRDS, TANAGERS CARDINALS, GROSBEAKS, BUNTINGS, JUNCOES, SPARROWS, TOWHEES, Family Emberizidae.

1. WOOD WARBLERS, Subfamily Parulinae. These birds are usually bright-colored with thin bills for insect feeding; most have yellow coloring. Similar vireos are much duller. No warblers actually warble.

164. YELLOW-RUMPED AUDUBON'S WARBLER (AUDUBON'S RACE), *Dendroica coronata.* **[oak, str.wd.]** Sparrow size. Slate-blue, black streaked above; bright yellow rump; yellow cap. In winter both are brownish above with streaky white breast and yellow throat; male shows his white wing patches in spring. Flocks together to feed on ground and in foliage. Hab: coniferous forests; in winter open woods, brush thickets, gardens. WR: all our area. Res: in some areas. **a. YELLOW-RUMPED WARBLER (MYRTLE RACE),** *Dendroica coronata*, is similar in size with a white throat. Frequents same area.

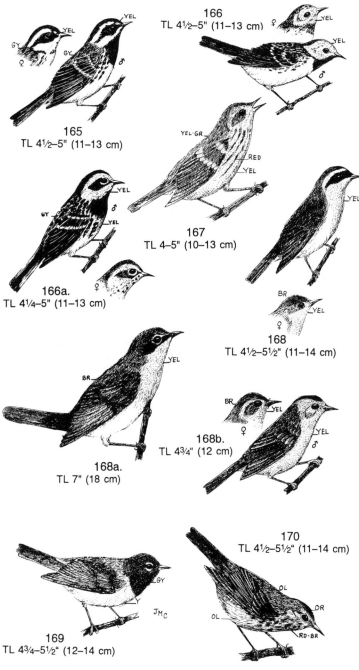

166
TL 4½–5" (11–13 cm)

165
TL 4½–5" (11–13 cm)

167
TL 4–5" (10–13 cm)

166a.
TL 4¼–5" (11–13 cm)

168
TL 4½–5½" (11–14 cm)

168a.
TL 7" (18 cm)

168b.
TL 4¾" (12 cm)

170
TL 4½–5½" (11–14 cm)

169
TL 4¾–5½" (12–14 cm)

165. BLACK-THROATED GRAY WARBLER, *Dendroica nigrescens.* **[oak, shrub, str.wd.]** Warbler size. Male with distinctive black and white face-design, black throat, and a gray back faintly dark marked. Voice: song-chant, beginning "zeedle seedle zeedle zseet chee." Hab: open coniferous, or oak woods with brush, piñon-juniper, chaparral. BR: coastal mountains of C, nC mountains. WR: coastal sC, Baja. M: widespread.

166. HERMIT WARBLER, *Dendroica occidentalis.* **[str.wd.]** Warbler size. Male has all yellow head and black throat; dark gray back; whitish underparts. Difficult to observe since they live in the upper parts of the tallest trees. Hab: coniferous forests; migrates and winters in lower montane forests and pine-oak woods. BR: Coast Ranges to Santa Cruz Co. WR: coastal C from Sonoma Co. south. **a. TOWNSEND'S WARBLER,** *Dendroica townsendi.* Black crown, cheek patch and throat; also tree-top tenants. WR: coastal C and Baja. M: widespread.

167. YELLOW WARBLER, *Dendroica petechia.* **[str.wd.]** Warbler size. Most yellow of the warblers; locally called "wild canary." Male has a red streaked breast; female's faintly streaked; yellow tail spots and wing-bars. Forages at mid-height in trees. Hab: cultivated areas, garden shrubs, shade trees, marshes, thickets, usually near water; in migration and during winter it likes woods' edges, scrub growth. BR: C except Central Valley and seC. WR: sC, Baja.

168. COMMON YELLOWTHROAT, *Geothlypis trichas.* **[str.wd.]** Warbler size. Yellow throat and breast; whitish belly; greenish brown cap, back, wings, and tail; male has black mask with a white strip above. Forages and nests close to the ground; rarely in sight. Voice: "whichity whichity" song; Hab: swamps, bogs, wet thickets, humid forest undergrowth. Res: San Francisco Bay area south to nBaja. BR: extends to nC. **a. YELLOW-BREASTED CHAT,** *Icteria virens.* **[str.wd.]** Our largest warbler. Has white eye-ring and black stripe below eye instead of mask. BR: C and Baja, except high mountains, Central Valley, and deserts. **b. WILSON'S WARBLER (PILEOLATED WARBLER),** *Wilsonia pusilla.* **[str.wd.]** Has a black cap instead of a mask or eye streak; all yellow belly; forage and nest near the ground in tangled underbrush. BR: coastal.

169. MACGILLIVRAY'S WARBLER, *Oporornis tolmiei.* **[shrub, str.wd.]** Warbler size. Olive above, yellow below. Male gray-hooded with black marks on throat; female paler; white eye-ring broken behind and in front. Nests and forages close to the ground. Very elusive and rapidly slips through the brush. Hab: dense coniferous forest undergrowth of berries, poison oak, and fern; shady damp thickets, streamside woods. BR: coast from San Luis Obispo north, also San Diego Co. M: widespread.

170. ORANGE-CROWNED WARBLER, *Vermivora celata.* **[shrub, oak, str.wd.]** Warbler size. Plain greenish gray above and olive-yellowish below; light yellow stripe over the eye; orange crown rarely seen; faint red-brown streaks on breast. Hunts insects while moving quietly in outermost foliage. Hab: streamside woods with alder and willow thickets, mixed coniferous-deciduous forests. WR: Central Valley. Res: coastal C.

171
TL 7–9½" (18–24 cm)

171a.
TL 7½–9" (19–23 cm)

172
TL 8–10" (20–25 cm)

173
TL 8–11" (20–28 cm)

175
TL 8½–11" (22–28 cm)

174
TL 6–8" (15–20 cm)

176
TL 7–8" (18–20 cm)

2. ORIOLES AND BLACKBIRDS, Subfamily Icterinae. These strongly-billed birds are medium to large sized. Most show iridescent black or purple colors, also orange and yellow. This varied group includes bobolinks and meadowlarks.

171. RED-WINGED BLACKBIRD, *Agelaius phoeniceus.* **[water, grass]** Robin size. Male has bright red wing patch; females and juvenile males are brown-streaked. Voice: song is gurgling, squeaky, hingelike "onk-ka-la-reeee." Hab: marshes, hay fields; forages cultivated lands, edges of water. During migration and winter it likes open fields, pastures, prairies. Res: most of our area. **a. TRICOLORED BLACKBIRD,** *Agelaius tricolor.* Similar, distinguished by white below red shoulder patch; females brown with streaked throat. Res: interior valleys of cC, sC coast.

172. BREWER'S BLACKBIRD, *Euphagus cyanocephalus.* **[grass, oak, str.wd.]** Robin size. Male shiny black; breeding plumage shows a white eye, green body tint, and purple sheen on head; female pale brown-gray below, dark brown above, with a dark eye. These birds do not hop but have a stately walk. Hab: suburban shrubby areas near water, marshes, streamside woods, farms, parks. Res: throughout our area.

173. YELLOW-HEADED BLACKBIRD, *Xanthocephalus xanthocephalus.* **[water]** Robin size. Yellow-orange breast and head in male. Shows white patch on black wings in flight; female brown with yellow on throat and breast. Walks very stately; colonial; a flock nests close together, usually in the center of a large marsh; their nest is woven sedge grass attached to reed stalks. Hab: marshes, irrigated or freshly plowed fields. WR: most of our area. BR: in valleys of cC and sC.

174. BROWN-HEADED COWBIRD, *Molothrus ater.*[str.wd. grass] Sparrow size. Male has brown head and glossy green-black body; female, grayish brown; short heavy bill. Does not pair or make nests; the female lays eggs one at a time in the nests of other species, then goes on her merry way. When hatched the baby cowbird demands so much food and care from the host bird that usually her fledglings starve. Frequently with cattle, sitting on backs or walking under and around them, feeding on insects. Hab: pastures, farms, woods' edges, streamside woods. Res: most of our area.

175. WESTERN MEADOWLARK, *Sturnella neglecta.* **[grass]** Robin size. Mottled brown above; yellow throat and belly with a wide black "V" on breast; sides of tail white; brown lateral crown stripes, one through the eye, the other above. An "early riser," their cheerful song is heard long before sunup. They walk, hunting grasshoppers and other insects on the ground. Likes to perch on fenceposts along roadsides. Hab: prairie, meadows, pasture, grassland, farmland. Res: all our area.

176. HOODED ORIOLE, *Icterus cucullatus.* **[str.wd. sav.]** Robin(-). Male has orange to orange-yellow head and body; black throat, wings,

177
TL 7–8½" (18–22 cm)

178
TL 7–8½" (18–22 cm)

179
TL 6–7½" (15–19 cm)

179a.
TL 7–7¾" (18–19 cm)

180
TL 7½–9" (19–23 cm)

181
TL 6½–8" (17–20 cm)

and tail; female greenish gray above, underparts yellowish. Head lowers nervously when it watches strangers. They favor palms for hanging their basket-shaped nest of woven fiber. Hab: mesquite scrub, palm groves, deciduous streamside woods, farms and towns. BR: coastal C from Marin Co. south, Central Valley, sC, south into Baja.

177. NORTHERN ORIOLE (BULLOCK'S ORIOLE), *Icterus galbula bullockii.* **[str.wd. oak, grass]** Sparrow(+). Bulk of body to base of wings and sides of tail in male orange; black elsewhere with large white blotch on wing; female, pale yellow breast, whitish belly, olive-gray back. Nest is suspended from the tip of a branch, which they vigorously defend. Hab: river groves, savanna, streamside and oak woods, towns, farms. BR: most of C, nwBaja. Res: coastal swC.

178. SCOTT'S ORIOLE, *Icterus parisorum.* **[des. shrub]** Robin size. Yellow body with black head, breast, upper back, and tip of tail; white wing-bar in male; female yellow with brownish above. Climbs, rather than flies, along drooping outer branches. Prefer yuccas for hanging their woven nest pouches. Voice: deep warbling whistles like a meadowlark's. Hab: oak scrub, yucca, piñon-juniper, palm oases. BR: from csC north to Santa Barbara Co. and east to Sierra Nevada. Res: scC, ncBaja.

3. TANAGERS, Subfamily Thraupinae. These brilliantly-colored, thrush-sized birds prefer a woods environment. Males usually sing from a high twig in a tree.

179. WESTERN TANAGER, *Piranga ludoviciana.* **[oak]** Sparrow(+). Male has bright red head and throat; yellow elsewhere except black on shoulders, wings, and tail; yellow and white bars on wings; female generally greenish gray above to yellowish below. Eats insects and fruit. Hab: summer in coniferous or deciduous forests in mountains; during migration, more open woods. Res: coastal C to nwBaja. BR: extends inland from coast. **a. SUMMER TANAGER,** *Piranga rubra.* **[str.wd.]** Rose red all over with yellow bill. BR: a few locations in sC.

4. CARDINALS, GROSBEAKS AND ALLIES, Subfamily Cardinalinae. Finchlike birds with thick, short conical bills adapted for seed cracking.

180. NORTHERN CARDINAL, *Cardinalis cardinalis.* **[str.wd.]** Robin size. Unique bright red crested male with black around base of bill; female with dull red on crest, wings, and tail; body is fawn-colored except for black at base of bill. Hab: woodland edges, suburban gardens. Feeds and nests in thickets. Res: introduced in sC (Los Angeles Co.).

181. BLUE GROSBEAK, *Guiraca caerulea.* **[str.wd.]** Sparrow(+). Male blue all over except for 2 red-brown bars on wings; wings and tail nearly black. Feeds on insects and seeds mostly on the ground. After breeding season, it forms small flocks, often mixing with other birds. Hab: forest edges, cultivated fields, clearings, brushy weedy places, fairly dense

182
TL 5–5½" (13–14 cm)

183
TL 6½–8" (17–20 cm)

184
TL 5–6" (13–15 cm)

185
TL 4–5" (10–13 cm)

186
TL 5–6" (13–15 cm)

187
TL 5½–6½" (14–17 cm)

streamside thickets. BR: Central Valley, coastal C from Santa Barbara Co. south, locations in sC and nBaja.

182. LAZULI BUNTING, *Passerina amoena.* **[shrub, grass, str.wd.]** Warbler size. Male light blue on head, throat, and lower back; gray-streaked on upper back; reddish brown on breast; white wing-bars; female and juveniles pale brownish on back to yellow-brown on breast. Hab: broken brushy slopes, streamsides, chaparral, open woods; during migration, open woods with grass. BR: all our area except cseC.

183. BLACK-HEADED GROSBEAK, *Pheucticus melanocephalus.* **[str.wd. oak]** Robin(-). Male with sharply delineated black head; white bars on black wings; black tail; reddish brown body with black stripes on upper back; white belly; female paler, with white stripes on head. Ground feeder that often looks for hand-outs in public campgrounds. Hab: diverse vegetation: streamside cottonwoods and willows, piñon-juniper, oak woods, mixed forests, cultivated areas, oak scrub, orchards. BR: all our area except cseC.

5. NEW WORLD SPARROWS AND ALLIES, Subfamily Emberizinae. These seed-eaters have conical bills for cracking seeds. To save repetition, the sparrows listed here are assumed to be a shade of brown with some darker streaking unless otherwise noted; size varies from 4½ to 7½ inches (refer to illus.). Towhees, juncos, longspurs, and buntings are also in this family.

184. RUFOUS-CROWNED SPARROW, *Aimophila ruficeps.* **[shrub. grass]** Black whisker patch on side of throat, reddish brown crown, and plain grayish breast are distinctive; juveniles have red-brown streaks on breast. Hab: grassy slopes, rocky areas with brush, often chaparral. Res: along C coast from San Francisco Bay area south, foothills of Sierra Nevada.

185. GRASSHOPPER SPARROW, *Ammodramus savannarum.* **[grass]** Light streaked yellow-brown breast of adult, pale stripe on top of head, and light yellow shoulder are distinctive. Hab: lower elevations; grassland, hay meadows, prairies, cultivated fields. BR: coastal C and Central Valley.

186. SAGE SPARROW (BELL'S SPARROW), *Amphispiza belli.* **[des. shrub]** Black whiskers on each side of white throat; white line over eye; dark facial and body pattern, streaked with white on sides; dark breast spot. Frequently flicks dark tail. Hab: dry brushy foothills, open deserts, shrub and sagebrush; dry lowlands and midlands. Res: most of our area except central part of state.

187. LARK SPARROW, *Chondestes grammacus.* **[shrub, grass, oak]** Chestnut head marks, black spot on gray breast, and rounded white-tipped tail are distinctive. Male may have two mates with nests close together. They feed as a flock. Hab: prairies, woods' edges, cultivated areas, orchards, grassland, farms. Res: most of our area.

188
TL 5½–6¼" (14–16 cm)

189
TL 5–6" (13–15 cm)

190
TL 5–7" (13–18 cm)

191
TL 6½–7½" (17–19 cm)

192
TL 5–6" (13–15 cm)

193
TL 6¼–7" (16–18 cm)

194
TL 8–10" (20–25 cm)

188. DARK-EYED (OREGON JUNCO), *Junco hyemalis oregonus.*
[str.wd. oak] Black cap over head, neck, and breast; reddish brown upper back; dark tail with white sides and tip; white belly with rusty sides; female has dark gray on head; used to be called snowbirds because they arrive early before winter is over while snow is still on the ground. Big flocks feed on weed seeds keeping in contact by a constant "tek tek" call. Hab: mostly in understory and edges of coniferous, deciduous, and mixed forests; in winter, roadsides, weeded pastures, parks, gardens. Res: w coast. WR: extends to the rest of our area.

189. LINCOLN'S SPARROW, *Melospiza lincolnii.* **[grass]** Looks like a song sparrow, usually without central breast spot; sides of face are grayer; creamy brown-yellow band across breast. Voice: song starts with low, sweet gurgling notes, rising abruptly and then falling; juncolike "tsip" note. A shy bird that keeps hidden under low brush cover when not feeding on the ground. Hab: in winter it prefers mixed shrubs and grassland; in summer, it likes streamside meadows. WR: throughout our area.

190. SONG SPARROW, *Melospiza melodia.* **[str.wd. shrub]** Strong breast streaks join together in a dark central spot in adult. Feeds close to brushy vegetation. This well known singer selects part of a tree as a perch, throws his head back and pours forth his repertoire of songs. Hab: streamside woods, marshes, thickets, cultivated areas, brush, grass, sea coasts, gardens, pastures. BR: C except seC desert area.

191. FOX SPARROW, *Passerella iliaca.* **[shrub, str.wd.]** "Fox" red rump and tail; breast streaked with inverted V's, often with a central spot. Rustles dry leaves under bushes like the towhee. Voice: brilliant and musical song, very loud and clear. Hab: likes protection of brushy undergrowth, forest edges, streamside woods; in winter, open and deciduous woods, lowland thickets. WR: most of our area except secC.

192. SAVANNAH SPARROW, *Passerculus sandwichensis.* **[grass, water, shrub]** Strongly streaked with brown, showing distinctive yellowish stripe above the eye and a white stripe atop the head. Hops and runs; flies only short distances. Likes grassy places. Hab: prairies, savanna, salt marshes, shores. Res: coastal C. WR: most of our area.

193. GREEN-TAILED TOWHEE, *Pipilo chlorurus.* **[shrub, str.wd.]** White throat with dark whisker mark, reddish cap, gray face and sides are distinctive; greenish to olive-gray elsewhere. Voice: slight "mew" call. Spends most of the time on or near the ground, scratching in the brush. Avoids danger by running into brush rather than flying. Hab: dry brushy mountain slopes, low chaparral, sage, streamside thickets. BR: inland from Santa Barbara to San Diego cos., csC. WR: sC.

194. CALIFORNIA TOWHEE (BROWN TOWHEE), *Pipilo crissalis.* **[shrub, oak, str.wd.]** Dark brown above; rusty throat and undertail; gray belly. Forages by scratching through debris on the ground. Hab: brushy stony areas, coastal foothill chaparral, suburban backyards, mesquite, streamside thickets, farms. Res: most of our area.

RE B
RD - BR

195
TL 7–8½" (18–22 cm)

196
TL 5¼–6" (13–15 cm)

GY
BR
GY
GY

197
TL 5–5½" (13–14 cm)

RD-BR
438a

198
TL 5–5½" (13–14 cm)

BR

198a
TL 5¼" (13 cm)

GY

199
TL 6–7" (15–18 cm)

YEL
BR
GY

199a.
TL 6½–7" (16–18 cm)

GY
YEL
YEL

200
TL 4–4½" (10–11 cm)

YEL

199b.
TL 6–7" (15–18 cm)

195. RUFOUS-SIDED TOWHEE, *Pipilo erythrophthalmus.* **[shrub, str.wd. oak]** Overall dark color; distinct rufous sides contrast sharply with white belly; males are black above with white markings on wings and back; females are brown with some white on wings; red eyes. Often heard scratching noisily among dry leaves. Hab: streamside thickets, brush, chaparral, undergrowth, forest edges, city parks, and gardens. Res: most of our area.

196. VESPER SPARROW, *Pooecetes gramineus.* **[shrub, grass]** Wide white outer tail feathers, notched tail, and reddish brown patch on shoulder are distinctive. Similar to the Song Sparrow and likewise known for the beauty and spontaneity of its singing, especially its vesper songs. Feeds and nests on the ground. Hab: fields, open grass country, sagebrush, rural roadsides, clearings in woods. WR: Central Valley, scC, Baja.

197. BLACK-CHINNED SPARROW, *Spizella atrogularis.* **[shrub, des.]** Very unique, almost juncolike sparrow with black chin and mask against otherwise unmarked blue-gray head and breast; tail mainly brownish; back and wings brown streaked and black bordered; females lack the black chin. Forages and nests close to the ground in dense brush. Very shy. Hab: sagebrush, chaparral, brushy hillsides, arid scrub. BR: foothills on both sides of Central Valley, cwC, swC, nwBaja.

198. CHIPPING SPARROW, *Spizella passerina.* **[oak]** Black eye-stripe with a white line above, bright reddish brown cap, black bill, and gray breast are distinctive. Often in yards where it appears as confident of man as the robin. Lines its nests with hair, preferring horse hair if available. Hab: open coniferous forests, pine-oak woods, parks. In migration, brushy pastures, farms and suburban areas, woods. BR: most of our area except for Central Valley. WR: sC south to Baja. **a. BREWER'S SPARROW,** *Spizella breweri.* **[shrub]** Similar to Chipping Sparrow, but crown is finely streaked. BR: sC mountains.

199. WHITE-CROWNED SPARROW, *Zonotrichia leucophrys.* **[shrub, grass]** Brown back with darker brown streaks; gray breast; yellow spot between eye and bill; bright white and black stripes on crown distinctive; 2 white wing stripes. Hab: edges of woodland forests, parks, gardens. In migration and winter, cultivated lands and arid brush. Res: Santa Barbara north along C coast. WR: throughout our area below snow line. **a. WHITE-THROATED SPARROW,** *Zonotrichia albicollis.* **[str.wd. shrub]** Similar except for white throat patch. WR: coastal C. **b. GOLDEN-CROWNED SPARROW,** *Zonotrichia atricapilla.* **[shrub]** Has a gold crown. WR: most of our area except cseC.

T. FINCHES, Family Fringillidae. Fringillidae are seed-eaters; almost all have comparatively short, thick bills capable of cracking seeds. A few species have bright-colored males.

200. LAWRENCE'S GOLDFINCH, *Carduelis lawrencei.* **[oak, grass, shrub]** Warbler size. Male has distinctive black face, cap and chin; gray on back, except yellow rump and breast; blackish wings marked with

201
TL 3½–4½" (9–11 cm)

202
TL 4½–5½" (11–14 cm)

203
TL 4½–5" (11–13 cm)

204
TL 5–6" (13–15 cm)

204a
TL 6–6½" (15–16 cm)

205
TL 5–6" (13–15 cm)

206
TL 7–8½" (18–22 cm)

yellow; white and black tail; female all grayish above. Nests near the end of spring when weeds have seeded, especially dandelions, to feed their young. Hab: open oak or oak-pine woods, weedy areas, arid areas near water, dry chaparral. BR: cC bordering Central Valley. Res: swC, nwBaja.

201. LESSER GOLDFINCH (GREEN-BACKED GOLDFINCH), *Carduelis psaltria.* **[oak, str.wd. shrub, grass]** Warbler(-). Greenish gray above with dark streaks and black cap; wings and tail blackish with white bars or streaks; yellow below. Feeds almost entirely on seeds, dandelion is favored to feed the young. Typically in flocks, after nesting, often mixed with other goldfinches. Hab: open bushy country, wooded streams, suburban gardens, open oak woods, pastures. Res: in most of our area, except high mountains and hot deserts.

202. AMERICAN GOLDFINCH, *Carduelis tristis.* **[str.wd. shrub, grass]** Warbler size. Breeding male is the only small, yellow bird with a black fore-cap, wings, and tail, plus a white patch at the base of tail; female is more greenish olive above and has no black cap; winter male is browner without a black cap. Common in flocks wherever seed plants are found, especially thistles and dandelions. Voice: canarylike bright, soft song. Flocks often sing in chorus. Hab: river groves, weedy fields, woods' edges, orchards, roadsides, farms and feeders. Res: C, west of Sierra Nevada and deserts. WR: extends east, nBaja.

203. PINE SISKIN, *Carduelis pinus* **[oak, grass]** Warbler size. Heavily streaked with a bit of yellow on wings. Travels in large flocks. If startled they rise as a unit, changing from a tight group to a spread-out "cloud" of birds, then back to a tight formation as they wing off to another feeding ground. Hab: coniferous and mixed woodlands at higher elevations, weedy areas. Res: nC. WR: all our area except seC deserts.

204. HOUSE FINCH, *Carpodacus mexicanus.* **[most habitats]** Sparrow size. Male has a bright red forehead, breast, and rump, with brown streaks on belly; female without red. Voice: bright warbling song sung at length from a high perch. Hab: from low to middle altitudes in country and towns, savanna, canyons, deserts, woods, arid brush and scrub. Res: most of C and Baja, except high mountains. **a. CASSIN'S FINCH,** *Carpodacus cassinii.* Similar in appearance; male has bright red crown. Res: all our area, nwBaja.

205. PURPLE FINCH, *Carpodacus purpureus.* **[oak, str.wd.]** Sparrow size. Wine-red colored male has more red than other finches; brown on wings and tail; brown-streaked on red back; female brown-streaked. Voice: deep, lively, loud and long-warbling song. Hab: open fir-spruce forests, deciduous and coniferous woods, tall shrubs, weedy areas, cultivated lands, towns. Res: coastal mountain ranges of C and nwBaja. WR: extends inland.

206. EVENING GROSBEAK, *Coccothraustes vespertinus.* **[str.wd.]** Robin(-). Male has yellow across forehead, on lower back, and along side; head brown, shading to yellow on back; tail and wings are black, except for white wing patches; female is grayish to yellow-gray with similar markings. Hab: coniferous forests, especially fir. In winter, they feed in flocks on seeds from box elders, maples, fruiting shrubs, and feeders. Res: nC, Sierra Nevada. WR: C, except for sw corner.

207. RED CROSSBILL, *Loxia curvirostra.* **[str.wd.]** Sparrow size. Crossed mandibles and bright red color (except for dark brown wings and tail) of male are distinctive; some brown streaks on back; female brown-streaked on olive-yellow. May often be seen clinging to a pine cone, pine nuts being their main diet and easily extracted by their specialized crossed bill. Hab: pine forests, pine savanna. Res: in summer, higher elevations in nC and Cascades; in winter, lower elevations in mixed woods from Santa Barbara to Los Angeles cos. inland.

U. WEAVER FINCHES, Family Passeridae. This Old World family eats seeds and insects.

208. HOUSE SPARROW (ENGLISH SPARROW), *Passer domesticus.* **[bldg. grass]** Sparrow size. Male has a distinctive black bib and bill, chestnut stripe from eye to nape, and white cheeks; otherwise brown above and gray below; female has a tan streak over the eye and no bib. Voice: monotonous series of musical chirps; quarrelsome grating notes. Hab: cities, farms, suburbs. Res: throughout our area.

207
TL 5½–6½" (14–17 cm)

208
TL 5–6½" (13–17 cm)

Food foraging behavior

Bird kept aloft by warm air currents rising from the earth.

Soaring

Undulating

Bird kept aloft by wing-beats.

Deep Wing-beats

Upward

Rapid beat and glide

Jerky

Straight

Erratic

Irregular rapid beat and glide

Backward

Patterns of flight

Upward Burst

Chickadee

Hummingbird

Warbler

Wren-tit

Brewer Blackbirds

Nuthatch

Woodpecker

Hermit Thrush

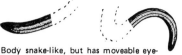

Body snake-like, but has moveable eyelids, and tail breaks off easily. *Legless Lizards.*

Large shell on back. *Turtles & Tortoises.*

Iguanid Lizards with horns on body and head. *Horned Lizards.*

Eye with pupil vertical. *Night Lizards Geckos*

Scales on belly are large, quadrangular and arranged in eight longitudinal rows; head with distinctive shape. *Whiptail or Racerunner Lizards.*

Iguanid Lizard without ear opening. *Earless Lizard.*

Eye with pupil round. Most *Lizards.*

Even, quadrangular scales on belly; head flat on top. *Night Lizards.*

Toes with side-scales. *Leaf-toed Gecko.*

Strong fold of skin between belly and back. *Alligator Lizards.*

Scales on back without keels in rest of Colubrids.

Small, almost useless eyes; belly scales same shape as back scales. *Blind Snakes.*

Heat-testing pit between nostril and eye. Rattle on tail. *Rattlesnakes.*

Keels down middle of back scales in Colubrids. *Garter, Gopher,*

Scales under chin of same general small size. *Boas.*

Two rows of scales under tail in most Colubrids; anal scale divided.

Two rows of scales under tail in Colubrids, but anal scale single. *Glossy, Garter, Gopher and King Snakes.*

Anal scale single, but scales under tail in only 1 row. *Long-nosed Snake.*

Typical Colubrid or common snake head; also found in *Coral Snake.*

6.

COMMON REPTILES

Reptiles have a covering of hard scales to protect them against enemies and against drying out, whereas amphibians, such as frogs and salamanders, have a smooth and moist skin. Reptiles appear mainly during the warm months of the year, going into winter sleep in various hiding places when cold weather comes because their blood remains the same temperature as the air, termed "cold blooded." No native reptile in California, except the rattlesnake, is dangerously poisonous. There are a few rare, small snakes with poisonous rear fangs here, but the poison is rather mild and these snakes never attack humans unless roughly handled. If you are struck by a rattlesnake, do not run, as this pumps the poison into your heart. Carry a snakebite kit on hikes.

The reptiles are divided into three orders: Turtles, Lizards, and Snakes. When you are trying to identify a reptile, study the pictures and descriptions until you find the one you see. Observe what kind of habitat or wildlife area (chaparral, grassland, etc.) you find it living in, also note if it is found in your part of the state.

TURTLES: ORDER TESTUDINES

A. BOX and WATER TURTLES, Family Emydidae. About 200 million years ago, before dinosaurs appeared, turtles dwelled on land and in aquatic environments. Their enlarged ribs are integrated into a hardened carapace with limb girdles inside the rib cage. They have dry scaly skin, a horny beak instead of teeth, and their body temperature is controlled by behavior. The aquatic species have webbed toes. All turtles lay eggs.

1. WESTERN POND TURTLE, *Clemmys marmorata.* Freshwater turtle family. **[water str.wd.]** Top shell (carapace) brownish yellow; bottom shell (plastron) light yellow. The grayish brown neck and head are flecked with dark spots or a network of black; limbs have prominent scales. Aquatic; it only leaves water to bask on logs or rocks in the sun; feeds on water plants, insects, and dead animals. Female digs a hole in a sunny spot near water to lay 5 to 11 eggs and covers them with soil. Hibernates in mud at bottom of pond. Hab: ponds, small lakes with

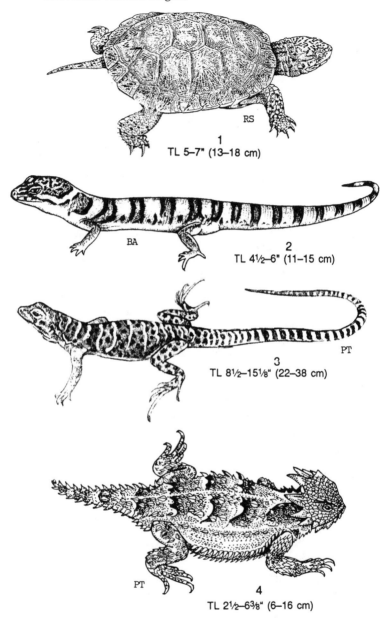

1
TL 5–7" (13–18 cm)

2
TL 4½–6" (11–15 cm)

3
TL 8½–15⅛" (22–38 cm)

4
TL 2½–6⅜" (6–16 cm)

abundant vegetation, marshes, slow moving streams. R: west of Sierra Nevada crest from nC to sC; wBaja.

NOTE: Eastern Painted Turtles, with bright-colored necks, have been freed in some areas of our region, after being imported from elsewhere.

LIZARDS: ORDER SQUAMATA. Tail usually breaks off and eyelids move.

A. GECKO, Family Gekkonidae. These lizards are marked by their delicate, soft granular skin. They have flattened bodies with short, clawed limbs and toe pads with minute bristles, each of which ends in minute suction cups allowing them to climb and cling to various surfaces. Most species lack movable eyelids except the American species *Coleonyx* which has eyelids. Geckos are very social and the most vocal of lizards, communicating in chirps and squeaks.

2. BANDED GECKO, *Coleonyx variegatus.* **[rocks, des. shrub]** Ground color spotted or banded brown against pale yellow; protruding, movable eyelids, and verticle pupils. Nocturnal, feeding at night on insects and spiders. May run with tail curled over back when stalking prey; sometimes makes a strange chirping, squeaking noise. Hab: rocky terrain, canyon walls, sand dunes, semi-arid areas. **a. SAN DIEGO BANDED GECKO,** *Coleonyx variegatus abbotti,* head spotted. R: coastal sC into nwBaja. **b. DESERT BANDED GECKO,** *Coleonyx variegatus variegatus.* Head not spotted, faint collar on neck. R: scC to Baja, not coastal.

B. INGUANID LIZARD, Family Iguanidae. Includes the majority of North American lizards. Their tough skin is scaled; shape and arrangement varies with species. Most visually communicate by a show of color and body language. Mates court; females lay eggs; defends territory by head bobbing push-ups and other signs of aggression.

3. LEOPARD LIZARD, *Gambelia wislizenii.* **[des. shrub, grass]** Gray body with white bands and dark leopard spots, capable of striking color change. During breeding season, females have red-orange spots and bars on sides. All scales on top of head are smaller than the ear opening. Runs swiftly with forelimbs raised when chasing insects and smaller lizards. Hab: semi-arid regions with sandy or gravelly soil and sparse vegetation. R: sC to Baja excluding coast. **a. BLUNT-NOSED LEOPARD LIZARD,** *Gambelia silus,* has a blunt nose. R: San Joaquin Valley.

4. COAST HORNED LIZARD, *Phrynosoma coronatum.* **[shrub, sav., rocks, des.]** Ground colored with dark markings on either side of spine; oval shaped, flat body; head crowned with spines, the center two longest ones appear to be horns; edge of sides fringed with pointed scales. Ferociously puffs up, opens mouth, and hisses. Eats ants and other insects. Hab: scrub and grass; common to washes with low shrubs; needs warmth for sunning and patches of loose soil for burying itself. R: most of our area.

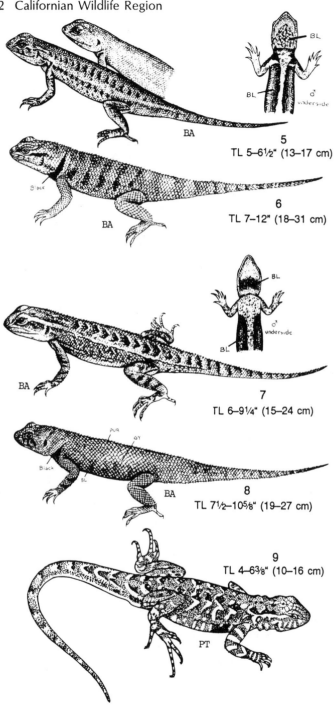

BA

5
TL 5–6½" (13–17 cm)

BA

6
TL 7–12" (18–31 cm)

BA

7
TL 6–9¼" (15–24 cm)

BA

8
TL 7½–10⅝" (19–27 cm)

9
TL 4–6⅜" (10–16 cm)

PT

5. WESTERN SAGEBRUSH LIZARD, *Sceloporus graciosus gracilis.* **[shrub, rocks, des.]** Gray or grayish brown, with light stripes between rows of dark blotches; rust colored at base of armpits; blue markings on belly and throat separated by white; female paler without blue on throat. Eats insects. Hab: sagebrush, gravelly soils, fine sand dunes. Rare in piñon-juniper woodland, coniferous forests, and river bottoms in coastal redwoods. R: our region except Central Valley and coastal sC.

6. YELLOW-BACKED SPINY LIZARD, *Sceloporus magister uniformis.* **[des. shrub, rocks, str.wd.]** Has very rough, sharp scales; the back is yellowish tan with a darker blotch in front of the shoulder; 5 to 7 large, pointed scales just in front of the ear opening (as shown). Feeds on insects and some plant food. Wary, agile, darts fast—hard to catch. Often bites when captured. Hab: arid and semi-arid regions with adequate vegetation and rocks for cover; along rivers in willows and cottonwoods. R: se portion of our area, also found in southern San Joaquin Valley.

7. NORTHWESTERN FENCE LIZARD (BLUEBELLY), *Sceloporus occidentalis occidentalis.* **[most habitats]** Spiny lizard, gray-brown with dark gray and light tan markings; blue patches on sides of whitish belly, used to court females or scare off other males; two blue patches on throat in male; yellowish orange undersurface of leg. Commonly seen on fence posts, logs, rocks, buildings. Wary of danger, it will quickly dart to the opposite side of the post, or as a last resort, scurry to safety. Stalks insects, often in wood or rock piles in daytime. Hab: variety of habitats excluding severe desert areas. R: most of our area from Santa Barbara area north. **a. GREAT BASIN FENCE LIZARD,** *Sceloporus occidentalis biseniatus.* Similar but only one blue patch on throat; belly gray. R: Santa Barbara Co. south in Baja.

8. GRANITE SPINY LIZARD, *Sceloporus orcutti.* **[rocks, des. shrub]** Coppery brown above; male with pale blue belly patch; no dark blotches; not so roughly scaled as Desert Spiny Lizard. Eats insects and some plants. Very wary and speedy once they warm up. Hab: large boulders, granite cliffs with mixed vegetation. R: sC, cBaja. Found in San Diego and Riverside cos.

9. SIDE-BLOTCHED LIZARD, *Uta stansburiana.* **[shrub, rocks, des.]** Brown back pattern over light tan; black or blue blotch behind front legs; skin folded on the throat; tail a little longer than head and body. Early risers; during the warm part of a winter day, they sun to limber up their small body, which is about 2 in. long, before hunting. Feeds on insects after carefully stalking them. Hab: semi-arid regions with various dry soils and scattered rocks; low, sparse vegetation. R: C, San Francisco Bay area through Baja.

C. NIGHT LIZARD, Family Xantusidae. Related to geckos with soft, often warty skin; flattened body; lidless, light sensitive eyes with vertical pupils. These lizards have small round scales on their backs and large squarish scales on the belly; shield on head. Toes end in claws. Live-bearing.

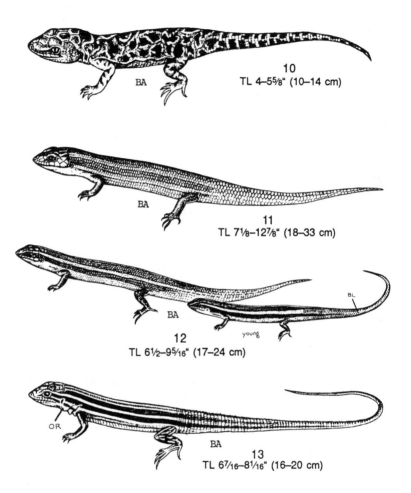

10
TL 4–5⅝" (10–14 cm)

11
TL 7⅛–12⅞" (18–33 cm)

12
TL 6½–9⁵⁄₁₆" (17–24 cm)

13
TL 6⁷⁄₁₆–8¹⁄₁₆" (16–20 cm)

10. GRANITE NIGHT LIZARD, *Xantusia henshawi.* **[rocks, des. shrub]** Has yellowish ground color covered with round blotches of dark brown or gray-brown; light color reduces to a network in dark phase; color change may occur rapidly; tail with dark bands. One or two young are born in fall, tail first and upside down. Hab: arid, semi-arid regions with rocky canyons and hills, preferring the shady side. R: lower swC to wBaja.

D. SKINK, Family Scincidae. Long, slender body has smooth, shiny scales; small head with large scales; legs small; no skin folds. Tail breaks off easily and is often brightly colored to draw a predator attack away from its body. Females lay eggs. More dependent on moisture than other lizards.

11. GILBERT'S SKINK, *Eumeces gilberti.* **[rocks, shrub, oak, grass, str.wd.]** Olive-brown with faint stripes that fade with age; the scales in the light lines are bordered by an indistinct or no margin. Young usually have a blue or yellow-pink tail which helps confuse attacking predators. Breeding adults may have a reddish head. Hides under boards, leaves, or rocks by day; hunts insects, moths, and worms. Hab: variety of habitats, open grassland, chaparral, piñon-juniper woodland; often in rocky areas where there is a water source. R: is comprised of 4 very similar subspecies which occupy interior C from the San Francisco Bay area into cBaja.

12. WESTERN SKINK, *Eumeces skiltonianus.* **[rocks, shrub, grass, oak, bldg.]** Striped horizontally; the wider middle stripe is brown bordered with two yellowish stripes down the back; scales in light stripes along sides bordered by a distinct dark margin. Young animals have blue tails. Found in daytime under rocks and logs; hunts insects at night. Female guards her nest until the 2 to 6 eggs hatch. Hab: piñon-juniper woodland, broken chaparral; prefers rocky habitat near streams, but also found on dry hillsides. R: nC southward along coast into Baja.

E. WHIPTAIL LIZARD, Family Teiidae. Slim-bodied with long, whiplike tails and well-developed legs. Head turns quickly from side to side while frequently flicking out tongue as they move in nervous jerks. All lay eggs. There exists a true unisexual species, *Cnemidophorus*, of which all individuals are female. A mature female will lay viable, but unfertilized eggs; all will hatch into females.

13. ORANGE-THROATED WHIPTAIL, *Cnemidophorus hyperythrus.* **[shrub, des. rocks]** Striped with orange throat; back with even beige stripes, separated by dark brown to black bands; belly light blue to white. Tail is gray, blue in juveniles, almost 3 times length of head and body. Makes sudden rushes to catch insects. Hab: arid and semi-arid regions in chaparral, canyons, and washes where sand, loose soil, or rocks are present that provide open spaces for running. R: lower sw corner of our area into Baja.

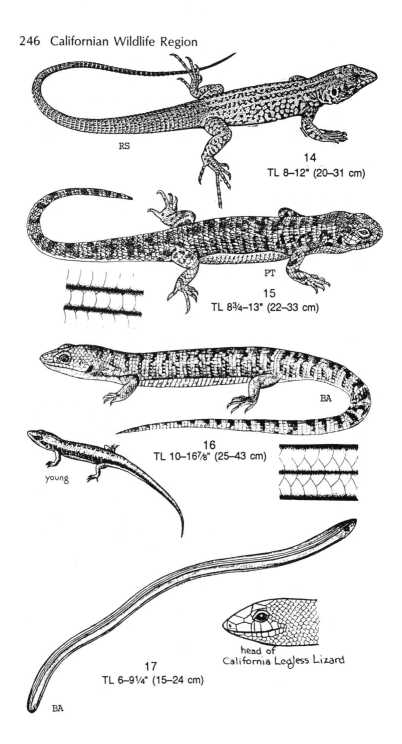

RS

14
TL 8–12" (20–31 cm)

PT

15
TL 8¾–13" (22–33 cm)

BA

16
TL 10–16⅞" (25–43 cm)

young

17
TL 6–9¼" (15–24 cm)

BA

head of
California Legless Lizard

14. CALIFORNIA WHIPTAIL, *Cnemidophorus tigris mundus.* **[grass, des. shrub, rocks, oak, str.wd.]** Tail is two and a half times length of body and head. Color light brownish yellow, with many irregular dark spots and bands, typically 8 light stripes, which may be faded or absent on lower back and base of tail. Tail bright blue in young. Hab: active runner that prefers open areas with sparse vegetation in desert or semi-arid regions. May also be found in woodlands and drier pine forests. R: nC south to Santa Barbara. **a. COASTAL WHIPTAIL,** *Cnemidophorus tigris multiscutatus,* similar. R: coastal sC and wBaja. **b. GREAT BASIN WHIPTAIL,** *Cnemidophorus tigris tigris,* has 4 instead of 8 light to obscure stripes on back. R: cC south to Baja except coastal area.

G. ALLIGATOR LIZARD, Family Anguidae. Bony plates embedded in the scales give these lizards long, shiny, stiff bodies and tails. Their skin is folded along the sides to allow for breathing and expansion. The tail breaks easily, but a new one grows back within a few weeks. When threatened it opens mouth and hisses at enemy; hunts insects and small mammals by day and night.

15. NORTHERN ALLIGATOR LIZARD, *Gerrhonotus coeruleus.* **[str.wd. oak]** Olive-gray to olive-brown back with dark, rectangular markings; dark lines on belly pass down sides of scales (as shown); eyes dark. Live-bearing of 2 to 15 young; prefers cooler temperatures and more moist places than most lizards. Hab: woodlands and forest under rotten logs, rocks, or loose bark, also grassland. R: including subspecies: nC along coast and Sierra Nevada foothills (Monterey Co. north, excluding Central Valley).

16. SOUTHERN ALLIGATOR LIZARD, *Gerrhonotus multicarinatus.* **[shrub, oak, str.wd. grass, bldg. rocks]** Light brown body usually has sharply-marked, even cross-bands on tail and back; belly scale-rows show dark stripes or broken lines down middle (as shown); tail is often twice the length of body, and somewhat prehensile, wrapping around twigs to help climb. During warm months, the female lays eggs, unlike the Northern, who gives live birth. Hab: chaparral, grassland, oak woods, pine forests; most often found in moist areas, and trash piles near homes. R, including subspecies: our entire area, except San Joaquin Valley.

G. LEGLESS LIZARD, Family Anniellidae. These long, slender lizards are legless, have movable eyelids, and no external ear openings. Scales are smooth and overlapping all over the body except the head, which has large symmetrical plates; tail blunt.

17. CALIFORNIA LEGLESS LIZARD, *Anniella pulchra.* **[str.wd. oak, grass, shrub]** Body has dark lines on silvery, shining skin. The presence of eyelids and a tail that grows back if broken indicates it is not a snake. Usually hunts ground-dwelling insects and worms as it burrows in loose soil. Hab: areas of loose soil; prefers some vegetation. Often found under leaf litter beneath bushes such as lupine. Normally has 2 young born in the fall. R: wC from San Francisco Bay to nBaja. **a. BLACK LEGLESS LIZARD,** *Anniella pulchra nigra.* **[str.wd. oak, grass, shrub]** Black and yellow belly. R: C coast—Monterey area.

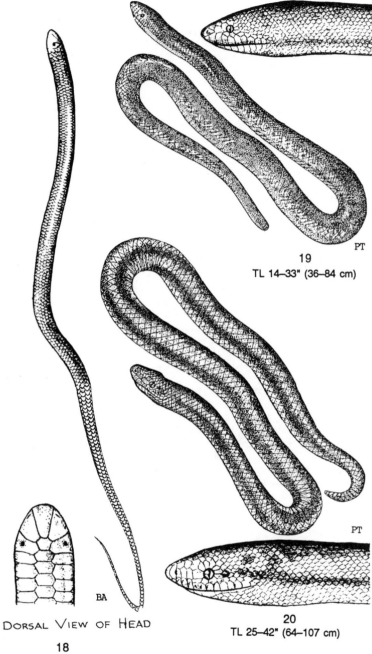

19
TL 14–33" (36–84 cm)

PT

DORSAL VIEW OF HEAD
18
TL 7–16" (18–41 cm)

BA

20
TL 25–42" (64–107 cm)

PT

SNAKES: ORDER SQUAMATA, SUBORDER SERPENTES. The tails of snakes do not break off easily, and they do not have movable eyelids or ears; the tongue both tastes and smells. All snakes feed on live animals, which they swallow whole, killed either by biting or crushing. They grow their entire life, but slowly after maturity.

A. SLENDER BLIND SNAKES, Family Leptotyphlopidae. These snakes look so much like earthworms that they are called "worm snakes." Their body is like a round pencil with no constricton at the neck; they have moist, circular scales and a spine at the tip of their tail. Although they have tiny eyes, these are nonfunctional and appear as black dots under an ocular scale. They burrow in sandy loam or moist soil and especially like to eat termites, ants, and their pupae.

18. WESTERN BLIND SNAKE, *Leptotyphlops humilis.* **[des. grass, rocks]** Blunt head and tail; eyes appear only as dark spots; upper parts brown, pink, or purple with silver sheen, paler below. May come out at night. Lays 2 to 6 eggs in late summer. Hab: slightly damp, loose beach soil where it can burrow; also under shrubs and roots searching for insects, millipedes, and spiders; in deserts and rocky, brush-covered mountains; often in washes and near streams. R: sC from Santa Barbara south to Baja.

B. BOAS, Family Boidae. Boas have heavy, thick, muscular bodies; eyes with vertical pupils; glossy smooth scales. Males may show small, spearlike projections on each side of their anal opening (vestige of an ancient leg). Their prey is killed by constriction (suffocation). They often roll into a ball, with their head hidden. Live-bearing.

19. RUBBER BOA, *Charina bottae.* **[str.wd. oak]** Feels and looks rubbery, with blunt tail-like head (called "two-headed snake" because the head and tail look alike); top of head has large, evenly-shaped plates; plain olive-brown above, yellowish below. Good climber, swimmer, and burrower. Hunts small mammals and salamanders. Hab: often near streams in woods, scattered chaparral, grassy areas, coniferous forests; hides beneath logs, rocks. R: nC and wC to Santa Barbara, except central part of state; scattered mountainous areas in sC.

20. DESERT ROSY BOA, *Lichanura trivirgata gracia.* **[des. shrub, rocks, str.wd.]** Head is a little wider than neck; 3 prominent, wide, reddish brown or rose stripes down the slate colored back; belly cream, spotted or blotched with gray; well-developed anal spine. Constricts lizards and small mammals. Nocturnal; expert climber. Hab: brushy, rocky areas, arid mountain slopes, chaparral, coastal sage. R: cseC. **a. COASTAL ROSY BOA,** *Lichanura trivirgata roseofusca.* Has 3 reddish brown stripes with irregular borders on bluish back. R: swC (from Los Angeles Co. south), nwBaja.

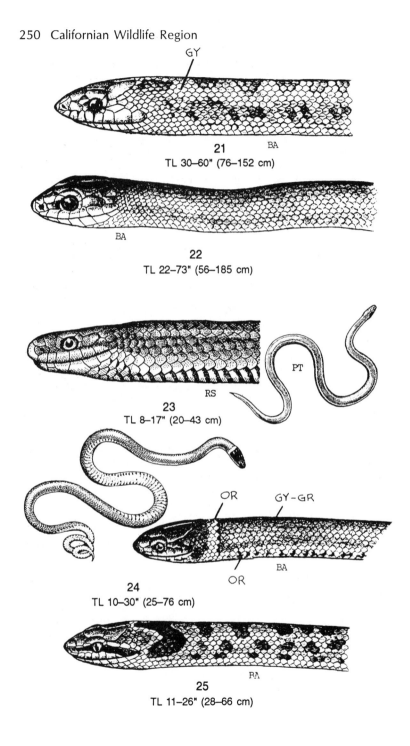

21
TL 30–60" (76–152 cm)

22
TL 22–73" (56–185 cm)

23
TL 8–17" (20–43 cm)

24
TL 10–30" (25–76 cm)

25
TL 11–26" (28–66 cm)

C. COLUBRIDS (COMMON SNAKES), Family   Colubridae.

These snakes have a large head plate, and most have no hollow, poisonous fangs. They catch small mammals, insects, lizards.

1. Common snakes without keeled scales.

21. GLOSSY SNAKE, *Arizona elegans.* **[grass, shrub, rocks des. oak]** Looks like a faded gopher snake with light brown blotches against white; head smaller; smooth, glossy scales. Is a good burrower and stays underground in the day. Eats mainly lizards. Lays an average of 8 large eggs. Hab: chaparral, desert, open woods, mountains. R: cC (except coast), sC, nBaja.

22. RACER, *Coluber constrictor.* **[grass, str.wd. shrub, oak]** Smooth-scaled, slim snake; plain olive, bluish, or brown above and light yellow below; juvenile with brown saddles on back. Very active, fast moving; when hunting, it holds its head well above the ground; fights if cornered. Lays soft, leathery eggs. Hibernates in large groups, often with other species, in rocky hillsides. Hab: open areas with thin brush, meadows, stream banks, prairies, piñon-juniper woods, forest glades; uses rocks and logs for basking. R: most of our area, except San Joaquin Valley and San Diego Co.

23. SHARP-TAILED SNAKE, *Contia tenuis.* **[str.wd. oak, grass. shrub]** Gray to red-brown on top with reddish near tail; may have faint reddish or yellowish line on each upper side; lower sides have distinctive crossbars of alternating cream and black; smooth scales; sharp spine on tail. Sometimes in groups, but seldom found as they forage at night under logs and rocks. Mainly feeds on slugs. Goes beneath ground in rodent holes when the weather is very dry. Lays 2 to 8 eggs. Hab: likes moist areas, grass, scattered chaparral, edges of coniferous forests and streamside woodlands. R: mainly in coastal hills or mountains of cC, nC, and Sierra Nevada foothills.

24. RINGNECK SNAKE, *Diadophis punctatus.* **[grass, str.wd. oak, shrub]** Slender blackish, bluish, or olive-colored snake with characteristic orange or yellow neck-ring; orange-yellow or reddish belly color startles enemies when tail is suddenly turned over and coiled to expose bright colors. Eats amphibians, lizards, and insects. Hab: moist areas, woods, grassland, coniferous forests, chaparral, gardens, farms; found under boards, in loose bark. R, including subspecies: most of our area except Central Valley.

25. NIGHT SNAKE, *Hypsiglena torquata.* **[oak, rocks, des. shrub]** Dark gray or gray-brown spots on a lighter gray or gray-brown background; blotches may be connected; butterfly-shaped dark area on neck and a dark stripe through the eyes are distinctive. Hunts at night for frogs and lizards, subduing them with poison from back teeth glands. Hab: plains, deserts, chaparral, sagebrush, woods; in crevices or under litter, rocks, boards. R: most of our area, except part of Central Valley.

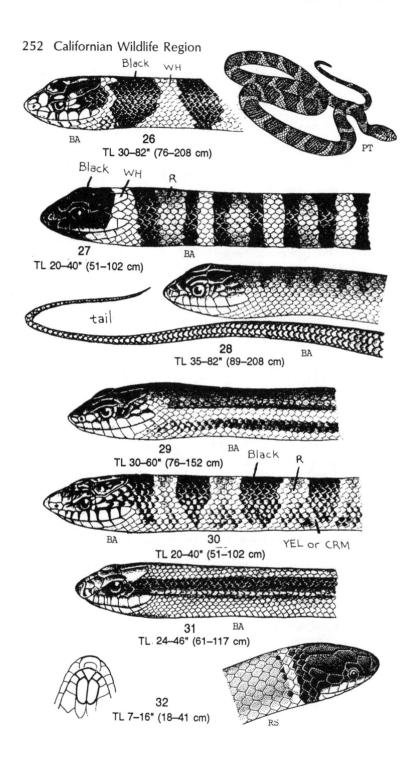

Black WH

BA **26**
TL 30–82" (76–208 cm)

PT

Black WH R

27
TL 20–40" (51–102 cm) BA

tail

28
TL 35–82" (89–208 cm) BA

29 BA
TL 30–60" (76–152 cm)

Black R

BA **30**
TL 20–40" (51–102 cm) YEL or CRM

31 BA
TL 24–46" (61–117 cm)

32
TL 7–16" (18–41 cm)

RS

26. COMMON KINGSNAKE, *Lampropeltis getulus.* **[shrub, oak, str.wd. grass, des.]** Black or dark brown rings alternate with pale yellow or white rings; pale bands broader on belly; may have a yellow stripe down back. Hab: rocky outcrops, rotting logs, coniferous forests, deciduous woods, thick brush, prairies, farms. R: most of C and nwBaja, except high mountains.

27. CALIFORNIA MOUNTAIN KINGSNAKE, *Lampropeltis zonata.* **[shrub, oak, des. str.wd.]** Beautiful black, white, and red rings, with red touched on each side by the black. Hab: moist coniferous and broadleaf woods, chaparral, rocky stream banks. R: mountains of coastal and interior C, ncBaja.

28. COACHWHIP (COMMON WHIPSNAKE), *Masticophis flagellum.* **[grass, shrub, sav. des.]** No stripes; great variation in color, usually gray, pink, or tan with dark crossbars on neck, rarely all black; tail looks like a braided whip. The fastest snake in our area; often climbs trees. Kills small animals by striking and biting. Feeds on rodents, birds, eggs, other snakes, and large insects. Hab: deserts, grassland, brushland, woods, farmland. R, including subspecies: San Francisco Bay area and cC, except coast and Central Valley, to Santa Barbara Co.; rest of our area into Baja including the coast.

29. CALIFORNIA WHIPSNAKE (STRIPED RACER), *Masticophis lateralis.* **[shrub, oak, des.]** Usually dark brown or black above, contrasting with a sharp, pale yellow stripe on each side; creamy on belly, often with coral pink under tail. Holds head high above grass when hunting for prey. Hab: chaparral with grassy patches, rocky canyons, hillsides, streams, especially oak woods, sometimes deserts. R, including subspecies: most of our region outside of the Central Valley.

30. LONG-NOSED SNAKE, *Rhinocheilus lecontei.* **[grass, des. shrub, rocks, str.wd. sav.]** Slender with alternating blackish and red saddles, outlined in white; blackish head with white areas on nose and below; whitish belly; white spots appear in black bands; pointed snout protrudes past lower jaw; usually single row of scales under tail. Hunts at night, often burrowing. Hab: deserts, brush, dry grassland. R: cC, except coast; sC, nBaja.

31. WESTERN PATCH-NOSED SNAKE, *Salvadora hexalepis.* **[shrub, rocks, des.]** Distinctive patchlike scale on nose; broad pale stripe down gray back, bordered by darker sides; whitish below. Eats small mammals, lizards, and eggs. A fast, daylight snake. Lays eggs. Hab: dry areas including chaparral, grassland, desert scrub of creosote bush, sagebrush, sandy and rocky areas, piñon-juniper woods. R (includes ssp., *Salvadora hexalepis mojavensis*: sC, Baja.

32. CALIFORNIA BLACK-HEADED SNAKE, *Tantilla planiceps eiseni.* **[grass, shrub, str.wd. des.]** May have a faint, narrow lighter stripe down its olive-gray back; light collar prominent behind distinct black head followed by black dots. Hides most of the time in burrows of animals or rock crevices; comes out at night to hunt. Hab: likes

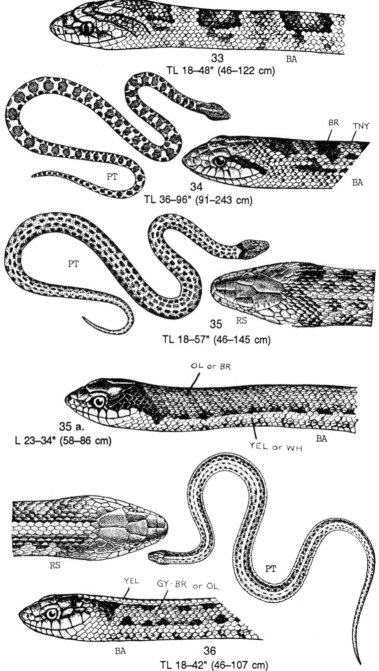

33
TL 18–48" (46–122 cm)

BR TNY

PT

BA

34
TL 36–96" (91–243 cm)

PT

RS

35
TL 18–57" (46–145 cm)

OL or BR

35 a.
L 23–34" (58–86 cm)

YEL or WH

BA

RS

PT

YEL   GY-BR or OL

BA   36
TL 18–42" (46–107 cm)

grassland, oak-pine or oak woods, edges of deserts, chaparral. R: spotty areas of coastal mountains from Livermore Valley to sC and Baja.

33. CALIFORNIA LYRE SNAKE, *Trimorphodon biscutatus vandenburghi.* **[rocks, des. shrub, oak]** Catlike eyes for seeing in the dark; slender neck; broad head. A lyre-shaped dark marking on the top of its head is distinctive. Light brownish gray with dark hexagonal blotches over the back with light or crossed centers; belly usually pale yellow or cream with a few brown spots. Climbs trees and goes into rock crevices after lizards and small mammals, using poison of back teeth; in daylight, it hides in rock holes. Hab: rock-loving snake of desert grasslands, creosote bush deserts, rocky canyons. R: swC, nwBaja.

2. Gopher and Garter Snakes (keeled scales on back).

34. PACIFIC GOPHER SNAKE, *Pituophis melanoleucus catenifer.* **[most habitats]** Known as "Pine Snake" in the East and "Bullsnake" in the Midwest, it is our largest native snake. Dark black-brown and reddish brown blotches on yellow or creamy-buff basal coloring are distinctive and separated. Hisses loudly and vibrates tail in dry leaves to give a rattling sound that may cause uninformed people to kill this very valuable snake. Active mostly in daylight; a great hunter of ground squirrels, rabbits, and mice, often entering burrows or climbing trees for birds or bird eggs. Kills by constriction. Lays as many as 24 large eggs. Hab: almost all habitats, but prefers grass and open brush. R: west and cC to Santa Barbara. **a. SAN DIEGO GOPHER SNAKE,** *Pituophis melanoleucus annectans.* Blotches on back are more or less joined together. R: Santa Barbara Co. south into Baja.

35. WESTERN AQUATIC GARTER SNAKE, *Thamnophis couchi.* **[water, str.wd. grass]** Head more pointed and narrower than western terrestrial garter snake; faint stripes down back; plain gray-olive or brownish above, with dark spots on sides. The western aquatic garter snake spends most of the time in water. An alert, timid snake; when frightened, it makes a dash for the water. Swims swiftly to catch frogs, toads, fish, and other aquatic prey. Hab: rocky streams or rivers with brush-protected pools, brackish marshes. R, including several subspecies: most of our area, spotty in places. **a. TWO-STRIPED GARTER SNAKE,** *Thamnophis couchi hammondi.* No back stripe; highly aquatic. R: south along C coast and inland from Monterey to nwBaja.

36. WESTERN TERRESTRIAL GARTER SNAKE, *Thamnophis elegans.* **[grass, str.wd. oak, shrub, water]** Dull yellow back stripe and side stripes separated by light reddish areas, more or less blotched with black, are distinctive. Eats slugs and frogs. When afraid, it wiggles into low ground cover for shelter. Live-bearing, from 4 to 19 young that are 6 to 9 in. long, in late summer. Hab: grass, brush, woods, coniferous forest, damp areas. R: nC to Santa Barbara, except Central Valley. **a. MOUNTAIN TERRESTRIAL GARTER SNAKE,** *Thamnophis elegans elegans.* Back stripe yellowish orange; pale belly. R: Sierra Nevada foothills and east slope of Coast Range.

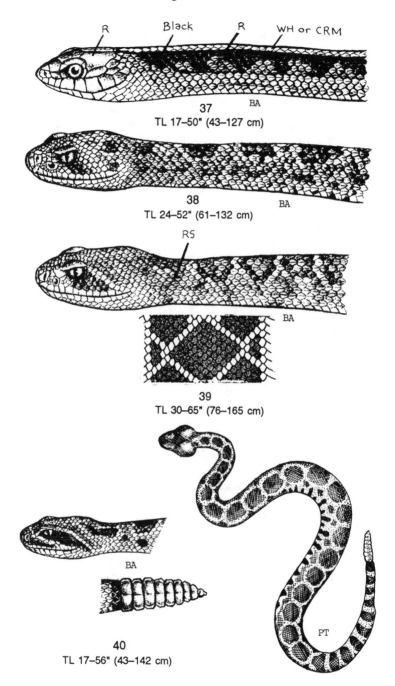

37
TL 17–50" (43–127 cm)

38
TL 24–52" (61–132 cm)

39
TL 30–65" (76–165 cm)

40
TL 17–56" (43–142 cm)

37. CALIFORNIA RED-SIDED GARTER SNAKE, *Thamnophis sirtalis infernalis.* **[grass, water, str.wd.]** Similar to other garter snakes, but red on head is stronger and ground color darker; narrow side stripes are bright greenish yellow. An energetic and efficient hunter; devours slugs, leeches, worms, fish, tadpoles, frogs, lizards, newts, rodents. Hab: in or near streams, ponds, marshes, cultivated wet fields, gardens. R: C coast from Humboldt Co. to San Diego Co. **a. VALLEY GARTER SNAKE,** *Thamnophis sirtalis fitchi.* R: cC to nC, except for coast (lower part of San Joaquin Valley northwards).

D. VIPERS, Family Viperidae

1. PIT VIPERS, Subfamily Crotalinae. Rattlesnakes, cottonmouths, and the copperhead are all venomous snakes with a pit near each nostril used for sensing the heat of their warm-blooded prey. Hollow, movable fangs in front of the mouth carry poison; the fangs swing out on their hinges and stab. They eat all varieties of rodents and rabbits. The biggest snakes kill jackrabbits.

38. SPECKLED RATTLESNAKE, *Crotalus mitchelli.* **[rocks, des. shrub]** Has cross-bands of vague dark blotches (groupings of dots) against light ground color; sharp black and white rings on tail above rattles. Nocturnal. Feeds mainly on rodents and birds. Young are 9 to 11 in. at birth. Hab: mainly found in rocky, brushy places, creosote, sagebrush, piñon-juniper woods, chaparral. R: swC (interior L.A. Co. south to San Diego Co., except coast), nwBaja.

39. RED DIAMOND RATTLESNAKE, *Crotalus ruber.* **[shrub, rocks, des.]** Tan, reddish, or pinkish colored with sharply marked dark diamonds on back. Hab: rocky brush country, chaparral, woods, cultivated areas. R: swC, nwBaja.

40. NORTHERN PACIFIC RATTLESNAKE, *Crotalus viridis oreganus.* **[shrub, grass, oak, rocks, des.]** Body olive, grayish tan, often matches with soil color; brown rectangular blotches bordered by light color down back becoming dark bands near tail; light stripe reaches from eye to corner of mouth. Eats small animals and birds. Live-bearing; averages 12 young. Hibernates in large groups. The rattlesnake is the only serpent that has interlocking segments (rattles) at the end of the tail. A segment is added each time the snake sheds its skin. R: nC south to Santa Barbara vicinity. **a. SOUTHERN PACIFIC RATTLESNAKE,** *Crotalus viridis helleri.* Tail bands are broader and not as defined. R: from Santa Barbara vicinity south into Baja.

PACIFIC RATTLESNAKE

Warts all over body.
Hind legs long. *Toads.*

Hind legs long, but no
warts on body. *Frogs.*

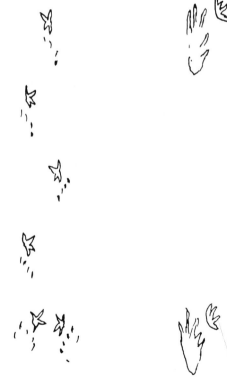

Toad   **Frog**

COMMON AMPHIBIANS

Frogs, toads and salamanders appear mainly during damp, mild weather or near permanent water. All have smooth, clammy skins, which cannot stand much heat or direct sunlight. None in our region are poisonous. All go through three stages of life called metamorhposis. First is the egg, second the larva (called "tadpole" or "pollywog"), and third the adult. The larvae usually have gills and may or may not live in water. Amphibians live mainly on insects and worms; some larvae eat plant food.

CLASS: AMPHIBIA. This class is comprised of cold-blooded, mainly 4-legged animals, with smooth moist skins.

SALAMANDERS AND NEWTS: ORDER CAUDATA. The tooth pattern of transverse rows on the upper mouth is distinctive.

    A. LARGEST SALAMANDERS, Family Dicamptodontidae. These are very aquatic salamanders found in or near water all year. The smallest salamander is also included in this family.

1. PACIFIC GIANT SALAMANDER, *Dicamptodon ensatus*. **[water, str.wd.]** Body is brown, gray, or purplish with black marbled markings; strong legs; large head; sleek skin; tail with narrow ridge on upper side. Most salamanders make no sound, but when caught, this one has a barking cry. Hab: moist woodlands close to cold, clear shallows of streams, lakes, ponds; under rocks, logs. R: wC, coastal woodlands from Monterey north.

    B. MOLE SALAMANDERS, Family Ambystomatidae. Mole salamanders are mainly active at night. Their teeth form a distinctive row across the roof of their mouth. They eat insects and mice, also other salamanders and garter snakes.

2. CALIFORNIA TIGER SALAMANDER *Ambystoma tigrinum californiense*. **[grass, water, str.wd. oak]** This largest land-dwelling salamander has a stocky body, small eyes, and tubercles that line the bottom of the feet. Color black or gray-black with yellowish or whitish spots; individuals vary from very dark with a few light markings to very light sides with a few dark markings on back. In dry weather, it lives in

Abbreviations: Hab = habitat; R = range; TL = length from nose to base of tail; C = California; B = Baja; w = western; c = central; n = northern; s = southern; nw = northwestern; etc.

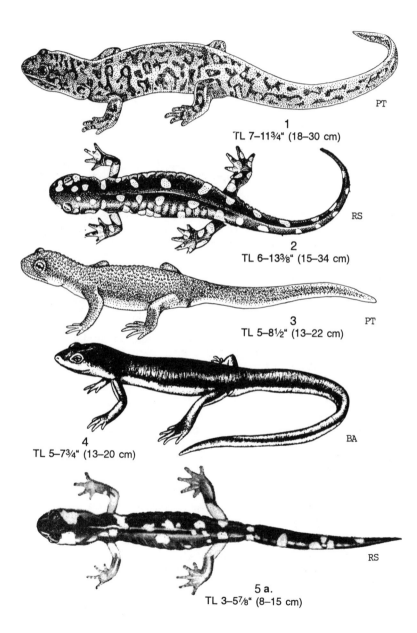

PT

1
TL 7–11¾" (18–30 cm)

RS

2
TL 6–13⅜" (15–34 cm)

PT

3
TL 5–8½" (13–22 cm)

BA

4
TL 5–7¾" (13–20 cm)

RS

5 a.
TL 3–5⅞" (8–15 cm)

animal burrows (squirrel, badger), crevices, and holes in logs and stumps, but comes out after rain when the ground is damp. Big groups migrate at night to breed near lakes and streams. Hab: sagebrush areas to grass, mountain meadows, woods. R: central coast and Central Valley.

C. NEWTS, Family Salamandridae. Most of the year Pacific newts are not aquatic and have tough, grainy skin. The males become sleek-skinned during mating season when they must enter the water to breed.

3. ROUGH-SKINNED NEWT, *Taricha granulosa.* **[water, str.wd. grass]** Dark brown color on back blends into light belly color; light colored area above mouth does not reach to lower eyelid; eyes are small; dark lower eyelids are distinctive. Y-shaped teeth are not found in this species. When threatened, it shows off bright tail and belly colors. If captured, its potent skin secretion usually allows it to go free uneaten. Hab: ponds and slow streams with water plants near grassland and burned forests. R: cwC, Santa Cruz north to Mendocino Co.; portions of Siskiyou Co.

4. CALIFORNIA NEWT, *Taricha torosa.* **[oak, str.wd. water]** The large eyes have light-colored lower eyelids; body dark brown above, orange-brown below; teeth are in a distinctive "Y" shape; skin rough in land-traveling specimens, smooth in breeding males. Hab: grass, woods, coniferous forests (except redwoods) sea level to 5000 ft. (1524 m); hides under logs, rocks and bark near slow streams, ponds, and reservoirs. R: wC coast, San Diego north to Mendocino Co., cC in Sierra Nevada foothills south to Fresno. **a. RED-BELLIED NEWT,** *Taricha rivularis.* Similar to California newt, but darker colors. R: northwest coast.

D. LUNGLESS SALAMANDERS, Family Plethodontidae. Lungless salamanders are land-dwellers, breathing through the skin and lining of the mouth and throat.

5. ENSATINA, *Ensatina eschscholtzii.* **[oak, str.wd. shrub]** Most ensatinas hybridize with each other and are of varied colors and ranges (see subspecies). Very distinctive swollen tail that is constricted at base. When touched it becomes rigid with stiff legs and swayed back. Hab: deciduous woods and coniferous forests, especially shaded canyons with water; also in grass of old chaparral; when cold or dry it hides deep in rotted logs or holes in the ground. **a. YELLOW-BLOTCHED ENSATINA,** *Ensatina eschscholtzii croceator.* **[oak, str.wd. shrub]** Upper part is black with large yellow, greenish-yellow, or cream spots. R: sC (mountains of Kern and Ventura cos.). **b. MONTEREY ENSATINA,** *Ensatina eschscholtzii eschscholtzii.* **[oak, str.wd. shrub]** Dark brown above, yellowish or whitish below. R: wC, nwBaja. (Monterey Co. to edge of San Diego Co., down coast to nwBaja). **c. LARGE-BLOTCHED ENSATINA,** *Ensatina eschscholtzii klauberi.* **[oak, str.wd. shrub]** Blackish on back with very large orange or yellowish pink blotches. R: sC (San Jacinto Mts. and mountains of San Diego

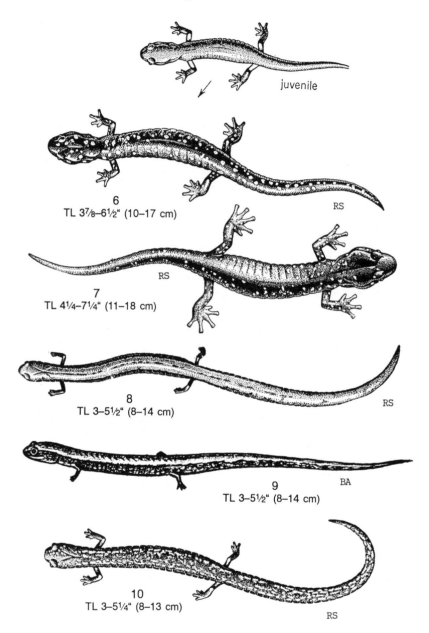

juvenile

6
TL 3⅞–6½" (10–17 cm)

RS

RS

7
TL 4¼–7¼" (11–18 cm)

8
TL 3–5½" (8–14 cm)

RS

9
TL 3–5½" (8–14 cm)

BA

10
TL 3–5¼" (8–13 cm)

RS

Co.) **d. OREGON ENSATINA,** *Ensatina eschscholtzii oregonensis.* **[oak, str.wd. shrub]** Plain brown (some nearly black) above, pale belly, sometimes with tiny black specks. R: nwC (Sonoma Co. northwards), cnC. **e. YELLOW-EYED ENSATINA,** *Ensatina eschscholtzii xanthoptica.* **[oak, str.wd. shrub]** Yellow patch in eye; orange color below, brownish yellow above. R: cC (east San Francisco Bay area and cental foothills of the Sierra Nevada).

6. BLACK SALAMANDER, *Aneides flavipunctatus.* **[str.wd. oak]** Usually black or blackish, but may be pale olive or green, with numerous white flecks in northern areas; black with large white spots south of San Francisco; head triangular; males have a heart-shaped head gland. In summer female lays 4 to 6 eggs and guards her nest until the tiny salamander hatches, bypasssing the larval stage in the fall. Hab: deciduous woods and coniferous forests or coastal grasslands. R: nwC south to Santa Cruz Co., cC northeast to foothills near Mt. Shasta.

7. ARBOREAL SALAMANDER, *Aneides lugubris.* **[oak, str.wd.]** Male has unusually large, triangular-shaped head; prominent eyes; brown body with small yellow spots; whitish, unmarked belly. Female broods eggs. May squeak and is the champion salamander tree-climber. Hab: live oak, black oak, or pine woods. R: wC along coast to nwBaja; also found in foothills of cC Sierra Nevada.

8. CALIFORNIA SLENDER SALAMANDER, *Batrachoseps attenuatus.* **[oak, str.wd. shrub, grass]** Has a very long, slender, wormlike body with short legs and tiny feet. Usually a uniform brownish color with a broad yellowish buff stripe down the back (varies to blotched); dark, dusky belly finely speckled with white. Commonly seen during the rainy season. Spends daytime buried under rocks or moist forest duff coiled up like a snake. Writhes violently if picked up by its tail, which easily breaks off. Hunts at night for worms and other types of insect life. The nest, often communal, is placed under soil, rocks, or wood and contains an average of 12 eggs. Young hatch as tiny salamanders without a larval stage. Hab: coastal mountains, chaparral, open woods, redwood forests, suburban areas. R: nC coast and inland to Central Valley and Sierra Nevada foothills.

NOTE: The four species of slender salamanders below are quite similar to the California Slender Salamander in overall appearance, habits, and habitat preference. They differ mostly in color variations and the range where they are found.

9. BLACK-BELLIED SLENDER SALAMANDER, *Batrachoseps nigriventris.* R: scC coast inland including Coast Range, foothills of the Sierra Nevada.

10. PACIFIC SLENDER SALAMANDER, *Batrachoseps pacificus.* R: swC from Los Angeles Co. south nwBaja; Monterey region to San Luis Obispo Co. **a. CHANNEL ISLANDS SLENDER SALAMANDER,** *Batrachoseps pacificus pacifucus.* R: found on the Channel Islands.

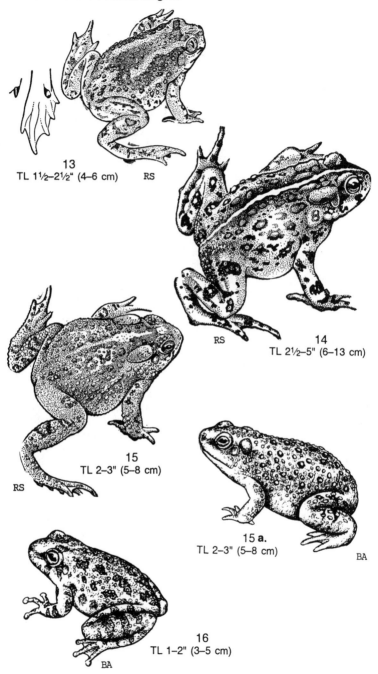

13
TL 1½–2½" (4–6 cm)   RS

14
TL 2½–5" (6–13 cm)

RS

15
TL 2–3" (5–8 cm)

RS

15 a.
TL 2–3" (5–8 cm)   BA

16
TL 1–2" (3–5 cm)

BA

11. KERN CANYON SLENDER SALAMANDER, *Batrachoseps simatus.*
R: Kern River drainage of scC.

12. TEHACHAPI SLENDER SALAMANDER, *Batrachoseps stebbinsi.*
R: sC Tehachapi Mts., Kern Co.

FROG AND TOADS: ORDER SALIENTIA

A. SPADEFOOT TOAD, Family Pelobatidae. The hind feet have a
toe with a sharp spur used to dig burrows; have upper teeth, fairly
smooth skin, and vertical eye pupils.

13. WESTERN SPADEFOOT, *Scaphiopus hammondi.* **[grass, sav.
water, des.]** Body is dusky brown, green, or gray with 4 irregular light
stripes on the back, whitish and unmarked below; large, protuberant
eyes without a bony bulge between them. Voice: sounds like stroking a
comb. Exudes a wet, smelly liquid when handled. Hab: favorable
burrowing soil in low flat areas, flood plains; sometimes higher in
arroyos and hills with sandy soil, short grass, or scattered bushes;
breeds in temperate pools or slow moving streams. R: ncC south to
nwBaja excluding coastline above Santa Barbara.

B. TRUE TOADS, Family Bufonidae. Toads generally come out at
dusk to hunt at night, returning regularly to the same burrow to hide
during the day. They burrow deeper if moisture or warmth are needed.

14. CALIFORNIA WESTERN TOAD, *Bufo boreas halophilus.* **[grass,
water, str.wd. oak, shrub]** Light colored warts are set in dark blotches,
surrounded by gray-green body color with a white or cream colored
back stripe; fold of skin on foot. It catches insects by shooting out its
long, hinged tongue. Active at daylight in mountains; at night in
lowlands. Voice: male chirps or peeps, much like a baby chick. Lives in
burrows. Hab: in or near grassland streams, rivers, springs, mountain
meadows, woods near water. R: most of our region.

15. SOUTHWESTERN ARROYO TOAD, *Bufo microscaphus
californicus.* **[str.wd. water, des.]** Warty and regularly stocky; greenish
gray to olive body; pale stripe across the head and dark spots on the
back are distinctive; paratoid glands on neck are widely separated and
egg-shaped. Hops more than walks. Voice: male gives melodious trill,
ending sharply. Hab: likes semi-arid arroyos, streams, washes, sandy
banks with cottonwoods. R: swC, nwBaja coast extending inland. **a.
RED-SPOTTED TOAD,** *Bufo punctatus.* Olive color with orange or red
warts. R: on southeast fringe of our area.

G. TREEFROGS, Family Hylidae. These frogs are small,
slim-waisted, and long-legged with toe pads for climbing.

16. CALIFORNIA TREEFROG, *Hyla cadaverina.* **[rocks, water, des.
str.wd.]** Generally gray with dark blotches; whitish to yellow below; male
has dusky throat; rarely has an eye-stripe. Beautifully camouflages with
environment. Usually only a few jumps away from water's edge. Voice:

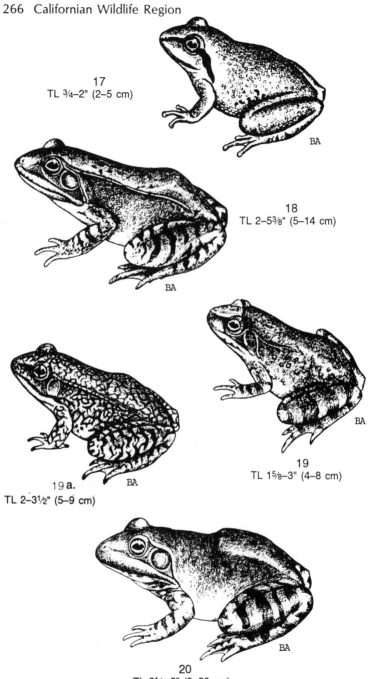

17
TL ¾–2" (2–5 cm)

BA

18
TL 2–5⅜" (5–14 cm)

BA

19
TL 1⅝–3" (4–8 cm)

BA

19 a.
TL 2–3½" (5–9 cm)

BA

20
TL 3½–8" (9–20 cm)

BA

male gives a ducklike quack, rapidly repeated. Hab: canyon washes and streams; prefers quiet pools with rocks and shade ranging from desert edges to pine belt in mountains. R: swC extending inland from Santa Barbara Co. south to nwBaja.

17. PACIFIC TREEFROG, *Hyla regilla*. **[usually most habitats]** Distinctive solid black eye-stripe down to shoulder; greenish gray color above (color can change in a few minutes), with or without dark elongated blotches on body; yellowish or cream belly; may have a spot on the head; suction pads on toes. Voice: male gives loud "krk-ek" call, repeated rapidly. Hab: sea level to mountain tops, usually near water in a wide variety of habitats. R: most of our region.

D. TRUE FROGS, Family Ranidae

18. CALIFORNIA RED-LEGGED FROG, *Rana aurora draytonii*. **[water. grass, str.wd.]** Large size with groin mottled red; red on lower belly; hind legs red with broad dark bands; dark mask touches whitish jaw stripe. Jumps about 3 ft. at a leap. Deposits up to 4000 eggs under water attached to vegetation, hatching into tadpoles. Voice: male gives stuttered "r-r-r-rowr." Hab: likes slow streams, lakes, ponds, grassland, marshes, humid wooded areas at low altitudes. R: most of our area except Central Valley where it no longer exists.

19. FOOTHILL YELLOW-LEGGED FROG, *Rana boylii*. **[water, str.wd.]** Bright yellow lower belly and hind legs are distinctive; brown, gray, reddish, or olive above, mottled or spotted with dusky color; pale triangle above the nose. Likes to sun on the shore. Dives when frightened. Eggs like a cluster of jelly-like grapes with up to 1000 in each one. Hab: woods, coniferous forests, near streams and rivers with sandy or gravelly soil. R: Santa Barbara Co. north excluding the Central Valley. **a. MOUNTAIN YELLOW-LEGGED FROG,** *Rana muscosa*. Likes plants near water for hiding. R: mountains of swC.

20. BULLFROG, *Rana catesbeiana*. **[water]** The largest frog; conspicuously large eardrums surrounded by fold of skin; brown, olive, or green in color; male with yellow throat. Remains as large olive green tadpoles (4 to 6 in.) for up to 2 years before turning into frogs. Usually eats insects, minnows, other frogs; also small birds and snakes. Voice: male gives deep-pitched "jug-o-rum" or "burr-wum" bull-like bellow; may "miaow" like a cat when attacked. Hab: permanent water edges with thick plant growth. R: most of our area.

E. TONGUELESS FROGS, Family Pipidae

21. AFRICAN CLAWED FROG, *Xenopus laevis*. **[water]** No eyelids or side folds; no teeth or tongue; lateral line on side has a stitched appearance; sharp black claws appear on inner toes. Voice 2-parted, faint trill. Hab: extremely aquatic; in ponds, lakes, reservoirs. R: swC (introduced in several counties).

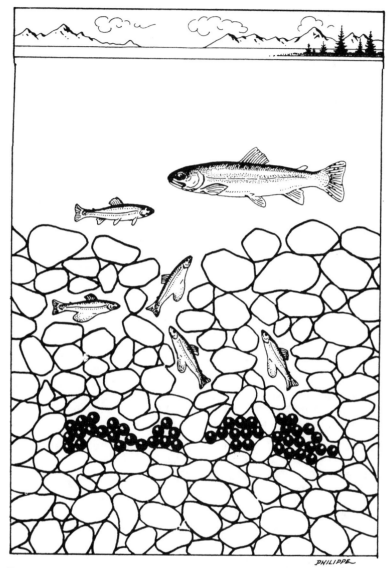

PHILIPPE

Trout eggs are buried in the gravel of a stream bed, usually lying several inches beneath the surface. When they hatch, The fry (or alevins) remain in the spaces between the gravel until the yolk sac is absorbed. At that time they work their way up to the surface and escape.

From *Trout of California* with permission of California Department of Fish and Game.

8.

COMMON FISHES

By far the largest number of fishes in the Californian Wildlife Region are found in the San Joaquin and Sacramento River systems. Most of the fishes found in the coastal streams are ocean fish, such as the steelhead trout, which spends part of its life in fresh water. Because so many kinds of fish have been brought in from outside the state or transplanted within the state, the picture is rather confusing. For this reason the ranges given are only general.

It will be helpful to study the drawing of a generalized fish below to learn the names of the different parts of the body. In identifying a fish, make sure it is close to the description and illustration given, as you might have a less common fish not described here. Scientific identying details are lengthy and outside the scope of this general guide.

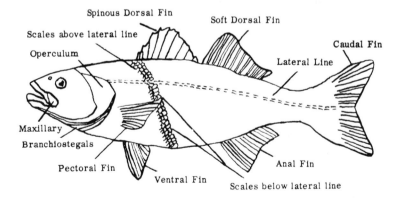

Used by permission from *A Key to the Fishes of the Sacramento-San Joaquin Basin*, by Garth Murphy.

Abbreviations used for this chapter: Hab = habitat; R = range; TL = total length; WT = weight; lbs. = pounds. **NOTE** The lengths and weight given with the fish illustrations are at best an average as fish continue to grow until they die, albeit much more slowly after reaching maturity. Also habitat and food supply greatly affect sizes.

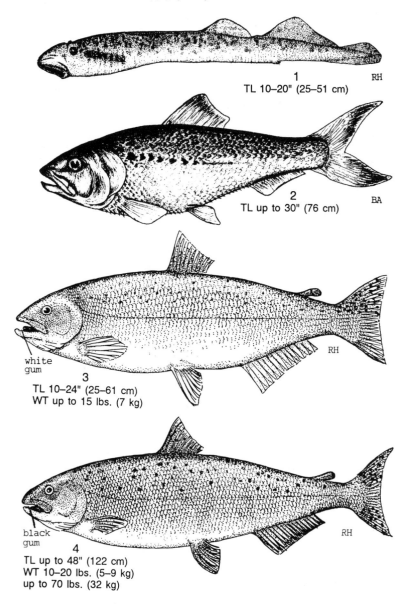

1   RH
TL 10–20" (25–51 cm)

2   BA
TL up to 30" (76 cm)

white
gum
3
TL 10–24" (25–61 cm)
WT up to 15 lbs. (7 kg)
                                         RH

black
gum   **4**
                                         RH
TL up to 48" (122 cm)
WT 10–20 lbs. (5–9 kg)
up to 70 lbs. (32 kg)

SUPERCLASS: PISCES

LAMPREY EELS: ORDER PETROMYZONTIFORMES

A. **LAMPREY EEL, Family Petromyzontidae.** Eels are primitive fish without jawbones or scales. They have undeveloped eyes, a circular suctorial mouth, and spines as teeth. They spawn in the gravel bottoms of clear streams; larvae mature to adults in 3 to 8 years.

1. **PACIFIC LAMPREY,** *Lampetra tridentata.* Dark grayish brown color, often mottled with some darker or lighter shades; sucker mouth. Hab: partly an ocean fish, coming up most rivers. R: most of our area. **a. RIVER LAMPREY,** *Lampetra ayresi,* and **b. PACIFIC BROOK LAMPREY,** *Lampetra pacifica,* come up the Sacramento-San Joaquin river drainage, but are uncommon.

BONY (TELEOSTEAN) FISHES: ORDER CLUPEIFORMES

A. **HERRING, Family Clupeidae.** Herrings are thin, silvery scaled fishes with bluish backs and a belly with a saw-toothed edge.

2. **AMERICAN SHAD,** *Alosa sapidissima.* Color lightens gradually from dark blue-gray on the back to pale silver underneath; thin, leaflike scales and saw-tooth keel on belly; usually has several dark spots in a row in back of upper gill flap. Fine tasting fish. Hab: fresh water for spawning, otherwise ocean-going. R: rivers the extent of our area, some in Millerton Lake in Fresno and Madera cos.; mainly in the Sacramento River drainages.

SALMON and TROUT: ORDER SALMONIFORMES

A. **SALMON AND TROUT, Family Salmonidae.** All have a fleshy, finlike bump on the back behind the rayed dorsal fin. Usually large, swift fish, they are excellent game. Ventral fins are always on the middle of the body, never just below the pectoral fin. Some species are solely freshwater fish, and others like the steelhead are anadromous, migrating up rivers to spawn. All require clear, cold, swift water for its oxygen content. The young of the anadromous fish migrate to the ocean where they grow for several years, and when ready to spawn they come back, often facing many obstacles, to the same stream where they had hatched.

3. **COHO (SILVER SALMON),** *Oncorhynchus kisutch.* Silvery color darkens in fresh water; black dots on the back and upper lobe of caudal fin. Hatchlings spend about 1 year in their stream before migrating to the ocean and become powerful fish by the time they return "home" to spawn 2 or 3 years later; dying afterward. Hab: ocean and fresh water. R: wC north of Monterey and inland.

4. **KING or CHINOOK SALMON,** *Oncorhynchus tshawytscha.* Silvery, bluish color; a long anal fin; dorsal fin without black spots, though sometimes blotched. Hab: ocean-going; freshwater cold rivers and

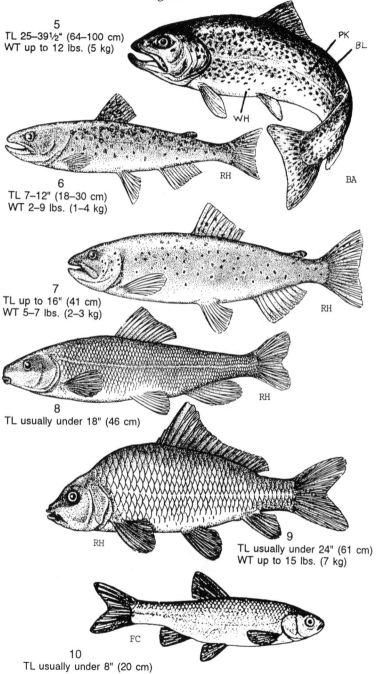

5
TL 25–39½" (64–100 cm)
WT up to 12 lbs. (5 kg)

6
TL 7–12" (18–30 cm)
WT 2–9 lbs. (1–4 kg)

7
TL up to 16" (41 cm)
WT 5–7 lbs. (2–3 kg)

8
TL usually under 18" (46 cm)

9
TL usually under 24" (61 cm)
WT up to 15 lbs. (7 kg)

10
TL usually under 8" (20 cm)

streams to spawn. R: cwC north, cC inland to San Joaquin and Sacramento river systems.

5. RAINBOW TROUT, *Oncorhynchus mykiss.* Black spots cover most of the body; reddish or purplish band extends along speckled sides; anal and dorsal fins speckled; spawning males may be rich mauve with a gray-black luster. **Steelhead** is the anadromous form of rainbow trout. Prefer insects, crustaceans, and smaller fish for food. Brilliantly colored rainbow are found in our foothill streams. Hab: rivers, streams, lakes, trout farms. R: in most western rivers, especially in the mountains.

6. BROOK TROUT, *Salvelinus fontinalis.* Back mottled with olive and black; has light spots on a dark background; usually some red spots; scales of body very tiny; white edge of fins distinctive. Hab: cold freshwater streams below 50 degrees F; may go to sea in some places. R: introduced to C, mostly in Sierra Nevada drainage.

7. BROWN TROUT, *Salmo trutta.* Body has red and black spots, the red spots fewer on the lower sides; back dark or greenish brown, sides yellowish brown, and the undersides whitish. Hab: rivers and streams. R: widely introduced in our area.

CHARACINS: ORDER CYPRINIFORMES

A. SUCKERS, Family Catostomidae. Bottom feeders; thick-lipped mouth is underslung for sucking up aquatic insects as they browse streambeds.

8. SACRAMENTO SUCKER, *Catostomus occidentalis.* Dorsal fin with 11 to 15 rays, gray to olive on the back; yellowish belly. Hab: rivers, streams, slow moving water. R: most common in Sacramento-San Joaquin river system, also other nC waters.

B. MINNOWS AND CARPS, Family Cyprinidae. The true minnows lack sucking mouth parts, but some look like suckers. They usually have long, slender scaled bodies; small mouths; teeth are in their throat and no teeth elsewhere. These teeth are useful in identifying the species. Carp are the biggest minnows.

9. CARP, *Cyprinus carpio.* The color is greenish brown; dorsal fin with a sawlike spine in the front. A scavenger; too bony for good eating. They go through a larval stage; live up to 18 years. Hab: slow streams, shallow, weedy ponds, lakes. R: introduced and widespread throughout our area.

10. TUI CHUB, *Gila bicolor.* Olive to brassy color on back; silvery belly; mouth small; fins rounded; anal fin rays 7 to 9. Most abundant of the minnows. Hab: shallow, slow-moving waters of lakes and rivers with vegetation. R: throughout C. **a. ARROYO CHUB (SOUTHERN CALIFORNIA CHUB),** *Gila orcutti.* Usually less than 4¾" (12 cm). Silvery or dark gray above, whitish below. R: swC (Santa Barbara Co. south to San Diego Co.).

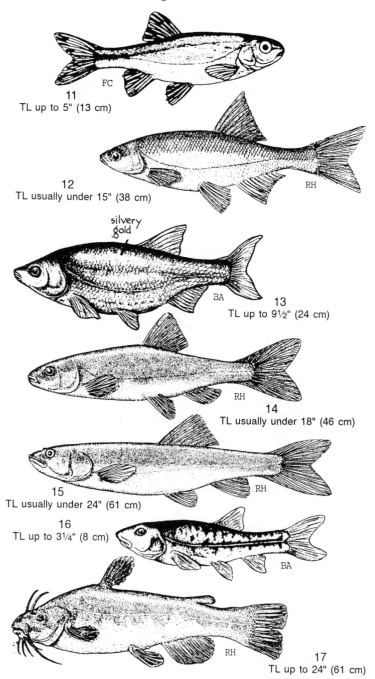

11
TL up to 5" (13 cm)
FC

12
TL usually under 15" (38 cm)
RH

silvery gold

13
TL up to 9½" (24 cm)
BA

14
TL usually under 18" (46 cm)
RH

15
TL usually under 24" (61 cm)
RH

16
TL up to 3¼" (8 cm)
BA

17
TL up to 24" (61 cm)
RH

11. CALIFORNIA ROACH, *Hesperoleucus symmetricus.* Widely distributed native minnow; dusky gray to steel blue above; dull silvery sides with a dark stripe along sides. Breeding male has red-orange chin and gill cover. Large head and eyes; low, small mouth. Mainly found in tributary streams; it is able to survive a decreasing volume of water through summer in shallow, warm pools. R: Sacramento and San Joaquin drainages.

12. HITCH, *Lavinia exilicauda.* Dark colored and speckled above, with silvery sides; rays of anal fin 10 to 14; body very compressed; head and mouth small; mouth upturned. Hab: slow streams, ponds, lakes, sloughs. R: cC.

13. GOLDEN SHINER, *Notemigonus crysoleucas.* Body deeply compressed; head small; anal fin rays 10 or more; silvery gold generally; eye and gill covers golden; lateral line curves deeply downward. Hab: lakes, warm, muddy bottoms of streams and sloughs; sometimes in cold water. R: cC, sC.

14. SACRAMENTO BLACKFISH, *Orthodon microlepidotus.* A fine-scaled and slender fish looking like a carp, but plain, light olive-colored. Herbivorous. The very prolific females secrete an adhesive to stick eggs to shallow water vegetation. Hab: warm, shallow river waters. R: cC, cwC, abundant in Sacramento-San Joaquin river system, and Clear Lake.

15. SACRAMENTO SQUAWFISH, *Ptychocheilus grandis.* Back greenish gray color; belly dirty yellow; mouth large, maxillary reaching to just below the front edge of the eye. Hab: prefers clear streams, deep pools. R: cC, abundant in Sierra Nevada foothill drainage.

16. SPECKLED DACE, *Rhinichthys osculus.* Variable in color, nose long, body slender, and has protractile lower jaw. Usually dark olive above, heavily speckled with black, some gold flecks; dark stripe runs along side through the eye to the mouth; barbels at corners. In breeding season the fins of both sexes turn red or orange. Hab: cool to warm streams, lakes, outflows of springs; prefers rocky areas. R: most of our area.

CATFISH: ORDER SILURIFORMES

A. CATFISH, Family Ictaluridae. Their bodies are distinctively scaleless; heads are flat and broad; pectoral and dorsal spines are strong and sharp; long barbels show about the mouth; bristlelike teeth fill the lower jaw. They are bottom-feeders and prefer slow moving or still water with muddy bottoms. Both parents guard the nest and young after finding a suitable spawning area sheltered under a log or undercut bank. Hundreds of fry, like a dense school of fish, remain close to the parents until 1 or 2 inches long.

17. WHITE CATFISH (FORK-TAILED CATFISH), *Ameiurus catus.* Similar to brown bullhead, but gets larger and tail fin is forked; some are colored blue on back with a silver belly. Hab: coastal streams. R: widely introduced in wC.

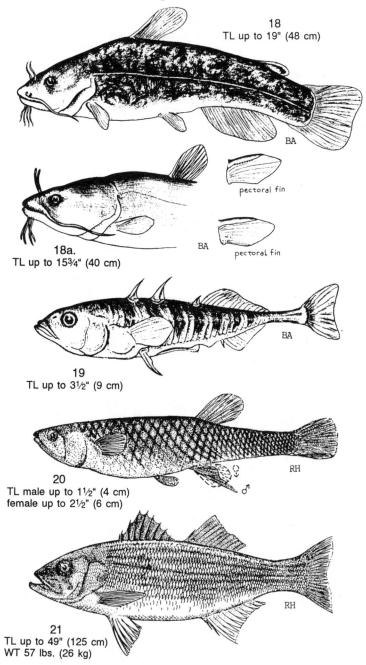

18
TL up to 19" (48 cm)

BA

pectoral fin

18a.
TL up to 15¾" (40 cm)

BA

pectoral fin

19
TL up to 3½" (9 cm)

BA

20
TL male up to 1½" (4 cm)
female up to 2½" (6 cm)

RH

21
TL up to 49" (125 cm)
WT 57 lbs. (26 kg)

RH

18. BROWN BULLHEAD (SQUARE-TAILED CATFISH), *Ameiurus nebulosus.* Anal fin rays 21 to 24; dark barbels under jaw; dark brown back, yellowish undersides; tail fin square. Hab: moderately clear to somewhat muddy waters with abundant plant life. R: coastal C streams from Salinas south to nwBaja (introduced in most C warm water rivers). **a. BLACK BULLHEAD,** *Ameiurus melas.* Similar to brown bullhead without mottling. R: introduced to California waters.

STICKLEBACKS: ORDER GASTEROSTEIFORMES

A. STICKLEBACKS, Family Gasterosteidae. Sticklebacks are small fish without scales; they have large eyes and their pelvic fins are reduced to heavy spines. An elaborate grass nest is built by the male, with a tunnel for the female to enter and lay eggs; the male is very pugnacious when guarding the young and the stick nest.

19. THREESPINE STICKLEBACK, *Gasterosteus aculeatus.* Large eyes; body fairly high for sticklebacks, but compressed from side to side; 3 sharp spines in front of soft dorsal fin; greenish brown on back, whitish below heavily speckled with black. Hab: common in coastal streams, grassy shallows near shore; also inland streams to the foothills of the Sierra Nevada. R: streams in most of our area.

KILLIFISHES: ORDER ATHERINIFORMES

A. LIVEBEARERS, Family Poeciliidae. The female gives birth to live young; the male has a modified anal fin, used in sexual reproduction.

20. GAMBUSIA (MOSQUITO FISH), *Gambusia affinis.* Has a stout body, small mouth, and flat head; male has a spinelike anal fin; usually light olive color but each scale edged with dark; lower jaw partly projects. Eaters of mosquito larvae. Hab: warm, vegetated, shallow pools; brackish sloughs; warm, sluggish streams. R: throughout C (introduced).

SPINY-RAYED FISHES: ORDER PERCIFORMES

A. TEMPERATE BASSES, Family Percichthyidae. Temperate basses are distinguished by slender dark stripes down their sides.

21. STRIPED BASS, *Morone saxatilis.* Body with very narrow, longitudinal stripes; 2 separate dorsal fins; a beautiful and light bluish purple in color. Hab: sea-going, entering freshwater streams to spawn; prefers estuaries. R: wC (introduced and now common along the coast).

B. SUNFISHES, Family Centrarchidae. This family includes also black basses and crappies, all of which are game or pan fishes. They have lateraly compressed bodies, small head, and medium to large scales. These fish like warm lakes and streams. The male scoops out a nest where the female lays her eggs, and he guards the eggs and the newly hatched fry.

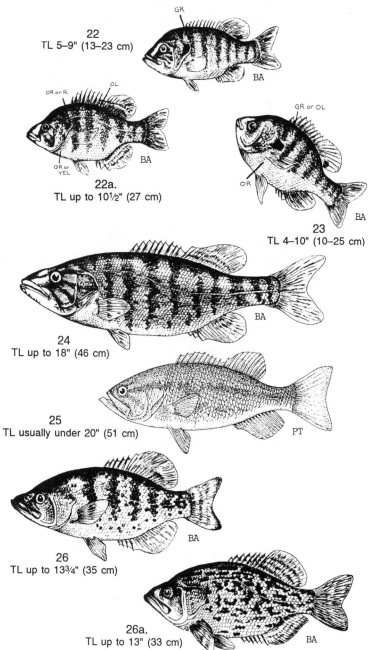

22
TL 5–9" (13–23 cm)

GR

BA

22a.
TL up to 10½" (27 cm)

OR or R

OL

OR or YEL

BA

23
TL 4–10" (10–25 cm)

GR or OL

OR

BA

24
TL up to 18" (46 cm)

BA

25
TL usually under 20" (51 cm)

PT

26
TL up to 13¾" (35 cm)

BA

26a.
TL up to 13" (33 cm)

BA

22. GREEN SUNFISH, *Lepomis cyanellus.* Robust fish with oblong body; brass-green above; upper sides have vertical bands; pale to olive-yellow on belly; black spot on large ear flap. Hab: ponds, shallows of lakes, small, warm turbid streams to cool, clear lakes. R: (introduced) presently distributed in waters throughout C. **a. REDEAR SUNFISH,** *Lepomis microlophus.* Ear margined with orange or red color. R: cC, sC.

23. BLUEGILL, *Lepomis macrochirus.* Body olive-green, somewhat hued with blue; dark vertical bands on sides; gills bluish color on sides of head; breeding male has an orange breast; flexible blue or black flap on ear; dark spot on rear end of dorsal fin. Very prolific; dense nesting colonies; male may have several females; they use the same nest each spawning season. Hab: shallows of lakes, ponds, rivers, generally at low elevations. R: non-native introduction well established in our area.

24. SMALLMOUTH BASS, *Micropterus dolomieui.* Dark olive to greenish above; irregular dark bars or mottling on yellow-green sides; smoky silver below; mouth does not reach beyond the eyes. Spawns on sandy bottoms or gravel beds. Males usually have more than one female. He stays to care for eggs and young several days, keeping them at the nest site. The same nest is re-used each time they spawn. All bass are heavy eaters of small fish, insects, and crayfish. Hab: widespread at mid-to-low elevations in large, clear streams and lakes. R: wC from Mendocino Co. south, cC to foothills of Sierra Nevada.

25. LARGEMOUTH BASS, *Micropterus salmoides.* Brownish green on the back; dark lateral band may break up in old individuals; belly and sides silver; scales are larger than in the smallmouth bass; large mouth with upper jaw reaching beyond the eyes. Male prepares nests that are 2 to 3 feet wide in weedy water; will stay to guard fry for up to 1 month. Hab: slow-moving, clear water of moderate temperatures with aquatic plant life in ponds, lakes, streams. R: introduced and widespread throughout our area.

26. WHITE CRAPPIE, *Pomoxis annularis.* Similar to the black crappie: light greenish brown markings above, white sides, yellow on belly; dark vertical bars appear on sides; fins are darkly speckled. Both crappies spawn in deep water over gravel in early summer; both feed on aquatic insects. Crappies are good to eat. Hab: large, warm, deep lakes and reservoirs; warm rivers and streams; more tolerant of turbid waters than the black crappie. R: throughout our area. **a. BLACK CRAPPIE,** *Pomoxis nigromaculatus.* Body color is mainly dense black spotting on dark greenish brown back. R: introduced and well established in waters throughout C and nwBaja.

C. SURFPERCH, Family Embiotocidae. Live-bearing fishes; they have spiny rays and a scaled ridge at the base of the dorsal fin.

27. TULE PERCH, *Hysterocarpus traski.* Back is dark bluish or purplish; belly whitish; often has dark narrow bars on sides and a hump behind the head. The young are born alive. Prefers muddy to gravel bottoms of lakes with aquatic plants. Hab: large streams, lower elevations. R: nC, cC.

D. SCULPINS, Family Cottidae. Sculpins have a scaleless body, smooth or covered with outgrowths of prickles. They have large, flat heads with eyes close together, and slender bodies. Males make the nest and guard eggs and fry.

28. COAST RANGE SCULPIN, *Cottus aleuticus.* Color on the back greenish brown and spotted; belly white; fins usually barred; prickles only behind pectoral fins. Hab: bottoms near mouths of coastal streams. R: wC south to San Luis Obispo Co.

29. PRICKLY SCULPIN, *Cottus asper.* Mottled dark on grayish olive; prickly all over body; black spot in back of spiny dorsal fin. Lays orange egg masses under stones. Hab: extremely various; prefers bottoms of quiet pools or coastal streams. R: wC south to Ventura Co., cC inland to San Joaquin and Sacramento river systems.

30. RIFFLE SCULPIN, *Cottus gulosus.* Mottled dark brown on grayish olive; spiny dorsal fin with black spot in back; prickles only behind the pectoral fins. Hab: cool coastal streams, headwaters; prefers gravelly bottoms. R: cwC, inland throughout the Sacramento-San Joaquin river systems.

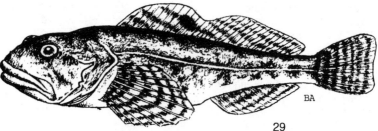

29
TL up to 10½" (27 cm)

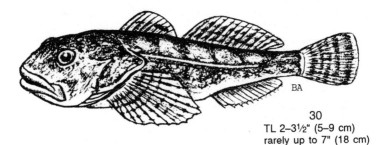

30
TL 2–3½" (5–9 cm)
rarely up to 7" (18 cm)

Suggested References

Plants

Abrams, Leroy. *Illustrated Flora of the Pacific States*, 4 volumes. Stanford: Stanford University Press, 1960.

Hickman, James C. *The Jepson Manual. Higher Plants of California*. Berkeley: University of California Press, 1993.

Munz, Phillip, and David Keck. *A California Flora*. Berkeley: University of California Press, 1963.

Mammals

Burt, William H., and Richard P. Grossenheider. *A Field Guide to the Mammals: Fieldmarks of all North American species found north of Mexico*, Third Edition. Boston: Houghton Mifflin Co., 1976.

California's Wildlife, Vol. 3, Mammals. Sacramento, CA: Department of Fish & Game, 1990.

Ingles, Lloyd G. *Mammals of the Pacific States: California, Oregon, and Washington*. Stanford: Stanford University Press, 1965.

Jaeger, Edmond C. *Desert Wildlife*. Stanford: Stanford University Press, 1961.

Jameson Jr. E.W., and Hans J. Peeters. *California Mammals*. Berkeley: University of California Press, 1988.

Whitaker Jr., John O. *National Audubon Society Field Guide to North American Mammals*. New York: Alfred A. Knopf, 1997.

Birds

Brown, Vinson, Henry Weston Jr., and Jerry Buzzell. *Handbook of California Birds*. Happy Camp, CA: Naturegraph, 1986.

Clarke, Herbert. *An Introduction to Southern California Birds*. Missoula, MT: Mountain Press, 1989.

Dickey, Florence V. *Familiar Birds of the Pacific Southwest*. Stanford: Stanford University Press, 1958.

Peterson, Roger Tory. *Western Birds*. Boston: Houghton Mifflin, 1990.

Udvardy, Miklos D.F. *The Audubon Society Field Guide to North American Birds: Western Region*, third edition. New York: Alfred A. Knopf, 1995.

Reptiles and Amphibians

Behler, John L. and F. Wayne King. *The Audubon Society Field Guide to North American Reptiles and Amphibians*. New York: Alfred A. Knopf, 1995.

Brown, Vinson. *Reptiles and Amphibians of the West*. Happy Camp, CA: Naturegraph, 1974.

Savage, Jay. *An Illustrated Key to Lizards, Snakes and Turtles of the West*. Happy Camp, CA: Naturegraph, 1989.

Stebbins, Robert C. *A Field Guide to Western Reptiles and Amphibians*, 2nd Revised Edition. Boston: Houghton Mifflin, 1985.

Fish

LaRivers, Ira. *Fishes and Fisheries of Nevada*. Carson City, NV: Nevada State Fish and Game Commission, 1962.

McGinnis, Samuel M. *Freshwater Fishes of California*. Berkeley: University of California Press, 1984.

Page, Lawrence M. and Brooks M. Burr. *A Field Guide to Freshwater Fishes, North America North of Mexico*. Boston: Houghton Mifflin, 1991.

Thompson, Peter. *Thompson's Guide to Freshwater Fishes*. Boston: Houghton Mifflin, 1985.

Wales, J.H. *Trout of California*. Sacramento, CA: Department of Fish and Game.

Williams, James D., et. al. *The Audubon Society Field Guide to North American Fishes, Whales, and Dolphins*. New York: Alfred A. Knopf, 1983.

Index

NOTES

NOTES